Praise for *Hollowed Out*

"When will we learn that an economy that works just for the wealthy just
doesn't work? David Madland, one of the nation's wisest young scholars,
explains with clarity and eloquence why trickle-down economics can't
keep its promise of rapid growth—and why a more just economy will
provide better results for everyone. This is a truly important book that
should shape our debate for many years to come."

—E. J. Dionne Jr., Senior Fellow, Brookings Institution, Professor,
  McCourt School of Public Policy, Georgetown University, and author
  of *Our Divided Political Heart: The Battle for the American Idea in an Age of
  Discontent*

"David Madland marshals reams of data, economic analysis, and social
science to make a deeply persuasive case for middle-class economics—
not only as a means of achieving sustainable, equitable economic growth,
but as the absolutely crucial foundation of American society. *Hollowed Out*
patiently walks us through the factors leading to the recent decline in
middle-class income and stability and, crucially, shows how to get the
economy back on the right track."

—John Podesta, former Counselor to President Barack Obama and former
  Chief of Staff to President Bill Clinton

"Trickle-down economics is the biggest economic lie ever told, and David Madland expertly and authoritatively shows us why. Meticulously researched and thoughtfully argued, *Hollowed Out* explains in plain language why growth and prosperity are always built from the middle out, not the top down. This should be required reading for economic policymakers."

—Nick Hanauer, Seattle-based entrepreneur who has helped launch more than twenty companies, including aQuantive Inc. and Amazon.com

"The dose is the difference between medicine and poison in economics as in healthcare. *Hollowed Out* makes the case that US inequality has gone beyond supply-siders' medicine for growth to poisoning our economy via loss of trust, political polarization, debt-driven consumer demand, and self-perpetuating aristocracy of wealth. Every member of Congress should read this before voting on the next tax cut for the wealthy."

—Richard Freeman, Professor of Economics, Harvard University

"Ideas are a powerful force in politics, and David Madland develops a very big and important one. Madland shows that the hollowing out of the American middle class has deeply damaged our economy, and in order to get back on track we need to make the economy work for everyone, not just the rich. *Hollowed Out* provides an important road map for anyone who wants to understand what is wrong with our economy and what needs to be done to fix it."

—Neera Tanden, President, Center for American Progress

Hollowed Out

The publisher gratefully acknowledges the generous support of the Anne G. Lipow Endowment Fund for Social Justice and Human Rights of the University of California Press Foundation, which was established by Stephen M. Silberstein.

Hollowed Out

*Why the Economy Doesn't Work
without a Strong Middle Class*

David Madland

UNIVERSITY OF CALIFORNIA PRESS

University of California Press, one of the most distinguished university presses in the United States, enriches
lives around the world by advancing scholarship in the
humanities, social sciences, and natural sciences. Its
activities are supported by the UC Press Foundation and
by philanthropic contributions from individuals and
institutions. For more information, visit www.ucpress.edu.

University of California Press
Oakland, California

Library of Congress Cataloging-in-Publication Data

Madland, David, author.
    Hollowed out : why the economy doesn't work without
a strong middle class / David Madland.
        p.   cm.
    Includes bibliographical references and index.
    ISBN 978-0-520-28164-6 (cloth : alk. paper)
    ISBN 978-0-520-28652-8 (pbk. : alk. paper)
    ISBN 978-0-520-96170-8 (ebook)
    1. Middle class—United States—Economic
conditions—21st century.   2. Middle class—United
States—Economic policy—21st century.
3. Consumption (Economics)—United States—21st
century.   4. United States—Economic policy—21st
century.   5. United States—Economic conditions—21st
century.   I. Title.   II. Title: Why the economy doesn't
work without a strong middle class.
    HT690.U6M33   2015
    305.5'50973—dc23 2014040833

Manufactured in the United States of America

24   23   22   21   20   19   18   17   16   15
10   9   8   7   6   5   4   3   2   1

In keeping with a commitment to support environmen-
tally responsible and sustainable printing practices, UC
Press has printed this book on Natures Natural, a fiber
that contains 30% post-consumer waste and meets the
minimum requirements of ANSI/NISO Z39.48–1992 (R 1997)
(*Permanence of Paper*).

To Karin, Charlie, and Jasper

CONTENTS

ILLUSTRATIONS

CHAPTER ONE

Middle Out vs. Trickle Down

On April 30, 2012, Edward Conard, a former partner for the financial management company Bain Capital and multimillionaire who retired at age fifty-one, sat across from Jon Stewart, host of *The Daily Show,* to promote his new book. Conard smiled and stared intently through his black-rimmed glasses as Jon Stewart, the liberal host of the comedy show, held up his book and described its contents. Conard's book argued that America's economy would be stronger if people like Conard were even richer and the country had even higher levels of economic inequality.

Stewart was puzzled by Conard's argument and joked that it didn't seem right because inequality in the United States was approaching the level in countries with "kidnapping-based economies," generating laughter in the audience.[1] Then Stewart shifted to an opening that would give Conard a chance to explain himself. "My question to you about the premise of the book," Stewart stated, pausing for effect before setting up his punch line, "is huh?"

Conard laughed along with the audience, and then launched into his argument that great rewards for the "most talented" people were the secret to America's success. Making the rich richer is good for everyone, he claimed, because high levels of inequality provide strong incentives for risk taking and innovation that are essential for economic growth.

Though Conard's comments were provocative—indeed his book tour generated significant press, including a multipage feature in the *New York Times Magazine*—he was merely stating the barely hidden premise underlying supply-side economics.[2] Supply-side economics, the misguided theory that has controlled economic policymaking for the past three decades, is built on the idea that inequality is good. Tax cuts for the rich and less regulation of business supposedly provide incentives for the wealthy to invest and work more. Enabling "job creators" to get richer helps us all, the theory goes.

Conard's former boss at Bain, Mitt Romney, the 2012 Republican Party nominee for president, ran on a platform of supply-side policies, as have virtually all Republicans since Ronald Reagan was elected president. Even a number of prominent Democrats support supply-side policies and logic. Not only do these wrongheaded ideas about inequality have great political influence, but—until quite recently—they were largely shared by academic economists. For the past several decades, the idea that high levels of inequality were good for the economy dominated economic thought.

Fortunately, these flawed ideas are beginning to be challenged. Academics have begun to rethink their views about the decline of the middle class and progressive politicians are finally starting to openly contest the logic underlying supply side after years of failing to do so. It is about time because our economy is suffering deeply from a financial crash caused in large part by high levels of inequality. And though we may not have a kidnapping-based economy, as Stewart joked, the American middle class is so weakened that we are experiencing the kinds of problems that plague less-developed countries, including high levels of societal distrust that make it hard to do business, governmental favors for privileged elites that distort the economy, and fewer opportunities for children of the middle class and the poor to get ahead, wasting vast quantities of human potential.

This book explains the rethinking of inequality that is happening in academia and in politics. The American economy has been thrown off balance because the middle class is so weakened and inequality so high. An economy that works only for the rich simply doesn't work. To have strong and sustainable growth, the economy needs to work for everyone.

A strong middle class is not merely the result of a strong economy—as was previously thought—but rather a source of America's economic growth. Rebuilding the middle class would provide the stable base of consumer demand necessary to increase business investment and job creation. It would also enable the country to fully develop the human capital of its people, increase the social trust that makes transactions possible, and balance political power to produce a government that works for the whole country, not just those at the top.

Elements of this line of thinking date back to some of history's most prominent economists—from John Stuart Mill to John Maynard Keynes—but until the Great Recession of 2007–2009 snapped the field back to attention, most economists ignored the importance of the middle class. Now, as they revise their models and assumptions that failed to predict the financial crisis, economists are rediscovering classic scholars, opening their eyes to the work of researchers in other fields such as history, political science, and sociology, and developing promising new lines of inquiry to try to understand the role of the middle class.

Hollowed Out brings together this long-standing and recent research. The book shows how the hollowing out of the middle class has harmed the US economy, clarifies how previous thought got it so wrong, and illuminates how this new middle-out synthesis could shape economic policymaking for generations to come.

To some readers, the argument that America's economy grows from the middle out, not from the top down, might seem intuitive and uncontroversial. But the argument is a direct criticism of conventional wisdom in academia and in politics. That a relatively simple and commonsense approach to the economy presents a radical challenge to the status quo indicates just how far off base economists and politicians went over the past few decades, and it explains why this book is necessary.

TRICKLE-DOWN

Edward Conard is more explicit about the supposed benefits of inequality than most supporters of supply-side policies. But from its beginnings, supply-side proponents have argued that inequality is good for the economy. Jude Wanniski, an economist and editorial writer for the *Wall Street Journal*, who wrote the *The Way the World Works* in 1978, which helped put supply-side economics on the map, claimed that the "basic economic problem that for all time has confronted the global electorate ... is the tension between income growth and income distribution."[3] For the good of the country, Wanniski maintained, income growth was the right choice and that required reducing taxes, especially on the wealthy, and greater levels of inequality.

George Gilder, an early promoter of supply side, put it more bluntly in *Wealth and Poverty*, published in 1981: "Equality ... [is] inconsistent with the disciplines and investment of economic and technical advance."[4] Gilder was very clear that economic growth required a select group of people to become very rich. "Material progress is ineluctably elitist," he wrote. "It makes the rich richer and increases their numbers, exalting a few extraordinary men who can produce wealth over the democratic masses who consume it." President Ronald Reagan—the first powerful political proponent of trickle-down—frequently quoted Gilder and in a speech in 1982 put Gilder in his own words by arguing that "we're the party that wants to see an America in which people can still get rich."[5] Because of this belief that helping the rich get richer will cause economic benefits to drip onto the middle class and poor, detractors of supply-side economics often call it trickle-down.

For decades, academic economists helped provide cover for trickle-down economics and the obvious harm it was doing to the middle class and the economy. Most academics didn't buy into all of supply-side dogma—they rejected the idea that tax cuts pay for themselves, for example—but in general the logic of the theory fit with many of their preconceptions about inequality and economic incentives.[6] Until quite recently, the vast majority of the economics profession believed—like supply-siders do—that inequality helped the economy to function properly. Even those who were troubled by high levels of inequality generally felt it was necessary for the good of the economy. According to the standard view in economics, policymakers faced a trade-off between economic growth and economic equality.

This underpinning of economic thought was most clearly demonstrated by Arthur Okun, a Yale University economist and the chief economic advisor to President Lyndon Johnson, in his book *Equality and Efficiency: The Big Tradeoff*, published in 1975.[7] Inequality, according to Okun, provided positive incentives that encouraged people to work hard and invest, making the economy more efficient. Further, Okun claimed that efforts to reduce inequality generally involved some level of waste that hindered the economy. Though Okun argued that the trade-off between equity and growth was less than most economists thought, the fact that even a liberal economist believed that high levels of economic inequality were good for the economy underscores how ingrained the idea was in economics departments.

At the time Okun wrote, the American middle class was still relatively strong and inequality low. But soon after his book was published, inequality began rising and the middle class weakened. Most economists were untroubled. Some even defended the changes. Indeed, a keynote address at the American Economic Association conference in 1999—the main association for academic economics—was titled "In Defense of Inequality," and argued that "inequality is an economic 'good' that has received too much bad press."[8] The keynote speaker, Finis Welch, was later elected by his colleagues as vice president of the economics association.[9]

Economists thought this way about inequality because the kind of logic they used ignored many of the downsides of inequality. Economists generally believe that long-run economic growth is determined by the productive use of physical capital, such as buildings and factories, and human capital, the knowledge that people have. The key to economic growth, then, is to provide the right incentives to encourage people to increase the supply of human and physical capital and make more efficient use of them. A greater payoff for people who increase society's capital—holding everything else equal—seemingly provides the right incentives.[10]

Holding everything else equal is of course key to making this logic work. But, as inequality has risen to extreme levels in the United States, everything else has not remained equal: the foundations of the economy have weakened. Society has changed so that people trust one another less and are reluctant to do business with one another. Government has become captured by the elites. Opportunities for the less well off to get an education and develop their skills have weakened in comparison to the rich. And the nature of consumer demand has changed and become less stable.

Most economists got it so wrong because they were trained to think of individuals as untouched by institutional or social influences. In the economic worldview, individuals act based on their narrow self-interest. Supposedly, according to most economic models, this leads to efficient results without much need for social or legal constraints. As a result, economists generally ignored the importance of good government and societal trust to a properly functioning economy. On the rare occasions they did look at these issues, it was almost always to study developing countries—not the United States—and thus they missed that these basic underpinnings of growth in America were sharply deteriorating.

Even for factors that economists commonly studied, such as demand and human capital, they hardly considered how the economy was impacted by a weakened middle class. Economic analysis of consumer demand and its relationship to economic growth was generally based on a stylized version of a typical consumer and ignored the impact of growing differences in income, wealth, and debt.[11] As a result, on the eve of the Great Recession most economists failed to recognize that consumer demand was dependent on middle-class debt and thus unstable. In a similar vein, too many studies of human capital and economic growth assumed that because some inequality provides an incentive for individuals to acquire greater skills, extremely high levels of inequality must be a good thing.[12] Though some economists were able to recognize that inequality had the potential to hinder the development of human capital, the profession rarely reflected on whether this was harming America's growth. It didn't take much looking to see that inequality was so high that it was providing much greater opportunities for the children of the rich to develop their human capital while the children of the poor and middle class were falling behind. Nor did it take great insight to consider the broader impact this was having on the economy, but few made the connections.

Because of these widespread failures, in 2007, on the brink of the Great Recession, most economists were caught unaware that the ground supporting the American economy was collapsing.[13] They missed the forest for the trees.

Economists originally incorporated a broad conception of humanity and society in their study: Adam Smith, the founder of the discipline, was a moral philosopher as well as a political economist after all.[14] But, over the past five or six decades, economists who wanted to study the influence of government or cultural factors or challenge the hyperrational view of economic-man were relegated to the fringes.[15] As a result, the study of economics in recent decades has often been "asocial and ahistorical," according to Ben Fine, an economist at the University of London, and Dimitris Milonakis, an economist at the University of Crete.[16]

Criticisms of the excessively narrow and theoretical perspective of the economics profession have come not just from those on the outside, but also from some of the most credentialed economists in the world.[17] And since the Great Recession, criticism has been particularly forceful.[18] Nobel Prize–winning economist Ronald Coase, for example, wrote in an essay in 2012 that "ignoring the influences of society, history, culture and politics on the working of the economy" is "suicidal" for the field of economics.[19] Similarly, Thomas Piketty, the French economist who some leading economists think will win the Nobel Prize for his work on inequality, argues in *Capital in the Twenty-First Century,* published in 2014: "The discipline of economics has yet to get over its childish passion for mathematics and for purely theoretical and often highly ideological speculation at the expense of historical research and collaboration with the other social sciences."[20]

To be sure, economists—like all social scientists—need to make simplifications and set aside certain factors from analysis in order to try to understand the complex system they are studying. Yet the simplifications that economists made were fundamentally flawed because they ignored issues that were critical to the economy. As a result, they turned a blind eye—or even gave their blessings—as trickle-down policies and changes in the global economy drove inequality to record levels and significantly weakened the middle class.

THE WEAKENING MIDDLE CLASS

The United States was founded as a middle-class country. On the eve of the American Revolution, America's carpenters, shopkeepers, and farmers enjoyed a higher standard of living than workers in other parts of the world.[21] Further, economic inequality was lower in the United States than any place else. In an era of kings and peasants, America's middle class stood apart.

America had its share of rich people, and of course it had slavery. But even so, the rich were not that much richer than the middle class. As Peter Lindert, an economic historian at UC Davis, explains: "Compared to any other country from which we have data, America in that era was more equal."[22] Those who lived during America's founding sensed that the country's economic equality was special. Thomas Jefferson noted in a letter that "we have no paupers.... The great mass of our population ... possess property [and] cultivate their own lands.... The wealthy, on the other hand, and those at their ease, know nothing of what the Europeans call luxury."[23]

The strength of America's middle class ebbed and flowed over time, especially as industrialization took hold.[24] But after World War II, America returned to its roots and built a mass middle class that was the envy of the world, with rapidly rising incomes and decreasing inequality.[25] The mid-1940s to the mid-1970s was a period "without extremes of wealth or poverty," as Nobel Prize–winning economist Paul Krugman explains.[26] To be clear, America in this era had rich people and poor people, but the bulk of society formed a prosperous middle class that was in relatively close proximity to both the top and the bottom.

Yet, over the past three to four decades, middle-class America has come undone. The American middle class was already hurting when the Great Recession struck and is now in deep trouble. While there's no official definition of the middle class, it's not hard to see that it is in decline. By most every measure, most Americans are struggling.

First, there is the basic level of income earned by the typical American. Median household income—meaning half make more and half make less—was lower in 2013 than it was in 1989.[27] This means that middle-class households now earn less than they did two decades ago. Similarly, incomes for poor and even upper-middle-class households have also stagnated.[28] It is true that over an even longer time period, the middle class have seen some income gains. But these gains have been quite small: over the past four decades, median compensation, including both wages and benefits, has grown at a snail's pace of just 0.27 percent per year—far slower than the overall economy or output per worker.[29] The miniscule gains that households have made have largely come because women have increasingly entered the workforce—meaning families are working longer hours, as they run faster and faster to stay in place.[30] Indeed, the hourly wage earned by a typical man is less than it was in 1973.[31]

Even these gloomy figures may be too rosy because they show what is happening to the typical household—but the typical worker is getting older, and older workers generally make more than younger workers.[32] Income trends are even worse when workers are compared to those of a similar age from a few decades ago. Median incomes for male workers now in their thirties are about 12 percent lower than the income was for their fathers' generation at the same age.[33]

While incomes have been stagnant for most Americans, the cost of middle-class basics like healthcare and gas have risen much faster than inflation, and some basics like housing and college have risen at double the rate of inflation over the past four decades.[34] It costs a lot more to maintain a middle-class lifestyle, but no matter their efforts most families have not been able to earn much more income. Not surprisingly, debt levels have jumped sharply—the average debt of middle-class families has nearly doubled since 1983.[35]

In contrast to the middle class and the poor, incomes of the rich, especially the very rich, have grown by astronomical amounts over the past three decades: in 2007, the year the Great Recession started, the top 0.01 percent, the richest one in ten thousand, earned in today's dollars the equivalent of about $38.8 million, compared to $6.4 million per year in 1979.[36] Because of rapidly rising incomes for the rich and stagnating incomes for everyone else, the economic distance between the rich and the middle class has grown by leaps and bounds.[37] CEO compensation, for example, increased from less than 30 times that of the average worker in 1978 to over 350 times what the average worker made in 2007.[38] Though incomes for the rich fell during the Great Recession more than they did for the middle class, incomes for the rich have come roaring back, while middle-class incomes have not—so much so that income differences are now back to near the prerecession levels.[39]

To picture how big these differences are, think of a strange building housing the middle class on the bottom floor and the very rich on the top story. In the late 1970s, the CEO's penthouse would have been on the thirtieth floor, making this apartment building a tall one, but one that would fit in many American cities. In 2007, the penthouse was 351 floors up, meaning the apartment building would need to be more than three times the size of the Empire State Building.

The rich now make so much more than the middle class because they captured the vast majority of the economy's gains over recent decades. The share of the nation's income going to the top 1 percent has approximately doubled over the past three decades, while the share of income going to the middle 60 percent of income earners has fallen precipitously and is now stagnating near the lowest level ever recorded since the government began keeping track of the statistic.[40] These changes in income share are "the equivalent of shifting $1.1 trillion of annual income to the top 1 percent of families," according to Princeton economist Alan Krueger.[41] Since the Great Recession ended, over 90 percent of the income gains have gone to the top 1 percent of income earners.[42]

And wealth differentials are even bigger than income differences. The bottom 90 percent of Americans have lost wealth over the past two and a half decades and now hold only about one-quarter of the country's wealth.[43] In contrast, the top 1 percent have seen dramatic gains in wealth and now hold 40 percent of total US wealth.[44] To put the wealth of the very rich in context, the average net worth of the 400 wealthiest Americans is "about the same as the gross domestic product of Brazil," according to Forbes Magazine.[45]

For most Americans, incomes are stagnant, debt levels are high, and they are taking home a smaller share of the pie than they once did and falling further behind the rich. This means, as economists put it, that the opportunities for the poor and middle class are increasingly constrained in comparison to those of the rich.

THE EMERGENCE OF MIDDLE OUT

As dramatic as these trends are, by themselves they were not enough to force economists to rethink their ideas about inequality. Rather, there were several developments that really pushed economists to pay serious attention to inequality and study its impact on the economy. Improved measurement of the incomes of the very rich helped, as did patterns of economic growth around the globe that didn't conform to expectations, but most important was the Great Recession.

Traditional measures showed that inequality in the United States had become higher than in many other countries, including notoriously unequal ones like the Philippines, Nigeria, and Russia.[46] But in recent years, economists such as Thomas Piketty and as UC Berkeley's Emmanuel Saez developed more accurate data about the incomes of the very rich over time which showed not only that the top 1 percent in America took home a much greater share of the nation's income than did the rich in most of the world, but also that the share the very rich received equaled record levels in American history.[47] The improved data not only elucidated these comparisons but also enabled economists to perform more nuanced analysis than they had been able to do before.

At the same time as income data was improving, growth trends in many countries were defying economists' models. Well before the Great Recession struck, it was becoming increasingly clear that the American economy grew more rapidly in the middle part of the twentieth century when the middle class was stronger than it did in recent, highly unequal decades.[48] Further, other rich countries that were more equal were growing at least as fast as the United States—and some actually had higher per capita growth rates.[49] Economists who studied growth, especially in the developing world, began to think that an important reason why countries like South Korea were growing much more rapidly than countries like the Philippines was because they had lower levels of inequality.[50] NYU's William Easterly, for example, argued that in countries around the world "middle-class societies have more income and growth."[51] In one of the more important papers in this line of research, Andrew Berg and Jonathan Ostry, economists at the International Monetary Fund, found that more equal countries tend to have significantly longer periods of growth while unequal countries had great trouble maintaining their growth for any sustained period.[52]

These observations about growth around the world didn't prove that inequality was harming the US economy, but they did at least suggest that the old ideas about inequality might be wrong and indicated the need for more research. This line of international comparative research became bogged down over data and methodological questions—and not every scholar came to similar conclusions—but the research clearly showed that simple assertions about inequality being good for the economy were not accurate and demonstrated that economists needed to think more deeply about exactly how inequality impacts economic growth.[53] As Heather Boushey, the executive director of the Washington Center for Equitable Growth, and Adam Hersh, a senior economist at the Center for American Progress, wrote, this cross-country analysis indicated that economists "need to understand the mechanisms through which inequality and the strength of the middle class affect the economy."[54] The actual experiences of countries around the world showed that scholars had to start looking at how inequality and the strength of the middle class impacted the underpinnings of growth. Especially before the Great Recession, these international comparisons were critical for challenging economists' preconceptions about inequality.

Then the Great Recession struck just as economic inequality in the United States was reaching the same level as had occurred right before the start of the Great Depression in 1929. The dramatic economic collapse forced many economists to look at inequality in a new way. Though the relationship between economic inequality and financial collapse is not as simple or direct as some have tried to claim, inequality and the weakness of the middle class clearly played a big part in driving the Great Recession.[55] The Great Recession began in the United States and was so severe in large part because our financial regulations were weakened by the political power of Wall Street and because the middle class was heavily indebted.[56] As Joseph Stiglitz, a Nobel Prize–winning economist, explained, "The most recent financial crisis has shown the errors" of ignoring inequality.[57]

When thinking critically about economic inequality and throwing off the blinders that have restricted the vision of economists, it is clear that America's economy depends upon a strong middle class. The middle-out theory of economic growth that emerges has deep historical roots in economics and other disciplines but also benefits from newer lines of research.[58]

A strong middle class performs four primary roles in the US economy. First, a strong middle class helps society function relatively smoothly, with higher levels of trust among people. Trust may seem a bit abstract, but it has a dramatic economic impact. People need to be able to trust one another enough to do business with one another. When there is little trust, the cost of doing business shoots up—or, as economists put it, transaction costs increase. As the middle class has weakened over the past few decades, trust has declined and transaction costs have risen sharply. Businesses and individuals, for example, have hired lawyers and security guards much more frequently than they previously did.[59] While these occupations may provide a valuable service, they don't increase the productivity of the economy, and merely add to the cost of doing business. Even worse, in part because of the decline in trust, businesses are increasingly focused on the short-term instead of long-term results.

Second, a strong middle class leads to better governance. A thriving economy depends on a well-functioning government that provides critical services, such as roads and schools, with relatively little corruption. But as the middle class has weakened and inequality risen, the wealthy have gained excessive political power and the middle class has become less civic-minded, leading to a host of governmental dysfunctions. The failures of American government over the past few decades have increasingly harmed the economy. America has underinvested in public goods like schools and roads in large part because the wealthy don't want to pay the taxes to fund them and has, for example, cut spending on infrastructure by $89 billion per year compared to what we spent several decades ago.[60] Corruption has increased sharply according to government data and surveys of experts. And the costs of special favors for business, especially for Wall Street, have risen to astronomical levels.

Third, the middle class is a source of stable demand. A stable and growing base of consumer demand enables businesses to invest in new products and hire additional workers, fueling growth. But because consumer demand in the years prior to the Great Recession was based heavily on middle-class debt, the economy was unstable. And now that the middle class is so weak, burdened by stagnant incomes, high debt levels, and underwater mortgages, they can't consume enough to keep the American economy going. In the aftermath of the Great Recession, the US economy has been stuck in a cycle of low demand and low growth.

Finally, a strong middle class creates more human capital. In the modern economy a skilled, healthy, and entrepreneurial workforce is a driver of economic growth, at least as much as the physical capital of factories and machines. But as inequality has risen and the middle class has weakened, America has not developed the full human potential of its middle class and poor. Our international competitors have passed us by on measures of human capital because the education and health outcomes for the middle class and poor have fallen sharply behind those of more affluent Americans.[61]

Further, entrepreneurship in America has declined as many would-be business leaders have been unable to take advantage of their human capital because members of the middle class no longer have the money necessary to start a business.[62]

In short, the decline of the American middle class has harmed the economy by restricting human capital, shrinking consumer demand, exacerbating governmental problems, and undermining trust.[63] The various ways the middle class is struggling affect these mechanisms of growth in slightly different ways. High levels of debt play a key role in reducing consumer demand, for example, while the declining position of the middle class compared to the rich undermines the quality of government. The middle class's lack of money is particularly important in explaining their inability to start a business, while extreme inequality has undermined societal trust. Stagnant incomes, rising debt, and record levels of inequality all impact growth and none can be ignored.

For people with economic models in their head, the weakness of the middle class can be thought of as harming the economy through both production (supply-side) and consumption (demand-side) mechanisms. Weak middle-class consumption has reduced aggregate demand, while declining trust and the inability of people to take full advantage of their human capital have limited the productive capacity of the economy. Inadequate government investments in infrastructure and education reduce the potential output of the country and are also part of why low levels of demand are holding back the economy in the aftermath of the Great Recession. As Robert Solow, who won the Nobel Prize for his analysis of economic growth, explained in a speech in 2013: "Any way you look at it, a highly unequal society is not exploiting its full potential for growth."[64] Further, these problems with demand, government, trust, and human capital that are fueled by the weakness of the middle class often reinforce one another. When government policies favored Wall Street interests, the new types of financial engineering that were allowed not only created great risks for the economy, but also contributed to the rise in debt that made the economy more fragile and reduced consumer spending in the wake of the Great Recession. America's college graduation rates have stagnated not only because middle-class and poor families have had a hard time affording college tuition when their incomes are declining but also because government investments in higher education have been inadequate because of the growing political power of the wealthy.

This growing understanding of how inequality harms our economy has set the stage for transformative political conflict. We are now at a sea-change moment in economic policymaking in the United States.

THE DEBATE OF OUR TIMES

After 30 years of political dominance, it is obvious that supply-side economics has failed in a number of ways and is thus vulnerable to a challenge from middle out. Supply side helped fuel the Great Recession of 2007–2009 by destabilizing consumer demand and encouraging the deregulation of Wall Street—costing the United States 8.7 million jobs and trillions of dollars in reduced economic growth.[65] The Great Recession alone is more than enough reason to get rid of supply side. But even excluding the Great Recession and its aftermath, growth was much slower over the past several decades, when trickle-down was ascendant, than it was in prior decades.[66] Even within the supply-side period, growth was weaker after President George W. Bush cut taxes for higher earners than it was after President Bill Clinton raised taxes on the rich.[67]

Moreover, trickle-down's supposed growth mechanisms haven't occurred the way the theory predicted. Savings, investment, employment, and productivity didn't increase after trickle-down policies were enacted, as a host of studies have shown.[68] And budget deficits skyrocketed when tax cuts didn't pay for themselves, contrary to the claims of trickle-down proponents.[69]

President Barack Obama has taken important first steps to take advantage of the opening provided by the failures of supply-side economics, arguing in several important speeches that "our economy doesn't grow from the top down; it grows from the middle out."[70] Importantly, President Obama has presented his argument as a direct challenge to the underpinnings of supply-side, stating that "we need to dispel the myth that the goals of growing the economy and reducing inequality are necessarily in conflict."[71] President Obama has even begun to explain some of the mechanisms of middle-out economics, noting, for example, the importance of middle-class consumer demand to the economy.[72] And a number of progressive governors and other rising political leaders have started to make similar arguments.[73]

These speeches have challenged supply-side economics in a way previous criticism has not. Previous criticism attacked supply-side indirectly—arguing, for example, that tax cuts make it harder to pay for important investments in education—but did not directly challenge the basic premise that the rich are job creators, or provide a comprehensive, alternative theory of economic growth.

But, even in the face of a direct challenge, supply side will not die easily because it is deeply ingrained in the thinking of both political parties. Supply side dominates the Republican Party and a number of leading independents and Democrats subscribe to its logic. Indeed, since the 1970s, taxes have been cut much more sharply for the rich than they have for the middle class, not just because of Republicans, but in large part because Democrats also supported these policies.[74] Certainly many Democrats opposed these changes, but Democrats often provided the critical support necessary for the proposals to become law.[75] President Bill Clinton, for example, signed into law a bill lowering capital gains taxes, which dramatically reduced taxes on the wealthy, especially the very wealthy, while doing little for the middle class—though he of course also increased income taxes in opposition to trickle-down orthodoxy.[76]

Further, trickle-down logic can frequently be heard in the statements of prominent politicians who are not part of the Republican Party. To take just a few examples: Andrew Cuomo, Democratic governor of New York, said that tax cuts for business and individuals are "the centerpiece" of his agenda, and his announcement of a commission to study how to do so was seen as the kickoff to his reelection campaign in 2014.[77] In 2013, Independent Michael Bloomberg argued that increasing the number of billionaires in New York City—even though it would increase inequality—would be a "godsend" because "they're the ones that spend a lot of money in the stores and restaurants and create a big chunk of our economy."[78] Douglas Gansler, a Democratic candidate for governor in Maryland in 2014, announced that he planned to cut taxes on business to help generate growth, according to his campaign.[79]

Trickle-down logic is also endlessly repeated in the media, where it is often accepted as fact. A recent study by Occidental College political scientist Peter Dreier and University of Northern Iowa communications professor Christopher Martin found that between 2009 and 2011 four elite media outlets (the *AP*, *Wall Street Journal*, *New York Times*, and *Washington Post*) frequently quoted people using the term "job killer" or used the term without attribution.[80] In over 90 percent of cases, the media failed to provide evidence to back the claim and simply bought into supply-side dogma. Leading issues portrayed as job killers were proposals to increase taxes on business and the wealthy or to raise the minimum wage. That proposals to raise revenue for schools and roads or put more money in the pockets of workers were portrayed in such a negative light is exactly what we would expect after over 30 years of trickle-down economics.

As a result, it is fair to say that the trickle-down worldview has impacted policymaking for more than three decades. Not only is trickle-down still lodged firmly in place, but since the Great Recession, adherents of supply side have doubled down on their policies. The rhetoric supply-siders use may be shifting to be more supportive of the middle class, but their policies have gotten more extreme.

Republican presidential candidate Mitt Romney ran against Obama in 2012 by proposing tax cuts for the wealthy that were far larger than the cuts enacted by President George W. Bush.[81] The budget proposal by the House Republicans in 2013 would have provided bigger tax cuts to the wealthy than even the Romney plan.[82] Further, these federal proposals for additional tax cuts for the rich would likely have required tax increases on the middle class, according to a number of analyses.[83] Similarly, Republican governors like North Carolina's Pat McCrory, Kansas's Sam Brownback, Wisconsin's Scott Walker, and New Jersey's Chris Christie have recently proposed policies that cut taxes for businesses and the wealthy, but raise them on the middle class.[84] In contrast, supply-side proposals of the past cut taxes most dramatically for the wealthy, but still reduced taxes for most everyone.[85]

That supply-side supporters have become even more dogmatic in the aftermath of the Great Recession is not particularly surprising. American history shows that proponents of the dominant theory often do not admit the error of their ways, but rather become even more strident as evidence mounts that their logic has failed.

The prevailing economic philosophy during the late 1800s and early 1900s was called laissez-faire. Like supply side, laissez-faire was based on a belief that high levels of inequality were morally just and economically beneficial.[86] Laissez-faire's proponents similarly pushed for big tax cuts for the wealthy and little regulation of business.[87] Andrew Mellon, a wealthy banker and treasury secretary to a line of Republican presidents from Warren Harding to Calvin Coolidge to Herbert Hoover, exemplified the dominant thinking of his era, arguing that "high rates inevitably put pressure upon the taxpayer to withdraw his capital from productive business."[88]

Even the complete economic failure of the economy during the Great Depression did not change the thinking of proponents of laissez-faire. After the economy collapsed in 1929, supporters of laissez-faire continued to push their favored policies. The Great Depression was an opportunity to "purge the rottenness out of the system" according to Mellon and "liquidate labor, liquidate stocks, liquidate farmers"—further extending the economic power of the remaining rich.[89]

It took John Maynard Keynes developing an alternative understanding of the economy in 1936—explaining how the favored policies of laissez-faire were counterproductive because low levels of demand were causing the economy to remain stuck in a prolonged depression—and years of political debate to finally establish broad, popular support for a new, working theory of the economy.[90] Once the Keynesian perspective was firmly in place after World War II, it dominated American economic policymaking for a generation or more. Beginning with President Franklin Roosevelt, and continuing through President Richard Nixon, the Keynesian perspective prevailed.[91]

But, in the late 1970s, high levels of inflation (fueled largely by external oil shocks), combined with a high unemployment rate, provided an opening to challenge Keynesian economics. Followers of Keynes were unprepared to deal with these problems and had lost credibility because they had helped exacerbate inflation by promoting governmental stimulus during times of full employment—contrary to Keynes's argument that government stimulus was only for recessions while balanced budgets should be maintained at other times.[92] As the economy soured in the late 1970s, supply side garnered a growing base of political supporters and seemed to have more compelling answers.[93] For several years, followers of Keynes and supply side battled, but with the election of Ronald Reagan as president and the passage of his economic agenda through Congress, supply side replaced Keynesian economics and became the prevailing view of policymakers.

Now, there is clearly an opening to challenge supply side. But the theory continues to have great political influence not just because it has powerful supporters, but more fundamentally because an alternative theory has not yet replaced it. Without a different way of understanding the economy, politicians hang on to what they know. Too many politicians today continue to push supply-side policies that exacerbate the economy's woes, just as politicians did in the aftermath of the Great Depression when they championed laissez-faire policies that further weakened the economy. As Keynes explained in the 1930s: "Practical men, who believe themselves to be quite exempt from any intellectual influences, are usually the slaves of some defunct economist."[94] Ideas—both when they are right and when they are wrong—are often more powerful than vested interests.[95]

Replacing supply side will of course take a fight. But more than that, it requires understanding why it hasn't worked and why middle out does a better job. Political speeches are an important part of this educational process, but they cannot convey the wealth of information supporting middle out.

This book explains what's behind middle-out economics.

A handful of important books have highlighted elements of middle out—most notably explaining how a strong middle class is critical to maintaining adequate demand—but the divergent research disciplines that contribute to middle-out economics have not been fully explored.[96] As this book explains, not only is inadequate consumer demand causing businesses to hold back on hiring, but the decline of the middle class is causing a host of other problems that for too long have been hidden from view. The decline of the middle class is undermining trust, driving poor government performance, and restricting human capital— all of which are harming the economy. Further, this book provides concrete examples of how the US economy has been harmed by extreme levels of inequality. The weakening of the middle class has led to a rapid rise in the percentage of security guards and lawyers, corporations increasingly focusing on short-term results, a measurable growth in corruption in government, reduced spending on public goods like infrastructure, and the United States falling behind our international competitors on a host of measures of human capital including education, health, entrepreneurship, and mobility, not to mention the collapse of the economy during the Great Recession. Moreover, *Hollowed Out* explains the political significance of these facts.

The claims of middle out are grounded in time and place. And the argument for middle-out economics is grounded in reality, rather than abstract theory.

Defenders of trickle-down often make universal claims—that tax cuts are needed no matter how low taxes are, that higher levels of inequality are good no matter the level. And to shut down debate, they sometimes resort to arguments about how perfect equality, where everyone has the same amount of money, would stifle growth. Indeed, Paul Ryan, Republican nominee for vice president in 2012 and current chair of the powerful House Ways and Means Committee, falsely argues that opponents of trickle-down maintain an "insistence on equality of outcome."[97] Similarly, "Imagine a society with perfect economic equality" is the first line of an article from 2013 titled "Defending the One Percent" by Greg Mankiw, a Harvard economist and the former chief economic advisor to President George W. Bush and Republican presidential nominee Mitt Romney.[98]

Of course, communism or absolute equality of conditions would reduce growth by stifling incentives. Just as perfect inequality, where one person held all of society's wealth, would reduce growth because no one would have any money to buy anything. Equality is good up to a point, just as inequality is good up to a point.

The real question is whether the current, extremely high levels of economic inequality are hurting the US economy. The answer is a resounding yes. As *Hollowed Out* will explain, the economy is an interrelated system of people, laws, and culture that has been destabilized by extreme levels of inequality and a weakened middle class. For the economy to work properly, we need to rebuild the middle class and make sure everyone has an opportunity to succeed.

CHAPTER TWO

Trust

The small town of Chiaromonte in southern Italy is nestled into the mountains, surrounded by fields, olive trees, small vineyards, and oak forests. The climate is quite mild, usually in the mid-80s in the summer and above freezing during the winter. Despite this postcard-perfect setting, life is bleak, as Harvard political scientist Edward Banfield explained in his classic book *The Moral Basis of a Backward Society*. Most residents are quite poor and have little chance to get ahead. Employees live in fear of being cheated by their employers. There are no banks in town or other sources of credit to help famers purchase fertilizer or irrigation equipment. Farmers refuse to seek out unused land to rent—even though doing so would be profitable—because they are afraid that the landowners would somehow gain an unfair advantage.

The problem is not lawlessness. The town has strong laws—indeed, cutting down a neighbors' tree could result in a six-month jail sentence—and police officers patrol the town to the enforce the laws. But laws and their enforcement are not enough to get over the hurdles necessary for people to do business together.

The problem in Chiaromonte is that residents don't trust one another. They do not trust others and are untrustworthy themselves. Inhabitants think only of their short-term gains, are willing to do anything to get ahead, and assume others will do likewise. Residents are, as Banfield explained, unable to join forces for "any end transcending the immediate material interest of the nuclear family."[1]

Trust is part of the foundation necessary for a strong economy because it enables people to cooperate. While the United States is not Chiaromonte by any stretch, trust has declined precipitously in America over the past several decades in significant part because economic inequality has risen so sharply.[2] High levels of economic inequality increase the social distances between people and social distance makes it harder for people to believe that people share the similar experiences and values that are the basis of trust.[3]

As people's income levels move further and further apart, they tend to live in different neighborhoods, shop at different stores, drive different cars, send their kids to different schools, vacation in different ways, and have different relationships to work, different concerns, and different lives. They do not relate to one another on as many levels as they did when income levels were more similar and, critically, they think that others are different from them. As Philip Keefer and Stephen Knack, economists at the World Bank, explain, "When social distance grows ... confidence in the inherent trustworthiness of others weakens."[4]

The decline of trust in America has had profoundly negative consequences on the country's economy. That's because virtually every economic transaction involves some degree of trust.

Employers must trust that workers will give a good effort and workers must trust that employers won't try to take advantage of them. The consumer needs to trust that the producer will provide a properly functioning product. The producer must trust that the consumer will pay for what they have ordered, and that their suppliers will deliver parts when needed. In turn, the suppliers must trust that the producer will pay their bills at the end of the month and not steal their intellectual property. The bank that lent the producer money must trust that the company will repay them. And investors must trust that the executive they hire will work in the best interests of the company.

Participants in these transactions can sometimes take actions to protect themselves if they fear the other side won't hold up its end of the bargain, but doing so is costly. A lawsuit, for example, would probably cost the consumer far more than the value of the product they purchased. Even where larger sums of money are involved—such as with a bank loan—lawsuits are still expensive and at times can be prohibitively so. Short of a lawsuit, participants can closely monitor the behavior of the other party for any sign of a breach. Or they can try to write an ironclad contract that addresses every possible contingency. But, as Nobel Prize–winning economist Oliver Williamson has pointed out, it is impossible to cover every important matter in a contract because something will always come up that wasn't fully and explicitly covered.[5]

All these actions—monitoring and writing contracts—take time and money.[6] Further, they can even lead to perverse outcomes, as only the actions that are rewarded with incentives or spelled out in a contract occur, while other important activities are ignored. And perhaps worst of all, lack of trust can make some transactions so costly as to preclude them from taking place.

Economists call these types of expenses transaction costs. Transaction costs are a bit like grit in the gears of a machine: grit slows the machine down, preventing it from operating at maximum efficiency, and can even completely clog up the gears, stopping the machine cold.

There are transaction costs in virtually all economic activities. Searching for a reliable product to purchase, negotiating a fair price, and making sure the other party does what they are supposed to all require time and money. As a result, reducing transaction costs has a big economic payoff.[7]

Lawyers provide a good illustration of transaction costs at work. While lawyers can supply critical services to businesses and individuals, their work is essentially a transaction cost. They are an expense that is necessary to complete a particular action, such as buying a business, but their involvement does not add new additional value to the transaction. Not surprisingly, as trust has declined in America, the use of lawyers has skyrocketed.

Trust lowers the cost of doing business and makes the economy more efficient by reducing transaction costs. Trust can even help facilitate innovation by reducing people's fear that they will be taken advantage of if they take a risk and try something new. That's because trust acts as a social lubricant that helps people do business together. As a *Wall Street Journal* column on the importance of trust put it: "You don't hand money or make promises to somebody unless you think that person is going to make good on his promises."[8] Thus, a culture of trust provides an essential underpinning to a well-functioning economy.

Unfortunately, the increased legalization of the economy is just the beginning of the considerable costs imposed by declining levels of trust. As the rest of this chapter will show, because of the decline in trust the percentage of security guards in the

US workforce has nearly doubled and short-termism among shareholders and CEOs has accelerated. But before getting to these examples, the chapter will first cover some basics about trust. It will explain in more detail what trust is and why economists typically ignored it. It will show that trust has decreased and that inequality is responsible for much of the decline.

WHAT IS TRUST AND WHERE DOES IT COME FROM?

While trust may feel like a bit of an amorphous concept to study, there is a large body of research on the subject. There are a number of different kinds of trust—trust in family members, for example. But the kind of trust with the most direct impact on the economy is trust in strangers—the kind of trust that was lacking in Chiaromonte. Trust in other people in society is what helps people work together beyond their close circle of friends and family and enables positive economic interactions. (Trust also impacts the economy through its role in improving the quality of governance, as will be discussed in chapter 3.)

Academics describe trust as the belief that most other people in a society will do right most of the time, behaving reliably and with integrity. As Stanford political economist Francis Fukuyama puts it, trust is the "expectation that arises within a community of regular, honest, cooperative behavior."[9]

To some economists—trained to think of humans as acting based purely on self-interest—the existence of trust is puzzling. Why don't people always cheat when they think they can get away with it? Why would anyone put themselves in a vulnerable position and trust that a stranger will behave fairly? In other words, why doesn't everyone act like the residents of Chiaromonte?

A partial answer comes from a branch of economics—often called game theory—that shows that people can take a longer-term view of their self-interest and cooperate with others. In relationships where people interact repeatedly, people often realize that their long-term interest is best served by coordinating with others. Still, even this more advanced view of human behavior by economists often misses some critical points. Humans are, of course, sometimes selfish, as the typical economic models maintain. But we also have other motivations—and these motivations are essential for trust to develop. Further, trust is more likely to develop under certain conditions, yet most economic theories have little to say about the underlying societal conditions that make trusting behaviors more likely.

Trust can exist because humans are wired to receive social cues and act in a reciprocal manner.[10] When people are treated fairly, they generally respond in kind, and when they are treated poorly, they retaliate. We are made in a way that enables trust to develop.

Scholars of evolution think that the process of acting reciprocally was a successful adaptation for societies.[11] When people acted in a reciprocal manner, they could work together—and societies that could work together had a survival advantage. This survival advantage, repeated over long periods of time in human evolution, embedded reciprocity into human behavior. As Peter Richerson and Robert Boyd, at UC Davis and Arizona State respectively, argue, evolutionary processes have made humans "contingent cooperators."[12] That is, reciprocity is not just a successful strategy in a game for self-interested individuals; reciprocity enabled humans to outcompete other species and is imprinted deep in human behavior.

It is worth quoting from Richerson and Boyd at length because they concisely explain how evolutionary forces created the conditions possible for trust to thrive. They note that humans are selfish, but also have a deep tendency toward reciprocal behavior: "Humans have evolved a social psychology that mixes a strong element of cooperative dispositions, deriving from group selection on cultural variation, with an equally strong selfish element deriving from more ancient primitive dispositions.... We are contingent cooperators. Few will continue cooperating when others do not. The effectiveness of our cooperation is *not* just a product of our social psychology; rather our social psychology creates evolutionary forces that build *cultural systems of morality and convention* that, in turn, make possible sophisticated systems of cooperation such as businesses." This human tendency for reciprocal action helps establish societal norms and values. Reciprocity encourages people to believe that other people are like them, share similar values, and will behave in a similar, moral fashion. Thus trust depends on the morality that is enabled by humans' reciprocal nature.[13]

Repaying a kindness with a kindness, of course, establishes trust. But to establish a culture of trust, where good reciprocal actions dominate, people also need to be willing to punish those who act in untrustworthy ways—reciprocating against the violation even when doing so may be against their self-interest because it involves a cost of time or money. Thus, self-interest alone is not enough to create a trusting environment. Without punishment, there would be a significant advantage to breaking the rules, and more and more people would act in this manner, creating conditions where trusting behaviors would make little sense.

Reciprocal actions are readily observed every day, where kindness is repaid with kindness and threats with threats.[14] Marketing companies are well aware of the tendency to reciprocate, and they often offer free trial products or send a small gift in a solicitation for donations, knowing that people feel some obligation to reciprocate.If humans were only motivated by self-interest, these inducements wouldn't work very well.

Economists Ernst Fehr and Simon Gachter argue that humans act based on reciprocity more frequently than they do based on pure self-interest—indeed, their analysis of a long line of experimental research found that about twice as many subjects acted based on reciprocity as behaved completely selfishly.[15] One of the key experiments Fehr and Gachter cite—one that has been repeated hundreds of times in a number of countries—is a bargaining game that requires subjects to agree on how to divide up a sum of money they are given. One person can propose how to divide up the money, and the other person can either accept or reject the offer. If the offer is rejected, neither party receives any money. If humans were purely self-interested, the recipient should accept any offer of free money, no matter how unequal the split. But in these experiments people commonly reject offers that they perceive as unfair. That's because people are reciprocal: they are quite willing to go against their own self-interest to punish their partner for an unfair split.

Other kinds of experiments find that people often trust others and reciprocate a kindness with a kindness. A common experimental "investment" game gives one person a sum of money and the opportunity to give some of it to their (typically unknown) partner.[16] Any money given to the partner will be doubled or tripled, according to the rules of the game, and any portion of that sum can be returned to the giver.

Whether the first person gives money to the second is considered a sign of trust, and whether the second person returns money is considered trustworthy behavior. The idea is that both parties can do well by working together, but individuals can also do quite well by behaving selfishly and keeping all the money to themselves. These kinds of studies have been repeated numerous times in a number of different settings with both large and small amounts of money. Researchers find that people frequently give money to their partner and the partner commonly returns a significant portion.

Importantly, the experiments Fehr and Gachter review often involved strangers in a single interaction, who never meet and can only observe the behaviors of the other subject, indicating that the reciprocal behaviors are not about a direct personal relationship, where people might expect some personal gain, or even about a longer-term view of their self-interest; rather, reciprocity is a general human orientation.

Because people are oriented toward both positive and negative reciprocity—repaying a kindness with a kindness, a slight with a slight—trust can thrive in some societies. Trust begets trust, as people act with reciprocity toward one another, helping create a virtuous circle. Yet trust does not thrive equally in all societies.

That is because trust is undermined by economic inequality, turning the virtuous circle into a vicious cycle where untrustworthy behaviors lead to even less trust. Certainly trust depends upon a number of factors—from individual experiences and background to the quality of a country's legal system and the level of racial and ethnic homogeneity—but inequality is of critical importance. Indeed, according to University of Maryland political scientist Eric Uslaner, inequality is the most important factor in determining the level of trust in others in a society.[17]

HOW INEQUALITY UNDERMINES TRUST

Inequality weakens the foundations of trust in a number of ways. Most fundamentally, economic inequality increases social separation and reduces the common values and experiences people share.[18] The more similarities individuals think they have and the more they interact, the more they are able to act based on reciprocity rather than pure self-interest and to trust one another.[19] When people have relatively similar economic situations, they think others are like them and act based on trust. But economic inequality pulls people apart socially and makes them less trusting and trustworthy, creating a cycle of lower trust begetting lower trust.

The attitudes and behaviors of people from all economic classes are affected by social separation, but the impact may be especially pronounced on the behaviors of those at the top, whose great economic resources can isolate them from the rest of society. "Greater resources, freedom, and independence from others among the upper class give rise to self-focused social-cognitive tendencies," according to research by University of California social psychologist Paul Piff and his colleagues that found affluent people more likely to lie in negotiations, cheat to win a prize, and endorse unethical behavior at work.[20]

One of the clearest ways to see that inequality harms trust is through laboratory experiments such as the investment game described above where a person is given a sum of money and the opportunity to give some of it to their (typically unknown) partner, who can in turn return some of the gift. In a particularly important study, the level of inequality was varied to tease out its effect on trust. In the study, participants were divided into three groups: in one group incomes were equal, in another incomes varied considerably but participants were unaware of these differences, and in the third participants were made aware of the differences in income. The researchers found that pairs with greater levels of economic inequality between them behaved more selfishly, giving and receiving less in the games. As the study authors explained: "Inequality, particularly when it is known, has a corrosive effect on trusting behaviors."[21]

We can also see that inequality reduces trust and trustworthiness through more realistic experiments, such as those that leave a wallet on the ground and observe whether it is returned. Places where a higher proportion of wallets are returned are thought to have more trustworthy people and to be more trusting. One such experiment placed wallets containing $50 worth of cash in dozens of different cities in Europe and the United States.[22] In countries with relative economic equality such as Norway and Denmark, 100 percent of the wallets were returned. In the United States, with its higher levels of inequality, around two-thirds of wallets were returned, about the same percentage as in Great Britain, where inequality is nearly as high as in the United States.[23] Real-world observations that are not part of an experiment also confirm that inequality is linked to lower levels of trust. Cheating on term papers, for example, is more likely in US states where economic inequality is high.[24]

But most studies of trust measure it through survey questions—asking respondents, for example, if they think most people can be trusted or whether cheating on taxes or failing to report an accident with a parked car can be justified. These studies then use advanced statistical analyses to control for other factors that affect trust, such as overall income and education levels as well as racial and ethnic diversity. In comparisons across countries, as well as US states, these studies consistently find that economic inequality is linked to lower levels of trust.[25]

Polls show, for example, that in US states with relatively strong middle classes, such as Minnesota and North Dakota, the percentage of residents who say that most people can be trusted is double that of those in less equal states such as Kentucky and Arkansas.[26] Polls also show that people in the relatively economically equal Scandinavian countries of Norway, Sweden, and Denmark express the highest levels of trust in the world, while the United States ranks below not only the top, but also other rich—but more equal—countries, such as Australia, the Netherlands, and Germany.[27]

Further, the trends over time also suggest that inequality shapes the level of trust in a society.[28] As the middle class has declined and inequality has risen over the past few decades in the United States, trust levels have fallen sharply. In 2012, only 32 percent of Americans thought that most people could be trusted, down from 47 percent in 1973.[29] Similarly, in Britain trust also fell over this time period as inequality rose almost as sharply as in the United States. In contrast, in countries where inequality remained flat or did not rise nearly as much—such as Sweden, Denmark, Australia, and Germany—trust levels remained steady and in some cases even increased.[30] Looking back even further than the early 1970s—which is difficult because there is very little polling about trust from this period—the evidence also suggests that economic equality and trust go together. In what may be the only cross-country survey of trust from the 1960s, America, when it was more equal, ranked higher on measures of trust than any of the other four countries surveyed—the United Kingdom, Germany, Mexico, and Italy.[31] Much further back, well before public polling, when Alexis de Tocqueville studied the United States in the early 1800s, he was struck by how America's relative economic equality helped people trust one another enough to work together to achieve larger, common goals—something that was quite unusual in his native France, where inequality was much higher.[32]

To be sure, the relationship between trust and inequality in the United States is not as simple as these results make it seem. Perceptions of inequality, as well as the actual level, matter.[33] There are also likely interaction effects between trust and inequality: inequality not only leads to lower levels of trust, but low levels of trust can exacerbate inequality. Without trust, those at the economic bottom of society are more likely to be marginalized and blocked from participating in the economy, further increasing inequality.

Further, inequality is not the sole cause of declining trust. There has been a dramatic increase in racial and ethnic diversity over the past several decades—fueled largely by immigration—that must be factored into the story. Growing racial and ethnic diversity makes it easier for people to think that others are not like them and thus are untrustworthy, and it has been critically important to the fall in trust, as a number of studies show.[34] But these studies not only typically find that both inequality and diversity are important factors that shape trust levels; growing diversity often affects trust through its interaction with economic inequality. As Christian Larsen, a professor of politics at Aalborg University in Denmark, explains, ethnic diversity doesn't have a large effect on its own; rather, "it is the interaction between ethnic divides and economic inequality that can lower trust levels."[35]

A closer look at the actual trends indicates that America's growing diversity is unlikely to explain the decline in trust by itself and that inequality has played a key role. In the early 1970s, the United States was among the more diverse countries in the developed world, but trust levels in the United States were quite high by international standards.[36] In addition, many other countries have experienced rising racial and ethnic diversity over recent decades, but not all have experienced a decline in trust. Trust declines have been most pronounced in those countries that have also had rising inequality. For example, over the past several decades, the United States and Britain have both become more diverse, more economically unequal, and less trusting. But Denmark and Sweden have seen increases in immigration at least as large as those in the United States and Britain, but have not experienced similar declines in trust. Over the past three decades, the share of the Danish population that was immigrants more than tripled and demographic changes were as dramatic in Sweden.[37] Indeed, Sweden now has a higher share of foreign-born residents than the United States.[38] If racial and ethnic diversity was the key driver of trust, these stark demographic changes should have led to a precipitous decline in trust. But because the level of economic equality in Denmark and Sweden remained high, trust levels did too.[39]

So while growing ethnic diversity is likely to explain some of the decline in trust in the United States over the past several decades, inequality was a key factor, as the survey and experimental evidence shows. Economic inequality—both on its own and through its interaction with increasing racial diversity—created social distances that made other people seem less trustworthy.

MEASURING THE ECONOMIC IMPORTANCE OF TRUST

The economic importance of trust was recognized by some of the most respected thinkers in the discipline's history. John Stuart Mill, the canonical nineteenth-century political economist, argued in *Principles of Political Economy,* published in 1848: "The advantage to mankind of being able to trust one another penetrates into every crevice and cranny of human life: the economical is perhaps the smallest part of it, yet even this is incalculable."[40] Similarly, Kenneth Arrow, who won the Nobel Prize in economics in 1972, wrote that the lack of trust can plausibly explain "much of the economic backwardness in the world."[41]

Unfortunately, these insights were largely ignored by economists over the past several decades. Instead, economists emphasized models based on self-interested individuals acting "rationally" that ignored societal influences on behavior and failed to accurately capture human nature. Cultural issues such as trust were "gradually pushed to the fringes or removed completely from the body of economic thought," as a review of the subject put it.[42] Just as trust was declining precipitously in the United States, this critical foundation of growth was ignored by many economists—not to mention many politicians.

Thankfully, in recent years a large and growing number of economists—as well as academics in other disciplines such as political science—have focused on measuring the economic importance of trust. And their research finds that trust makes a big economic impact.

Studies that look at individual behaviors show that people who live in higher trust areas are more likely to take economically beneficial actions, such as repaying their debts, investing their savings in the stock market rather than keeping it in cash, and using the more efficient formal banking sector rather than informal sources of credit.[43] Workers that trust their coworkers and superiors are more likely to engage in cooperative behavior that helps the firm, such as working harder.[44] There have also been a number of studies that find that companies with higher levels of trust are more economically successful, with higher levels of productivity, profitability, and stock returns.[45] Indeed, a review of 21 different academic studies on trust in firms and households found that the results were "unambiguous" that trust improves economic performance.[46]

Studies that look at economic growth across countries also find that trust is vital. For example, Philip Keefer and Stephen Knack, of the World Bank, compare economic growth in a number of countries and show that countries with higher levels of trust have greater economic growth, even when controlling for other factors that influence growth such as education and prior income levels. They argue that "the effects of trust on growth turn out to rival those of ... primary education."[47] Education is generally seen by economists as one of the most important contributors to growth, as will be discussed at length in chapter 5. So results like this suggest that trust packs a big punch.[48] Though not every study finds that trust is as economically important as education, even critical reviews of these cross-country studies tend to find that trust boosts economic growth.[49]

It is worth pointing out that most of the cross-country studies that find that trust has a particularly large impact include both rich and developing countries, and thus researchers, despite their best efforts, could be getting their results because of other differences between developed and developing countries. However, this possibility is unlikely because several studies focusing just on rich countries or regions in rich countries find that trust fosters economic growth.[50] Further, research that focuses only on the United States comes to the same conclusion. In studies of US states and counties, areas with higher levels of trust have stronger economies.[51] And a study of economic growth in America over the past century finds that changes in levels of trust explain "a substantial part" of the changes in growth.[52] Finally, most of the studies of firms and individuals discussed previously that find that trust is economically important were conducted in advanced countries.

HOW LOW LEVELS OF TRUST ARE HARMING THE US ECONOMY

While the research strongly suggests that declining levels of trust have harmed the US economy, it is worth digging deeper into some specific details to help illustrate the problem. Trust and its relationship to the economy can feel a bit amorphous without some concrete examples. Though attributing specific economic harm to a broad social change like the decline in trust is difficult, there are some telling examples that are highly likely to have been caused by the sharp reduction in trust over the past few decades. As mentioned in the introduction to this chapter, the increase in the use of lawyers in recent decades provides a simple illustration of how the decline in trust has harmed the economy. Lawyers are a transaction cost: for the most part, they don't increase the productivity of the economy or boost society's wealth; they simply help ensure that the rules are followed.[53] In this way, lawyers may do important work, but it is work that adds to the cost of doing business. Money spent on lawyers means less money for other, more productive transactions. And on occasion, lawyers can even prevent business transactions that would otherwise occur from happening. The costs of hiring a lawyer, for example, can completely block some business deals. Even worse, lawyers can sometimes do less admirable work. Frivolous lawsuits, for example, impose costs, and fear of them can shrink business opportunities.

An economy requires fewer lawyers when participants trust one another. When there is a degree of trust in society, people can spend less time and money monitoring the performance of others and expend less effort protecting themselves from being exploited. People feel that most other people—even if they don't know them—are likely to live up to their end of the bargain. In fact, a study by University of Wisconsin law professor Stewart Macaulay of business relationships in the 1960s—when societal trust was still relatively high—found lawyers frequently complaining that businesses trusted too much and did too many deals without a formal contract.[54] According to Macaulay's study of business practices, lawyers in the 1960s complained that they were "sick of being told, 'We can trust old Max.'"

But when people don't trust that the other side will act reciprocally and honor its obligations, they are likely to hire more lawyers. And once people stop trusting one another, the use of lawyers increases almost without end. Each party feels the need to protect themselves from the other side taking advantage of the rules—and once one party hires a lawyer, the other party is at a disadvantage unless they hire a lawyer. As Princeton University economist Orley Ashenfelter and his colleagues, Harvard's David Bloom and UC San Diego's Gordon Dahl, argue in their study of arbitration cases, the "use of lawyers becomes nearly universal, despite the fact that agreeing not to hire lawyers is cheaper and does not appear to alter arbitration outcomes."[55]

Not surprisingly, as trust has decreased over the past several decades, the number of lawyers has increased sharply. In 1970, there were 48 lawyers out of every 10,000 workers.[56] By 2012, 94 out of every 10,000 workers were lawyers, meaning that the number of lawyers doubled as a share of the workforce.

Over recent decades the economy has increasingly shifted away from manufacturing toward service and professional occupations, but the rise of lawyers stands out.[57] The doubling of the share of lawyers over the past 40 years is a dramatic change from previous trends and unlike what has happened to many other professions. The share of lawyers in the economy had been "rock-steady" since the early 1900s, according to Robert Putnam, a Harvard political scientist, but it started to increase "just as trust and social capital started to decline."[58] In contrast, other professions like doctors, airplane pilots, and engineers have not increased to a similar degree—indeed, the share of engineers in the workforce has declined.[59] As Putnam explains, "The jump in lawyers per capita is not simply a reflection of a general increase in professionals in America; it is unique to lawyers."

Still, it is important to note that there are many other possible reasons for the increase in lawyers besides the decline in societal trust, from changes in government regulation, to international trade, to growing urbanization and increasing ethnic and racial diversity.[60] Each of these alternative explanations has some merit and likely explains part of the trend. But there are holes in the alternative explanations that strongly suggest the decline in trust is an important part of the story.

Since 1970, government regulation has expanded into new areas, such as environmental protections, creating greater demand for lawyers.[61] However, at other times when government expanded into new areas—such as healthcare in the 1960s when Medicare and Medicaid were created—the share of lawyers in the workforce remained the same.[62] Similarly, the trend of increasing international trade created a greater need to understand rules in different countries and likely boosted the demand for lawyers.[63] Yet the data indicate that other countries with similar increases in global trade have not had as great a rise in the percentage of lawyers. International comparisons are tricky because the available data are not great and countries often categorize their legal professions differently, but the data suggest that during the mid-1980s the number of lawyers as a share of the population in the United States was in the middle of the pack of other developed countries, but by the 2000s the United States had pulled well ahead.[64] These trends indicate that trade was not solely responsible and instead indicate that something particular to the United States was a leading factor.

Likewise, the increasing urbanization of the country has brought people in closer contact, which may increase the demand for lawyers. But, even in urban areas, cities with greater levels of inequality tend to have more lawyers.[65] Cities such as Miami and New Orleans, for example, have far more lawyers as a share of their workforce than the more equal Portland and Indianapolis.[66]

The growing racial and ethnic diversity in the United States has created additional potential for conflict and likely increased the need for lawyers to resolve issues between groups. Growing diversity is part of the story, far more so than the other alternative explanations, but the data don't support it as a standalone cause. For example, some American states like New Mexico, Hawaii, and Arizona that have a very high percentage of nonwhite residents and have experienced dramatic increases in diversity over recent decades don't have particularly high percentages of lawyers in the workforce.[67] In contrast, some racially homogenous states like Vermont have a relatively high share of lawyers.

Not only do the data call into question the strength of alternative explanations, but the logic behind them also weakens on closer inspection. Changes in demographics, trade patterns, and regulation do not automatically lead people to hire so many more lawyers. If people trusted one another more, these changes could have been met, at least partly, with nonlegal responses. As Harvard Law professor Robert Clark explains, a complete answer to why the share of lawyers in the workforce has increased needs to explain why the demand was not satisfied by "non-legal sources of order, such as the family, informal social groups, market forces, and the major religions."[68] The decline in trust provides such an explanation, and certainly a better one than the alternatives.

The increase in the share of lawyers in the workforce has done great harm to the US economy. One way to think about the cost is that if lawyers were the same percentage of workers in the economy as they were in 1970, there would be 614,000 fewer lawyers today. Lawyers have an average salary of around $130,000, implying that the increased use of lawyers costs the economy approximately $80 billion a year.[69]

That's a lot of money. It represents not only an additional cost of doing business, but money that could be used for other purposes. It could, for example, pay for about one-quarter of all research and development done by US firms each year.[70] It could also be used to hire other kinds of workers that boost the productivity of the economy, such as scientists and engineers. Several studies go as far as to argue that the ratio of engineers to lawyers in a country is a significant determinant of their overall growth rate.[71] In other words, the opportunity costs of hiring additional lawyers are very high, as these skilled workers could be used to help the economy if they were employed in different professions.

But lawyers not only impose additional costs to complete regularly planned transactions; they sometimes engage in actions that directly hinder productive economic activities, such as patent trolling—suing companies for supposed patent infringements and then negotiating payoffs or other settlements. While patent trolling has been around for decades, research indicates that it has increased in recent years.[72]

Just as the percentage of lawyers in the workforce has sky-rocketed in recent decades, so too has the percentage of private security guards employed to watch office buildings and malls and perform other security work.[73] From 1970 to 2012, the share of security guards in the workforce increased by 73 percent.[74] The increase in the security guard workforce is much faster than the increase in other occupations such as truck drivers, waiters, and hairdressers.[75] Indeed, the increase in security guards is significantly faster than the general rise in service occupations that has occurred over the past four decades.[76]

Unfortunately, private security guards, like lawyers, are largely a transaction cost. They don't add to the productivity of, for example, office buildings, but rather are a necessary expense for building managers seeking to attract customers to lease space.

The cost of the additional security guards can be thought of in several ways. First, there are the additional dollars spent on security guards: if security guards were the same share of the workforce as they were in 1970, the approximately $8.9 billion extra we spend on private security guards could be put to other, more economically beneficial uses.[77] Then there are indirect costs, such as the additional time it takes to deliver a package because delivery people must sign in with a security guard and the resources that are spent training security guards. While this extra time may be quite small for an individual package, when multiplied by millions of deliveries it can add up. Similarly, the skills and time of people training guards could be used for more productive activities.

The increase in security guards is at least partly attributable to what has happened to trust in the United States. As people lose trust in others, they feel an additional need for security guards to help make sure others behave properly. While other factors have also played a role, they cannot fully explain the trends. Increased crime rates during the 1960s and 1970s almost certainly contributed to part of the rise in the number of private security guards. But crime rates have declined in recent decades. Property crimes, such as burglary, increased sharply between 1960 and 1980 but started to decrease after that period and are now back down to the same level they were in the mid-1960s, according to Federal Bureau of Investigation crime statistics.[78] Violent crime rates display a similar trajectory. Yet even as crime rates fell, the share of security guards in the workforce remained high throughout the 1980s, 1990s, and 2000s. Similarly, rising ethnic diversity likely made people more fearful of others and contributed to the increase in security guards. Diversity is important, but it is not the whole story either. Indeed, some fairly diverse states like Alaska and North Carolina have relatively modest percentages of security guards, while more ethnically homogenous states like West Virginia and Pennsylvania have greater percentages of their workforces in private security.[79]

Rising crime rates, growing racial and ethnic diversity, and declining trust all have led to a precipitous rise in the number of security guards. Studies on the determinants of the size of private and public police forces in US cities find that crime rates, racial and ethnic diversity, and inequality all have independent effects on the percentage of the workforce in security.[80] Studies of the United States in comparison to other rich countries come to similar conclusions.[81] Further, many of the studies find that inequality is more strongly linked to the size of the guard force than any other factor. All of which strongly suggests that the decline in trust is likely a significant reason that the share of security guards in the workforce has risen so precipitously.[82]

Perhaps the most significant economic damage that the decline of trust has inflicted on our economy is in changing how public companies now operate: they are increasingly focused on short-term measures instead of long-term results. Low levels of trust contributed to short-termism by helping drive a counter-productive reaction to the oversight issues that arise between investors and corporate managers.[83] Investors—through their power over the board of directors—hire CEOs.[84] But investors cannot observe all the actions and efforts that CEOs take. Further, what is best for the CEO may not be best for investors. Both investors and CEOs are interested in increasing the company's profit, but the investors' primary economic goal is to maximize the return on their capital at the lowest risk, while the CEO's primary economic motivation is to make money for themselves by maximizing their salary and making sure they keep their job. Economists call these differences in interests and information a principal-agent problem.

When people are trustworthy and trusted to act fairly, principal-agent problems can recede into the background. They are still there, but are less important because people tend to behave properly. Further, trust can help people to arrive at more efficient solutions to principal-agent problems.[85] When there are higher levels of trust, employers and employees can, for example, agree on relatively high but flat rates of pay that benefit both parties: employees get some security knowing that they will still do well even if events outside their control conspire against them to make their efforts less productive, and employers receive high levels of effort but do not have to give up so much of their profits to receive them.[86]

But as trust levels in the United States have declined, investors have responded to the principal-agent problem by providing additional incentives for "correct" behaviors and by more closely monitoring outputs. Unfortunately, this response has had disastrous effects.

CEO contracts now increasingly use "performance" pay, providing large stock grants and options to executives on the belief that this will help align the incentives of executives with those of investors. One study estimated that incentive pay increased from roughly 50 percent of CEO compensation in 1992 to 78 percent in 2008.[87] Similarly, investors have also monitored CEOs much more closely than before, firing CEOs more rapidly, and focusing on short-term earnings statements. Average CEO tenure has dropped from about 10 years in the 1970s to about six years in the 2000s.[88] The number of companies that offered earnings guidance increased 13-fold between 1994 and 2001, according to a review of large companies by McKinsey & Company, a management consulting firm.[89]

Greater monitoring of corporate executives and more closely aligning their incentives with that of investors has had pernicious effects. Put another way, the typical response to a low-trust environment—greater monitoring and a focus on incentives—has had a harmful effect on long-term growth.

Not surprisingly, corporate executives have sacrificed long-term growth prospects in order to meet quarterly earnings targets, because they know their pay and job depend on meeting these short-term goals. A number of studies have shown that corporations cut spending on research and development, capital investments, and even basic repairs to meet earnings expectations.[90] Studies also indicate that executives use accounting tricks to hit financial targets in their contracts.[91] In addition to these harmful but legal efforts to reach earnings targets and keep stock prices high, the increase in short-term pressures has led to the willingness of some executives to bend or even break the law, according to some analysts.[92]

Not only can academics observe short-termism in companies' financial documents, but corporate executives describe the system working in this manner. A particularly revealing survey of corporate executives by Duke University finance professor John Graham and his colleagues found respondents to be quite open about how they were motivated to meet short-term earnings goals.[93] In the survey, 80 percent of chief financial officers stated that they would be willing to cut spending on research and development to meet an earnings target and a majority of executives said they would not start a new project that they knew would be profitable if it meant falling short of the current quarter's earnings consensus.

In short, everyone understands that closer monitoring and additional incentives have led executives to behave in ways that are harmful to the long-term growth of companies. As Alfred Rappaport, emeritus professor at Northwestern University's business school, wrote in *Saving Capitalism from Short Termism,* "Short-termism is a rational choice for … corporate managers whose job security, labor-market reputation, and compensation are tied to near-term performance."[94]

Not surprisingly, the most recent full business cycle—the recovery from 2001 to 2007—had the lowest levels of net business investment of any business cycle on record, while share repurchases and dividend payouts, which boost short-term stock prices, hit historic highs.[95]

There are of course other factors at work, but the decline of trust has clearly contributed to the increase in short-termism.[96]

When there are low levels of trust, increased monitoring and greater use of incentives are the textbook responses to the principal-agent problem. In addition, low trust plays a supporting role in other explanations for short-termism.

Certainly, the rise of the belief that a corporation's role is to maximize shareholder value fueled short-termism.[97] But underlying the theory of shareholder value is the basic principal-agent problem between shareholders and CEOs and the problem of trust.[98] According to the theory of shareholder value, shareholders can't trust corporate managers to maximize corporate value and thus need to exert greater influence over the perceived interests of CEOs. Thus, shareholder value is largely about a lack of trust.

The increase in institutional—as opposed to individual— stock ownership also drove short-termism. But having institutional owners of stocks, such as mutual funds, makes trust between parties even more important because it adds an additional complication to the principal-agent relationship.[99] Investors are still the principals but their agents are now mutual fund managers, who in turn oversee CEOs. If investors trusted that mutual fund managers would act in their best interest, mutual fund managers, over the past few decades, would have been judged on their long-term performance. But investors focused on their short-term results.[100] And because mutual fund managers understood they were being judged based on the short-term, they also put short-term pressures on CEOs.[101]

CONCLUSION

While trust may seem like a soft concept, it has a real impact on economics, something that trickle-down theory ignores. Trust is the foundation of a well-functioning economy: it helps people work together and makes business more efficient by reducing transaction costs. Without trust, people act like the residents of Chiaromonte, focused solely on their short-term self-interest, unable to cooperate to produce mutually beneficial outcomes. Functioning economies need both self-interested and trusting behavior. As Edward Banfield explained in his study of the small Italian town, self-interest "is a very good thing from an economic standpoint, provided it is not so extreme as to render concerted action altogether impossible."[102]

Unfortunately, economic inequality undermines trust because it pulls people apart socially. With fewer social bonds, people believe they have less in common and are thus less likely to trust and behave in trustworthy ways. As a result, trust levels have fallen sharply as the American middle class has weakened and the country has grown more unequal.

This decline in trust has caused significant harm to the American economy, greatly increasing transaction costs. From the sharp increase in the percentage of lawyers and security guards, to the shift to corporations increasingly focusing on short-term results, the signs of declining trust and their economic costs are readily apparent. Even worse, the hidden costs of declining trust—such as business deals not done and innovative ideas stifled—are possibly even higher.

CHAPTER THREE

Good Governance

The United States was founded as a reaction against English elites making rules that harmed the interests of ordinary Americans. Not surprisingly, our country's founders recognized that the new, democratic government they were creating would not work properly if society was polarized into extremes of wealth and poverty. A well-functioning democracy, Thomas Jefferson believed, depended on a base of self-sufficient small landholders—middle-class, yeoman farmers—with enough economic freedom and independence to be good citizens.[1] Similarly, James Madison thought that a large gulf between the rich and the poor would cause political conflict that would harm the quality of America's governance. As Madison wrote in *The Federalist Papers:* "The most common and durable source of factions has been the various and unequal distribution of property."[2]

Madison, Jefferson, and others embedded these ideas about inequality in the US Constitution, which forbade the granting of any title of nobility in order to prevent a new privileged class from arising in America.[3] After the Revolution, states passed a wave of laws blocking land from passing to a single heir, forcing a wider distribution of wealth and warding off a hereditary aristocracy.[4] As Michael Thompson, a political science professor at William Paterson University, explains: "The American idea of a democratic republic had always been premised on an antipathy toward unequal divisions of property because early American thinkers saw in those unequal shares of economic power echoes of what had been historically overturned: a sociopolitical order of rank and privilege."[5]

Since the country's founding, our most respected leaders have also feared the threat inequality poses to American democracy: from Andrew Jackson's veto of a national bank because he worried that it would give wealthy bankers excessive economic and political power, to Abraham Lincoln's understanding that slavery and economic inequality were fundamentally linked, to Theodore Roosevelt's fear that the robber barons were using their great wealth to control government, to Franklin Roosevelt's recognition during the Great Depression that "necessitous men are not free men."[6] Clearly, the worry that extreme economic inequality will undermine democracy is long-standing, and as American as apple pie.

What is new, however, is the growing recognition that by harming our democracy, inequality has weakened our economy.

For too many years, academic economists largely ignored the role that government plays in providing a foundation for the economy. Government, often called an "institution" by economists, did not fit neatly with theoretical models of how individuals acted and thus didn't receive much attention.[7] It was "left out" of economic analysis, as Douglass North, winner of the Nobel Prize in economics, explained.[8] Even worse than simply ignoring government, a number of economists rejected the idea that government regulations were needed to ensure certain markets functioned properly. For example, up until the financial collapse in 2007 and 2008, many economists mistakenly believed that government oversight of Wall Street was unnecessary because financial markets would efficiently police themselves.[9] This thinking was of course nonsense, but too many academics believed it.

Political supporters of supply-side economics have perhaps been even more blind to the critical role good government plays in making the economy work. Though supply-side supporters sometimes acknowledge that some types of government spending, such as on roads and schools, are important to the economy, they frequently denigrate all government—the good and the bad. As Ronald Reagan put it: "Government is not the solution to our problem; government is the problem."[10] Republican Senate Majority Leader Mitch McConnell echoes the same sentiment today when he says: "big government has made our economy worse."[11] Supply-siders also insist on tax cuts, especially for the wealthy, which reduces the amount of money available for these critical public goods—no matter the occasional lip service paid to them.

The obvious failures of many economists to properly understand that the quality of government is critical in determining the performance of an economy made room in the discipline for "new institutional economics," a growing branch of economics that looks closely at the rules of the economy set by government. Whose side the government is on—the wealthy elite's or the general public's—makes a big difference, determining, for example, whether people are educated, whether roads can move people and goods, and if rules are fair and adequately enforced. This basic point—that the quality of government strongly influences people and society and thus the economy—is finally gaining the attention it deserves in economics departments. As Douglass North, one of the founders of this growing movement, explains: "Institutions provide the framework within which human beings interact."[12]

There is now a large body of research showing that the quality of governance has a fundamental impact on economic growth.[13] To highlight just a few studies, the World Bank's Stephen Knack argues that "all of the evidence points in the same direction, i.e. that good governance is crucial for growth," while Princeton economist Dani Rodrik and his colleagues write that "the quality of institutions 'trumps' everything else" in determining a country's level of economic development.[14] Unfortunately, this research has generally been seen as relevant only to developing economies and not to the United States. But it is.

When economists study why government matters for economic growth, they find that some government actions, such as investments in education and infrastructure are quite helpful. Education and infrastructure increase economic productivity, but are underprovided by the private sector. So when the government spends money on these public goods, the whole economy tends to benefit. As Josh Bivens, an economist with the Economic Policy Institute, argues in his review of studies on public investments, there is "an enormous amount of economic evidence demonstrating that public investment is a significant long-run driver of productivity growth—and hence growth in average living standards."[15] Research by economists such as David Aschauer of Bates College and Alicia Munnell of Boston College, among others, finds that public investments in infrastructure complement private investments and boost economic growth.[16] Rather than crowding out private investment, public investment "crowds in" private capital and thus spurs growth. The economic importance of investments in education is similarly critical.[17] Princeton University economist Alan Krueger estimates that a year of schooling increases an individual's earnings by 10 percent, while Harvard economists Lawrence Katz and Claudia Goldin found that America's increasing educational attainment from 1915 to 1999 was responsible for a significant portion of GDP growth.[18]

Economists also note that some government actions can reduce growth. Here, they tend to focus on the harm done by "rent seeking"—special government help for special interests, such as purchasing things from government below cost, selling things to government above cost, selective enforcement of the law, and special protections.[19] These special favors waste tax dollars on unnecessary or inefficient projects, diverting economic resources away from more productive activities.[20] They can also block economic competition, for example, by giving monopoly power to politically connected companies. Finally, if rent seeking becomes pervasive, it can fundamentally alter the shape of the economy as economic resources are frequently marshaled in predatory ways instead of generating economic growth.

As Nobel Prize–winning economist Joseph Stiglitz writes: "In their simplest form, rents are nothing more than re-distributions from one part of society to the rent seekers.... But there is a broader economic consequence:... Efforts are directed toward getting a larger share of the pie rather than increasing the size of the pie. But it's worse than that: rent seeking distorts resource allocations and makes the economy weaker. It is a centripetal force: the rewards of rent seeking become so outsized that more and more energy is directed toward it, at the expense of everything else."[21]

An especially brazen and harmful form of rent seeking is corruption—the use of governmental powers by officials for self-enrichment.[22] Corruption stifles economic growth by making it much harder and more expensive to engage in ordinary economic activities such as opening a business or transporting goods.[23] Corruption is an extra burden on business transactions and, more maliciously, can protect certain businesses at the expense of potential competitors. Corruption particularly harms entrepreneurs who don't have the resources or the connections to grease the wheels of commerce with bribes.[24]

The problems of rent seeking and inadequate public investments are too often thought of as concerns for developing countries. Yet, if one looks at the United States with the same kind of scrutiny we give other countries, it is pretty easy to see they are problems here too. America's government is certainly better than in many other countries, but the same basic pattern of high levels of inequality leading to weak governance and inadequate growth so familiar in other parts of the world is playing out right here at home. Just as in developing countries, high levels of economic inequality have enabled wealthy elites to capture greater economic rents and decreased our ability to make adequate investments in schools and infrastructure.

Wall Street rent seeking is the emblematic example that suggests economic elites in the United States have power and influence approaching the level that in other countries we condemn and instantly recognize as economically harmful. Over the past few decades, Wall Street bankers used their wealth and power to successfully push for deregulation so they could enter into profitable but risky lines of business. But when this risk brought their large firms—and the economy—to the brink of collapse, they succeeded in getting the government to bail them out with nary a concession required, and against the recommendations the United States made for emerging market economies when they suffered banking crises.

The sad state of our roads, bridges, and public universities tells another critical part of the story of how inequality weakens the economy by undermining government. As the middle class has declined, the governments' ability make investments in public infrastructure has steadily diminished. Similarly, higher education spending has failed to keep pace with demand. Despite broad public support for spending on infrastructure and education and their significant economic benefits, America's political system has not made necessary investments because rising inequality has undermined the government's ability to respond to public needs. Just like in less developed countries, the rich have been able to secure policies that lock in the current level of development, while policies the middle class prefer would be good for the future of the whole country but haven't been enacted.

To make these arguments, this chapter will review the historical and international research showing how in highly unequal societies the wealthy have commonly used their disproportionate economic resources to control government and harm the economy. The chapter will then explain how in the United States today rising inequality has eroded the quality of governance by helping the rich gain political influence, increasing political polarization, and decreasing the country's "civicness." Finally, the chapter will show how these changes have led to special interest giveaways and inadequate public investments that have harmed the economy.

The idea that a strong middle class is important for a well-functioning government is central to a great deal of political science research, while the idea that the quality of governance has a profound impact on the economy has finally become well accepted in economics. Despite the obvious connections between these strands of research, they have rarely been brought together to examine government and economy in the United States. This chapter brings together these two well-established lines of research in a novel way to show how inequality has weakened the American government and economy.

INEQUALITY, UNDERMINING GOVERNMENT, AND THE ECONOMY THROUGHOUT HISTORY

In the early 1700s, when the New World was under the rule of colonial powers, the United States and Canada were poorer than many of the other colonies in the Americas, especially those in the Caribbean.[25] But over time the United States and Canada pulled far ahead of other countries in North and South America, presenting a great puzzle for economists to try to explain. Common explanations for the remarkable growth of the United States and Canada compared to their neighbors don't stand up to close scrutiny. Though the United States and Canada were both British colonies and thus shared similar structures and culture, this similarity is unlikely to explain their success because other British colonies in the region, such as Jamaica, Belize, and Guyana, grew very slowly. Similarly, both the United States and Canada have cooler climates than many other colonies. But so do countries like Argentina and Chile that did not grow until relatively recently and still lag behind.

Rather, what separated the United States and Canada from the other New World colonies was that they were more economically equal. Their economies (especially outside the US South) were based largely on small-scale farming and other small businesses, rather than, as in the other colonies, mass plantation agriculture and large-scale mining that fostered highly unequal societies. Because Canada and the United States were more equal, their governments evolved to be more democratic and thus provided greater access to public goods like education, which made all the difference for their future growth. The formerly wealthy but unequal colonies in other parts of the Americas remained stuck economically because elites controlled their governments and used their control to maintain power rather than invest in the development of the entire country. Put another way, because the United States and Canada were more economically equal, their governments were of much higher quality and thus their economies were able to grow much more rapidly, especially as the economy shifted away from an agricultural base.

As Kenneth Sokoloff, an economic historian at UCLA before he passed away, and Stanley Engerman, an economist at the University of Rochester, argue, the United States and Canada caught up to many of the other former colonies by the early 1800s and eventually far surpassed them because a greater share of their population was granted democratic rights and voters used their democratic rights to expand schooling and boost literacy, which enabled citizens to more fully participate in the economy.[26] The United States and Canada led the other former colonies in getting rid of wealth, property, and literacy restrictions that limited voting rights to a narrow elite and instead had much broader participation in their democracies. This greater participation by ordinary citizens led to much better policies on things like property rights protections, industrial development, access to land and other natural resources, and public provision of education. Public education was particularly important because it helped Canada and especially the United States have much higher literacy rates than the other former colonies. As Sokoloff and Engerman wrote: "Nearly all of the New World economies were sufficiently prosperous by the beginning of the nineteenth century to establish a widespread network of primary schools." But "few actually made investments on a scale sufficient to serve the general population." As a result, literacy rates in the United States and Canada reached 80 percent by the 1870s, over three times the rate of not only Cuba, but also Argentina, Brazil, Chile, and Jamaica—countries with much higher levels of economic inequality.

In the highly unequal colonies, elites used their power to create governments and economies that worked primarily for their benefit. As Sokoloff and Engerman explain: "Greater inequality in wealth contributed to the evolution of institutions that protected the privileges of the elites and restricted the opportunities for the broad mass of the population to participate fully in the commercial economy even after the abolition of slavery." Policies that the wealthy preferred tended to lock in the current level of development, while policies the middle class preferred—and was able to secure in the United States and Canada—were good for the future of the whole country.

MIT economist Daron Acemoglu and Harvard government professor James Robinson tell a similar story in their review of economic growth throughout the history of the world.[27] Venice, the authors argue, grew rich in the Middle Ages in part because it developed a financial contract that enabled ordinary citizens to raise money for sailing expeditions, and it prospered as these entrepreneurs developed markets. But it quickly sank back into obscurity as wealthy elites used their political power to curtail these contracts, pulling the ladder up with them to protect their profits by preventing new competitors. And in a more current example, the authors explain that Nogales, Arizona, has become relatively rich, while its neighbor Nogales, Sonora, has remained relatively poor, because over its history the government in the United States has been more responsive to its citizens' calls for better roads, schools, and public health than the Mexican government.

Research from economists using advanced statistical techniques comes to similar conclusions. These studies find that governments in unequal countries provide fewer public goods and give out more special favors, even when controlling for a host of factors that are also thought to be related to economic growth, such as current levels of income, geographic location, temperature, natural resources, and colonial history.[28] NYU economist William Easterly, for example, analyzed economic development over the past few decades to argue that in countries with weak middle classes, the "elite underinvest in human and infrastructure capital because they fear empowering the opposition."[29] In a related vein, Jong-Sung You, professor of international relations at UC San Diego, and Sanjeev Khagram, a public policy professor at Occidental College, argue that in unequal countries "the wealthy have both greater motivation and more opportunity to engage in corruption, whereas the poor are more vulnerable to extortion and less able to monitor and hold the rich and powerful accountable as inequality increases."[30]

Governments will always operate with some imperfections—underinvesting in public goods and enabling the rich to capture some economic rents. But the research demonstrates that high levels of inequality and a weak middle class make these problems much worse. As we observe across the world—from Russia's oligarchs to Sierra Leone's Krio—economic elites often use their power to shape government policy in ways that hinder long-run economic growth.[31]

INEQUALITY AND BAD GOVERNANCE IN AMERICAN HISTORY

Still, the United States may be different. The United States is among the world's oldest continuous democracies and also quite rich by international standards. As a result, our system of government may not be susceptible to these problems. But even a cursory review of our history—from the aristocratic, slaveholding South to the Gilded Age robber barons—shows that these abuses have happened in America. Certainly, American democracy has proved resilient in the face of a wealthy elite's desire to pervert government for its own purposes, responding and reasserting popular control of government. But we have not been immune to wealthy elites gaining disproportionate influence over government and harming our society and economy.

The richest slaveholders helped make the pre–Civil War South a very unequal society—even among whites—and much more unequal than the rest of the United States.[32] In 1860, only 25 percent of Southern households owned slaves.[33] But a mere 8,000 slaveholders—well less than 1 percent of the slaveholders—owned one million of the four million US slaves.[34] Such concentrated slave ownership helped the top 1 percent of income earners in the South take home twice the share of regional income as the top 1 percent in New England, and it made the South one of the more unequal societies in the world.[35]

The Southern slaveholding elite famously wielded its economic and political power to suppress blacks, denying them basic political and economic freedoms. But they also exerted strong influence over the government when dealing with less affluent whites, especially in state and local governments. And with their power, the slaveholding elite helped block the kinds of public investments the North made in schools and infrastructure that facilitated the region's greater prosperity. Just as elites in other countries often have done, Southern plantation owners used their economic and political power to block the majority's support for important economic investments.

By the 1850s, the United States enrolled a greater share of its children in primary schools than most other countries.[36] But this was purely a Northern achievement since the South sent its white children to school at only about one-third the rate the North did.[37] And school attendance was not even an option for most Southern blacks, as educating slaves was illegal in many Southern states.[38]

The North achieved this leadership in large part because its citizens voted to provide general taxpayer support for schools, significantly lessening the burden on families of paying for their children to attend school.[39] Public spending helped children of middle-class and poor families afford school. Local governments in the North raised more than three times as much for public schools per capita as local governments in the Southern states did and made schooling much more affordable for people with more modest means.[40] The South actually spent more per pupil than the North, but most of that money came from private tuition, which was not a problem for rich planters, though it was for most everyone else.[41] As Sun Go and Peter Lindert, economic historians at UC Davis, write: "The Northern states were ahead of Europe and the South in the reliance on public money and publicly run schools."[42]

Wealthy Southern slaveholders used a host of political maneuvers to prevent less wealthy citizens from raising taxes to fund public services like education, fearing that voters would heavily tax slaves.[43] From requiring very high levels of property ownership to hold elected office, to refusing to update state voting formulas to reflect the growth of population in areas where yeoman farmers lived, to requiring that any expansion in voting rights to the less wealthy be accompanied by constitutional protections against high taxes on slaves, Southern elites protected their power and prevented majorities from providing the public services they wanted.[44] As Robin Einhorn, an economic historian at UC Berkeley, writes: "Slaveholders simply would not allow nonslaveholding majorities to decide how to tax."[45] As a result, the South failed to make investments not only in education, but also in other public goods that foster economic growth, like roads and canals.[46] Einhorn explains that slaveholders "saw threats to their 'property' in any political action they did not control, even if yeoman were actually demanding roads, schools, and other mundane public services."[47]

Importantly, underinvestment in public goods continued well after the Civil War, meaning the economic harm wasn't easily reversed. Indeed, the governments in more equal regions of the United States led the country in creating public high schools in the early 1900s.[48]

The pre–Civil War South is not the only time in American history that high levels of economic inequality harmed the quality of governance and the functioning of the economy. During the Gilded Age—the era from roughly the end of the Civil War to the early 1900s—economic inequality was quite high, with one estimate finding that the wealthiest 12 percent of families owned 86 percent of the nation's wealth in 1890.[49] And during this period, wealthy business interests dominated government and overran the interests of the majority.[50] Historian Kevin

Phillips writes that during the Gilded Age "corporations and wealth" seized control of government.[51] Similarly, Harvard economist Edward Glaeser and his coauthors write that wealthy business leaders "subverted institutions as part of normal business practice."[52] To take but one example of the ways businesses used their power for private economic advantage in this period, large railroad, timber, and mining companies amassed huge swaths of formerly public land at giveaway prices, through a range of deceitful or fraudulent practices that largely went unchecked.[53]

It is not just hindsight that enabled people to see that extreme inequality was corrupting democracy. Rutherford B. Hayes, president from 1877 to 1881, wrote in his diary in retirement that "this is a government of the people, by the people, and for the people no longer. It is a government by the corporations, of the corporations, and for the corporations."[54] The level of influence the wealthy had in the Gilded Age was so normalized that Boies Penrose, a senator from Pennsylvania, said in 1896 of the relationship between business, money, and politics: "I believe in the division of labor. You send us to Congress; we pass laws under which you make money ... and out of your profits, you further contribute to our campaign funds to send us back again to pass more laws to enable you to make more money."[55]

How much control of government by the wealthy harmed the economy during the Gilded Age is difficult to parse out, because during this period the Industrial Revolution took hold in America, so the economy grew significantly even as it suffered a number of financial crises.[56] But it is hard to argue that so many special favors for the wealthy helped the economy. Most likely rapid growth occurred *in spite of* the disproportionate influence of the wealthy on government. Growth would have been greater if large corporations hadn't directed government resources to their coffers and blocked competition.

Indeed, economic growth was even faster right after the Gilded Age, when government was less controlled by economic elites. As the public gained political influence and reduced the special favors for the wealthy, the economy grew more quickly. A host of progressive policies—from antitrust laws, to campaign finance regulations, popular election of senators, direct referendums, and a progressive income tax—were implemented and tamed the influence of the wealthy and ended the Gilded Age. This reassertion of democratic control coincided with, and may have resulted in, even faster economic growth. As Harvard's Glaeser and his coauthors write: "This reputation for expansion should not obscure the fact that economic growth during 1860–1910 was much slower than that afterwards. . . . Institutional failures may have unduly limited the expansion."[57]

THE MIDDLE CLASS AND
GOOD GOVERNANCE

The question, of course, is whether the history of the Gilded Age and the aristocratic South is relevant to the United States today. Do a weak middle class and high levels of inequality undermine government today? And do they do so in ways that harm our economy? To answer these questions, we need to dig into the ways that a strong middle class and low levels of inequality make government work well.

A strong middle class and low levels of inequality do three beneficial things for democratic governance. First, these factors change the power dynamics in society, minimizing the power advantage of the wealthy. Second, they moderate political conflict.

Finally, they increase the "civicness" of citizens. All three work together to make government function properly. Unfortunately, the dramatic increase in income inequality in the United States has lead the wealthy to gain disproportionate political power, political conflict to intensify, and ordinary citizens to become less civic. These changes have made American government increasingly dysfunctional and increasingly looking like the governments of the pre–Civil War South and Gilded Age America.

The Rich Gain Power

Since Aristotle first wrote about government, scholars have understood that a strong middle class plays a key role in balancing power in a democracy between economic classes.[58] "Thus it is manifest," Aristotle wrote, "that the best political community is formed by citizens of the middle class ... for the addition of the middle class turns the scale, and prevents either of the extremes from being dominant."[59] US democracy does not risk unraveling into either of the poles of dictatorship or anarchy, as Aristotle and other authors feared would happen to countries without a middle class.[60] But the most relevant point these scholars make for the twenty-first-century United States is that a strong middle class reduces the ability of the elites to gain effective control of government.

As the middle class has weakened over the past thirty years, America's rich have gained far more influence over government than they previously had. While no single metric proves conclusively that the rich have increased their political power over recent decades, a number of signs indicate this is the case. The American public certainly thinks rich elites have gained power. In 1964, less than 30 percent of the public thought the federal government was run by "a few big interests," yet over the past few decades this percentage has significantly increased, so that in 2012, 78 percent of the public felt this way.[61]

More academic examinations of the power of the rich also tell a similar story. Several decades ago, when the United States was more equal economically, awards were frequently given to political scientists who wrote that the poor and middle class had significant political power. In 1961, Robert Dahl, now an emeritus professor of political science at Yale and often referred to as the "dean of American political scientists," wrote a book titled *Who Governs?*, arguing that American government was responsive to all its citizens.[62] Government may not have been equally responsive to rich and poor, but all groups enjoyed a significant degree of influence, according to Dahl.[63]

Despite some criticisms of the book at the time, political scientists generally praised the perspective of the book and it quickly became a canonical book in the field, winning the best book of the year award from the American Political Science Association.[64] Similarly, the political science book of the year from 1964 argued that business hardly, if ever, pushed politicians to alter their positions.[65] The book of the year from 1965 argued that political parties are "not a neatly pyramided bureaucracy, an elite class, or an oligarchy.... The party is an open, clientele-oriented structure, permeable at its base as well as its apex."[66]

Today, in sharp contrast, political scientists—not to mention journalists, historians, economists, and politicians themselves—frequently churn out well-received articles and books that explain how the wealthy dominate government.[67] Indeed, Benjamin Page, a political scientist at Northwestern University, and formerly a leading proponent of the view that ordinary citizens have great influence over government, published a paper in 2014 that reevaluated his prior argument and found that the opinions of rich individuals and business leaders largely determine how Congress acts. Page and his coauthor explain that today "economic elites and organized groups representing business interests have substantial independent impacts on U.S. government policy, while average citizens and mass-based interest groups have little or no independent influence."[68]

Many other recent studies tell a similar story. A particularly revealing study of the US Senate in 2009 by Vanderbilt University political scientist Larry Bartels, for example, compared senators' floor votes with the views of their constituents on a broad range of issues, including government spending, the minimum wage, civil rights, and abortion. Bartels found that senators' votes were vastly more responsive to the views of their affluent constituents than to those of their middle-class ones, and were completely disconnected from the views of their poorer constituents. "In almost every instance," Bartels wrote, "senators appear to be considerably more responsive to the opinions of affluent constituents than to the opinions of middle-class constituents, while the opinions of constituents in the bottom third of the income distribution have *no* apparent statistical effect on their senators' roll call votes."[69]

In 2012, Princeton political scientist Martin Gilens produced perhaps the most comprehensive study comparing the public's preferences with actual government policy.[70] Gilens examined 2,000 survey questions on a range of proposed policy changes, including taxes, government spending, and social issues, and found that the government is very responsive to the preferences of the affluent, but far less so to the preferences of the middle class and poor. Summarizing his findings, Gilens wrote: "The American government does respond to the public's preferences,

but that responsiveness is strongly tilted toward the most affluent citizens. Indeed, under most circumstances, the preferences
of the vast majority of Americans appear to have essentially no
impact on which policies the government does or doesn't adopt."

Gilens also found the influence of the rich had increased
compared to several decades ago. Gilens was careful to note that
many factors, such as whether Congress is under divided control, influence the responsiveness of government to citizens.
Still, he found the general trend has been away from the middle
class. As Gilens explains: "In recent decades the responsiveness
of policymakers to the preferences of the affluent has steadily
grown, but responsiveness to less-well-off Americans has not."
Several other studies also indicate that elected officials have
become less responsive to the preferences of the public.[71]

The political power of the wealthy has increased so dramatically in large part because money plays such a big role in American politics and the amount of money in politics has grown rapidly over recent decades. For example, the total amount spent on
presidential elections roughly doubled from 1970 to 2000, in inflation-adjusted dollars.[72] And contributions have since increased
even more rapidly in recent years, with the total amount spent on
presidential and congressional elections increasing by 50 percent
from 2000 to 2012.[73] As Thomas Mann, a senior fellow at the
Brookings Institution, puts it: "The cost of seeking office whether
it's for state legislature or a governorship or a member of the U.S.
House or Senate, these costs have been going up for decades. It's
kind of amusing to look back say to the 1970s, and you'll find many
members of Congress then were spending, oh, $75,000, $100,000,
$200,000—now that would almost be a rounding error."[74]

All this money in politics has given the rich greater influence.
As Martin Gilens bluntly explains, "Money—the 'mother's

milk' of politics—is the root of representational inequality."[75] Other factors besides inequality, such as the changing media environment, the increased use of expensive survey techniques, and evolving campaign finance rules, have clearly contributed to the rise of money in politics. But the basic point that, as inequality has increased, the rich have had even more money to spend than they previously did and that their money has been able to buy significant influence is not really in doubt.

Of all political activities—from voting to contacting public officials to volunteering on a campaign to attending a protest—those that involve money are where the rich have the greatest advantage.[76] Very few middle-class or poor people give money to politicians, and when they give, their contributions are fairly small. The vast majority of campaign contributions come from the wealthy, and the amount of money the rich contribute has increased rapidly over the past few decades.[77] To give but one example of the scale of the increase, the top 0.01 percent of donors—the biggest one in 10,000 donors—contributed over 40 percent of the money to campaigns in 2012, up dramatically from the early 1980s when they contributed a bit more than 10 percent.[78] And these totals only include the money we can see. Due to court rulings such as *Citizen's United v. FEC* and *Speech-Now.org v. FEC,* it has become much easier for wealthy individuals and businesses to avoid disclosing their campaign spending.[79] Then there is lobbying, where, just as with campaign contributions, expenditures have also rapidly increased in recent decades.[80] Lobbying spending accounts for a similar sum of money as campaign contributions and the dollar figures are at least as skewed toward business and other wealthy interests as contributions.[81] And similar to campaign contributions, not all lobbying needs to be disclosed.[82]

Certainly court rulings have played a part in the rise of giving by the wealthy, but the basic legal structure that allows for wealthy individuals to make large contributions has been in place for decades.[83] Rather, the growing wealth of the very rich is the main story. The trend of growing money in politics, as Adam Bonica, Nolan McCarty, Keith Poole, and Howard Rosenthal, political scientists from Stanford, Princeton, and Georgia, explain, "reflects the rising wealth of the super-rich and an increased willingness to spend large sums on elections."[84]

Some believe that all this money and lobbying explicitly buy votes—leading corrupt elected officials to do special favors for rich patrons in a quid pro quo—but the kind of corruption that breaks the law and leads to a politician's personal gain happens only on relatively rare occasions (though it appears to have increased along with inequality, as described later in this chapter). Campaign contributions, for example, generally don't go into politicians' pockets but rather are used to fund campaigns. A more accurate way to think about the amount of money currently in the political system is that it subtly corrupts the process, rather than overtly corrupting any particular individual. As Harvard Law professor Lawrence Lessig argues, the "core of the corruption in our present system of government" is that "the system induces the beneficiaries of Congress's acts to raise and give money to Congress to induce it to act."[85]

Most politicians attempt to serve the public interest, but they need money to run for office. This need for money changes who runs for office, how politicians spend their time, who they interact with, what arguments they hear, and even how they think and feel. Most candidates for office are now quite wealthy themselves—far more so than in previous decades—in part because they can finance elections by themselves or through their connections to similarly wealthy individuals.[86] And once they are elected, members of Congress now spend much of their time raising money, with the House Democratic leadership recently recommending that freshman members of Congress spend at least four hours per 10-hour workday fundraising.[87] Those politicians that are particularly good at raising money can give to the campaigns of allies, further extending their influence.

Political scientists are divided about how much influence campaign contributions and lobbying have. Some find fairly direct consequences, while others do not, but most understand that these expenditures have some degree of influence.[88] "What wealthy citizens and moneyed interests ... gain from their big contributions is influence over who runs for office," according to the report for the Task Force on Inequality and American Democracy from the American Political Science Association.[89] But contributions also help the wealthy gain access to elected officials and present their views to elected officials, something that few middle-class or poorer citizens do.[90] And there is good evidence that, at least at times, contributions and lobbying affect voting, writing letters to regulators, deciding whether to champion legislation, and other behaviors.[91] As the task force puts it: "Money does 'buy' something—privileged access for contributors and the special attention of members who reward them with vigorous help in minding their business in the committee process."

Then there are government officials passing through the revolving door of career opportunities to become lobbyists themselves. The lure of tripling their incomes by cashing in on knowledge and connections undoubtedly influences politicians' behavior when they are still in government—even if the politician believes in the causes they eventually go lobby for. Notorious lobbyist and convicted felon Jack Abramoff said that the best way to get a congressional staffer to do his bidding was to discuss the possibility of a job at a much higher salary.[92]

These days the revolving door seems to be spinning much more quickly. Estimates indicate that in the 1970s 3 percent of members of Congress became lobbyists when they left Congress, but by the 1990s this percentage had increased to over 22 percent, and since then it has continued to increase and is now estimated at over 40 percent.[93]

Just as political scientists through the ages have feared, high levels of inequality and a weakened middle class have enabled the rich to gain excessive influence over government. The evidence is clear that as inequality has risen, the rich have spent ever more money to shape politics and their efforts have been successful.

Polarization Increases

The second role a strong middle class plays in a democracy is to help reduce political polarization. So not only does a strong middle class help prevent the rich from dominating, it helps ensure that conflict between groups is manageable. In societies with relatively little economic inequality, people's economic interests converge and there are more bridges across classes so there is less to fight about and disagreements are less likely to polarize. As Seymour Martin Lipset, a past president of the American Political Science Association and former political sociologist at Stanford University, argued: "A large middle class in a country tempers conflict by penalizing extremist groups and rewarding moderacy."[94] And when there is conflict in a middle-class society, opposing sides are more likely to be able to work together. But, in recent decades, there has been less of a middle to create common ground and less trust to facilitate compromise, so political fighting has become more pronounced.[95]

It is not hard to see that partisan political fighting has become particularly bad. Norman Ornstein and Thomas Mann, senior fellows at the American Enterprise Institute and Brookings Institution and longtime students of the US Congress, argue that the level of partisan fighting and the willingness to take fights beyond acceptable levels and to distort rules have become much more pronounced in recent years. Fighting in Congress today, they argue, "more closely resembles . . . the Gilded Age . . . than the Cold War era."[96] In 2013, for example, the Congress and the president couldn't agree on a budget, which is a relatively common occurrence throughout history and hardly a sign of increased fighting. What was uncommon was that their disagreement led to a two-week shutdown of the federal government, furloughing 800,000 federal workers and many more from private companies that do business with the government, taking away an estimated $24 billion from the economy.[97] And because of a similar disagreement earlier in the year, the federal government nearly defaulted on its debt, which would have been unprecedented in American history.[98] While these few examples from one year by themselves don't prove that politics has become more polarized, they are highly suggestive.

When these anecdotes are combined with quantitative data, they make a convincing case that American politics has become increasingly polarized over the past several decades. The increased use of the filibuster is a good example: a total of seven filibusters were filed in the 1969–1970 Congress, but in the 2011–2012 Congress, *115* were filed.[99] And in perhaps the most comprehensive research on political fighting, Nolan McCarty, Keith Poole, and Howard Rosenthal studied congressional voting pat-

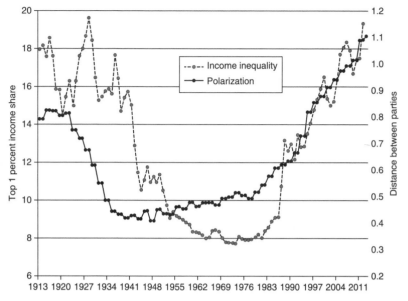

Figure 1. Top 1 percent income share and polarization in the US House of Representatives, 1913–2012. Source: Adapted from Adam Bonica and others, "Why Hasn't Democracy Slowed Rising Inequality?," *Journal of Economic Perspectives* 27, no. 3 (2013): 103–124.

terns from 1879 to the present. Their research shows not only that political polarization has increased dramatically over recent decades, but also that income inequality is correlated with a widening divide between the political parties.[100] Indeed, over the past century and a half the relationship between economic inequality and political polarization has been amazingly tight, as figure 1 shows.

Polarization is bad for any government, but especially so for American government, with all of its checks and balances. The checks and balances between the House, the Senate, and the president are designed to encourage compromise, but when opposing sides are unwilling to compromise, they lead the

American system of government to break down far more so than parliamentary systems.[101] As a result, growing polarization has rendered America's government increasingly unable to respond to the public's preferences or societal needs.

Civicness Declines

The third way a strong middle class improves the quality of governance is by increasing the "civicness" of citizens. For government to work well, people need to be able to work together, trust one another to act fairly and obey the law, and participate politically so they can make their desires known to elected officials and hold them accountable for achieving their goals.[102] A strong middle class and relative economic equality are essential for fostering these civic behaviors and attitudes. Civicness is built upon a foundation of economic equality.

Economic equality helps people feel they have shared bonds and are part of a similar community, which facilitates civic action. Alexis de Tocqueville, the Frenchman who came to the United States in the early 1800s and observed our democracy, noted that Americans frequently joined together in groups and worked together to accomplish large things.[103] Tocqueville attributed this civicness to the relative economic equality in the United States that enabled people to see their common interests.

More modern scholars such as Carles Boix and Daniel Posner, political scientists from Princeton and UCLA, make similar claims about the importance of equality for fostering civicness. "A community's cooperative capacity is a function of the degree of social and political inequality that a community has experienced over the course of its historical development," they argue.[104] Indeed, a host of studies from regions around the world show that places with lower levels of economic inequality are more civic, with higher levels of participation in politics and civic organizations.[105] Similarly, trust makes cooperation and compromise more likely among elected leaders and government officials, as well as ordinary citizens.[106] In order to work with one another effectively, people need to trust other people, and, as chapter 2 shows, economic equality is essential to developing trust.

These kinds of civic behaviors have been shown to produce better governance in settings around the world. Robert Putnam, a Harvard University political scientist, finds in his study of Italy that regions with higher levels of civicness—which he was one of the first to call "social capital"—have much more effective and accountable governments.[107] Putnam put regional governments through a series of tests—such as mailing letters or showing up at a government office building with an administrative problem—to demonstrate that those with high levels of civic engagement, even economically underdeveloped ones, have more effective governments that do things like quickly responding to citizens and providing quality services.[108] Similarly, Tom Rice, a political scientist at the University of Iowa, examined cities in Iowa and found that, in those with higher levels of social capital, citizens ranked the governments as more responsive and effective in surveys, and he also found that the governments did a better job maintaining public streets and parks, as measured by objective criteria.[109]

Trust has a similar effect on the quality of governance.[110] The World Bank's Stephen Knack reviewed the performance of US state governments on 35 technocratic measures such as the accuracy of revenue and expenditure forecasts, management of long-term debt, and timeliness of budget adoption, and found those with higher levels of trust performed significantly better.[111] As

University of Maryland political scientist Eric Uslaner argues: "Societies with higher levels of trust in turn have institutions that function better."[112]

But American citizens have become less civic as inequality has increased. Putnam created a stir in 2000 when he argued that "social capital" has declined sharply in recent decades as Americans join together less frequently in groups, volunteer less, and even socialize less. Instead of joining leagues to bowl, Americans are *Bowling Alone,* as Putnam titled his book.[113] Parent-teacher associations, for example, lost half a million members from 1990 to 1997 despite five million more kids in public schools, a decline that has continued since Putnam published his book.[114] Trust in others and in government has fallen sharply. Perhaps the most comprehensive measure of America's civicness was put together by the National Conference on Citizenship, an organization Congress created in 1953 to strengthen civic life. The index of dozens of different measures of civic participation and attitudes put together by the National Conference shows that civicness has fallen by 15 percentage points since the mid-1970s.[115] In a sign of the times, the 2014 mid-term elections had the lowest voter turnout since World War II, when many citizens were otherwise occupied.[116]

Not all measures of civicness have fallen so sharply, and some have hardly fallen at all. Voting in presidential elections has fallen only slightly since the 1970s—57 percent voted in the 2012 presidential election, down from 63 percent in the 1972 presidential election—because a number of other factors affect whether people participate in politics besides inequality. Education levels are especially important and so are whether people were asked to participate and the candidates' appeal.[117] Events such as the terrorist attack on September 11 that briefly inspire citizens to participate can also make a big difference. And high levels of inequality can sometimes temporarily spark anger and political engagement. But, all things being equal, higher levels of inequality reduce civic engagement. As Dora Costa and Matthew Kahn, both economics professors at UCLA, find, "the most important factor explaining the decline in social capital ... was rising income inequality."[118] Sometimes people can overcome obstacles to being civic, but much of the time, the obstacles win.

HOW BAD GOVERNMENT IS HARMING THE ECONOMY

As inequality has risen over the past three decades, political power has shifted toward the wealthy, politics has become more polarized, and civic engagement has suffered. These are all troubling signs for America's democracy. Still, by themselves these indicators do not necessarily undermine the quality of government in ways that harm the economy. It is still possible, though unlikely, that American government could still do a good job supporting economic growth.

To see how the decline in the quality of government has harmed the economy requires a closer look at its actual performance. Unfortunately, in recent decades American government has failed to provide the framework necessary to support strong economic growth. It has underinvested in essential public goods like education and infrastructure and become more prone to doling out benefits to the wealthy at the expense of the common good.

Underinvesting in Roads and Schools

Like the pre–Civil War South and the former colonies in South and Central America, the United States is failing to make investments in public goods that drive future growth. We have not made these investments because the middle class lacks the political power to translate its preferences into policy. Polls clearly show that most Americans would strongly prefer greater spending on education and infrastructure. But these public goods generally aren't as important for the wealthy as they are for the middle class. Though the wealthy often support spending on schools and roads, they have less interest in paying taxes to support them and often can afford private alternatives to these public goods. When push comes to shove and priorities are set—making choices about what to spend money on and at what level to set taxes—the priorities of the wealthy have held greater sway. And that has meant America has underinvested in infrastructure and education.

It is painfully obvious that American infrastructure is in rough shape. American bridges have collapsed in dramatic fashion and levees have failed spectacularly. More mundane but still very important are the problems of growing traffic delays, deteriorating energy grids, and less reliable transit. The American Society of Civil Engineers gives US infrastructure a D+, finding one in nine bridges is structurally deficient and 42 percent of major urban highways are congested.[119] They project that infrastructure expenditures will fall $1.1 trillion short of what the country needs by 2020.[120]

And the poor state of US infrastructure harms our economy. When a bridge north of Seattle collapsed in 2013—one that had long been classified as "functionally obsolescent," meaning it didn't meet modern building requirements—the state's department of commerce director estimated the state would lose $47 million in economic output while the bridge was being repaired, as approximately 70,000 vehicles per day were diverted and trade with Canada was rerouted elsewhere.[121] More commonplace costs include the impact of delays as commuters and goods are stuck in traffic—$121 billion in wasted time and fuel annually.[122] Similarly, failure to modernize an electricity grid that has barely changed since Thomas Edison built the first grid in 1882 could cost the country $197 billion in service interruptions over the next decade.[123] McKinsey & Company, the management consulting firm, estimates that additional infrastructure investments could create up to 1.8 million jobs and boost annual GDP by up to $320 billion by 2020.[124]

Similarly, a prosperous twenty-first-century economy demands a well-educated workforce—in fact, that is one of the few answers to inequality or "social mobility" that conservatives cite.[125] But at the moment when we need educational investment the most, the United States is falling behind.

The United States was once a world leader in sending its citizens to college, but our college graduation rates have stagnated over time and allowed other countries to pass us by. America simply has not increased its education levels very much over the past few decades while other countries have. Starting in the 1970s, education levels stopped increasing at a rapid rate.[126] Currently, just over four in 10 Americans between the ages of 25 and 34 have a college degree, nearly the same percentage as those between the ages of 55 and 64, meaning the college graduation rates have hardly budged in over a generation.[127] In contrast, countries like Canada have dramatically increased their graduation rates, so much so that 57 percent of young Canadians now have a college degree, which is up significantly from previous generations.[128] And Canada is not the only country to have passed us by. As recently as 1995, the United States was still tied for first in the world in the percentage of the population with a college degree, but now ranks only fourteenth.[129]

The failure of public spending on higher education to keep pace with demand explains at least some of this stagnation. Workers need ever more advanced training to compete in the international economy, but we aren't spending enough to help people prepare. Though the need for higher education has increased, total public spending on higher education as a share of the economy has remained roughly flat for the past three decades.[130] Even worse, the amount that students and their families must pay for a college education has risen dramatically. Indeed, the cost of attending a public university has jumped by over 250 percent over the past three decades.[131] In contrast, median family income has increased by only 16 percent during the same period.[132]

American colleges now receive roughly twice as much revenue from private tuition—as a share of total costs—as they did compared to just two decades ago.[133] All told, less than 40 percent of expenditures on higher education now come from public spending—compared to almost twice that for other advanced countries.[134] As Thomas Mortenson, a senior scholar at the Pell Institute for the Study of Opportunity in Higher Education, argues, "Public higher education is gradually being privatized."[135] This huge change in the affordability of college has made the cost of higher education a barrier that is too high for some families and created a large financial burden for other middle-class families. Because college is harder to afford, fewer are able to graduate.

And the level of public spending on colleges has only gotten worse since the Great Recession. State governments—the primary source of public funding for many schools—have not just failed to make adequate investments, but actually cut per pupil spending on colleges by an average of 28 percent between 2008 and 2013.[136] Of course, many factors, including the recession's effect on state budgets, are at work. But the declining political power of the middle class has played a role, especially since state tax revenues have started to recover and in 2013 were only 1.6 percent below their levels in 2008.[137] Budgets reflect choices about how much money to raise and what to spend that money on. And where the middle class is stronger, those choices have favored education. Indeed, two states with relatively strong middle classes—North Dakota and Wyoming—have actually increased spending on higher education since the Great Recession began.[138]

There are of course many factors that lead states to spend more on higher education—and these two states were fortunate to have relatively strong economies throughout the Great Recession—but a more rigorous look at the data also indicates that states with strong middle classes spend more on higher education. According to the author's previous research, states with stronger middle classes—defined by the share of income going to the middle 60 percent of households—spend a much greater share of their state income on higher education.[139] Critically, these results hold even when controlling for other factors that influence education spending such as state income levels, the share of the population comprising people of color, and the age distribution of the state.[140]

International comparisons also suggest that middle-class countries spend more public money on higher education. The United States ranks only sixteenth among rich countries in public spending for higher education as a share of the nation's economy.[141] And our rankings have declined as the middle class has weakened. In 1995, the earliest year for which comparable data exist, the United States was tied for seventh in public spending on higher education, but now has fallen behind more equal countries like Austria and Belgium.

Spending on elementary and secondary education tells a somewhat similar story as higher education, though with a few more caveats. The author's previous research on US states finds that states with a weaker middle class also spend less on elementary and secondary education, even when controlling for a host of other things that influence education spending.[142] Similarly, Matthias Doepke and David de la Croix, economists at Northwestern University and UC Louvain, show that across states in the United States and in countries around the world, inequality is associated with lower levels of public education spending.[143] They also find that a greater share of children attend private schools in US states and countries with higher levels of inequality, which suggests that the wealthy in these areas are opting out of the public system and have less interest in supporting public schools. Still, the research is not definitive and public spending on elementary and secondary education as a share of the economy has slightly increased over the past several decades, indicating that the relationship is complicated and many other factors besides inequality shape the level of spending.[144] But it is likely that spending on elementary and secondary education would have been higher if the middle class were stronger. Indeed, compared to other rich countries, the United States ranks sixteenth in spending on elementary and secondary education as a percentage of GDP, behind more middle-class countries like Norway and Denmark.[145] So while spending on elementary and secondary education has not been as clearly affected as spending on higher education, the basic story is that in part because of high levels of inequality, the United States has underinvested in public education.

Perhaps even more so than in education, the current level of public spending on infrastructure is particularly inadequate. As inequality has risen over the past several decades, public infra-

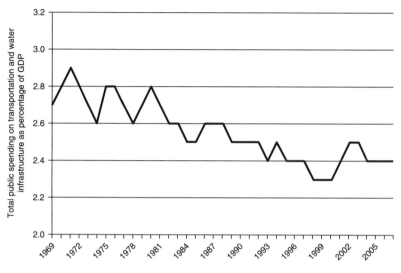

Figure 2. The significant decline of total public spending on infrastructure as a share of GDP. Source: Congressional Budget Office, "Public Spending on Transportation and Water Infrastructure" (2010). Total public spending includes spending at the federal, state, and local levels. Infrastructure in this instance is defined as transportation and water infrastructure.

structure investment has steadily declined, as figure 2 shows. The Congressional Budget Office reports that federal, state, and local spending on infrastructure totaled 2.4 percent of GDP in 2007, the most recent year for which comprehensive data were available.[146] If we had spent a similar amount to what we spent in the mid-1970s (2.8 percent), that would have come to almost $60 billion in additional infrastructure spending in 2007 alone.[147] We are now spending about the same dollar amount on infrastructure as we were four decades ago, even though our economy is much bigger than it was then.[148] In addition to the trend over time, analysis of state infrastructure spending also suggests that the middle class plays a role in supporting higher levels of investment. The 10 states with the strongest middle classes spent over 50 percent more on infrastructure as a share of state domestic product over the past decade than the 10 states with the weakest middle classes.[149]

Because of this downward trend, the United States now spends far less on infrastructure than our competitors. As *The Economist* notes: "Total public spending on transport and water infrastructure has fallen steadily since the 1960s and now stands at 2.4% of GDP. Europe, by contrast, invests 5% of GDP in its infrastructure, while China is racing into the future at 9%."[150] Surveys from the World Economic Forum rank US infrastructure quite poorly: The 2012–2013 report placed the US number 25 for quality of overall infrastructure, behind Barbados, Oman, and Bahrain. The US is thirtieth for air transportation infrastructure and thirty-third in quality of electricity supply (lack of interruptions and voltage fluctuations), behind Bosnia, Barbados, and Portugal.[151]

Beyond the numbers, the story of the most recent federal highway bill highlights how inequality harms government in a way that damages the economy. Inequality polarized politics and made agreement on even relatively uncontroversial issues quite difficult, so much so that a basic function of government, such as spending money on roads, is almost beyond the ability of Congress. That the bill in 2012 maintained spending at current inadequate levels and failed to reverse trends or meet infrastructure needs is almost beside the point.[152] The dysfunctional process that led to its passage tells the real story.

Breaking with a tradition of passing a long-term highway bill every five years, Congress could only agree to a series of temporary measures to buy time: Between September 30, 2009, and July 6, 2012, Congress passed 10 different "temporary" extensions to allow previously authorized spending levels to continue. Though temporary measures are better than no federal funding, they are a terrible way to deal with long-term infrastructure projects and make planning new projects virtually impossible. As Thomas Donahue, president of The US Chamber of Commerce, put it: "Nothing happens in the states and in the communities when you've got a 90-day or a 120-day extension."[153] Governors and mayors, Donahue continued, "can't write a contract [to build transportation infrastructure] in that amount of time, and jobs that could be had are not going to be had." Congress made a "breakthrough" in 2012 when it managed to authorize a two-year highway bill, but everyone recognized that three years of temporary measures followed by a two-year bill was an embarrassment that failed to address the country's needs.[154] Even worse, in the summer of 2014 when the fund that pays for highway projects was scheduled to run out of money, all Congress could do was provide another temporary fix for a few months.[155]

Behind not only the partisan gridlock, but also the general failure to make adequate investments in infrastructure and education is the decline of the middle class. The middle class does not have enough political power to get what they want from government. The public wants this spending, but because of the strong preferences of the rich for low taxes, we haven't made desired investments. A Brookings Institution/Northeastern University poll conducted in October 2012, for example, found that 81 percent of Americans believe the government needs to invest more in America's higher education system, with an even higher percentage saying that a college education is important for achieving the American Dream.[156] Other polls show similarly high figures: the General Social Survey, a long-standing academic survey, finds that roughly 75 percent of Americans support spending more on education.[157]

Infrastructure investments also garner high levels of support: 93 percent feel making improvements to infrastructure is important; 72 percent support "increasing federal spending to build and repair roads, bridges, and schools"; and 81 percent are prepared to pay more in taxes to do so.[158]

While the rich often support investments in infrastructure and education, they do not do so to the degree the middle class does. The middle class depends upon these basic public services in a way the rich do not. The wealthy can opt out of some public goods by, for example, sending their children to private schools. And when the wealthy can't completely opt out—they still have to use public roads and airports—they often can use their money to overcome some of these public goods' flaws. Paying for dramatically increased tuition for a public university burdens the wealthy less. First-class passengers for airline flights can enter an expedited line for security while other passengers wait in the normal line.[159] Some cities now offer the opportunity to buy a pass into the carpool lane even if you travel alone.[160] The luxury carmaker Audi promotes one of its models by stating, "The roads are underfunded by $450 billion. With the right car, you may never notice."[161]

Perhaps even more important than the different levels of need for public services are the sharp differences in attitudes about taxes and government spending. The rich have a much stronger desire to keep taxes low than the middle class. As Gilens found in his study of nearly 2,000 poll questions, more affluent people are less supportive of taxes and government spending than the middle class.[162]

A groundbreaking poll of roughly the top 1 percent of wealth holders—a notoriously difficult group to survey—highlights how the preferences of the wealthy and the middle class diverge. The authors of the study—political scientists Benjamin Page,

Larry Bartels, and Jason Seawright—found that the very wealthy wanted lower tax rates than the middle class did.[163] Critically, the study also found that the wealthy wanted low taxes more than their other political goals. For the rich, spending for education and infrastructure takes a backseat to low taxes. "Wealthy Americans ... in contrast to the general public," the authors found, "tend to favor dealing with budget deficits by cutting programs, even very popular social programs, rather than raising taxes."

A particularly revealing set of questions about education spending laid bare the differences between the wealthy and the middle class, showing that the middle class prioritizes education spending much more than the wealthy do. Page, Bartels, and Seawright found that only 28 percent of the wealthy agreed that the government should "make sure that everyone who wants to go to college can do so," compared to 78 percent of the general public. Similarly, only 35 percent of the wealthy felt that the "government should spend whatever is necessary to ensure that all children have really good public schools they can go to," compared to 87 percent of the general public.

As the polling makes clear, public goods just aren't as much of a priority for the wealthy as they are for the middle class. And when the rich have the political power to override the majority, the middle class and the economy pay the price. All told, the increased political power of the wealthy, combined with highly polarized politics and a disengaged public, has led to severe underinvestment in infrastructure and higher education.

Rent Seeking on the Rise

Even as our government has underinvested in infrastructure and education, it has increasingly doled out special favors for wealthy and powerful interests. When companies or individuals use their money and power to encourage government to provide them with special benefits, it is called rent seeking. Because rent seeking generally occurs behind closed doors, it is notoriously hard to measure. But the evidence strongly suggests that as the middle class has weakened over recent decades, the wealthy have been able to extract ever greater rents. Indeed, the level of rent seeking today may even approach that of the Gilded Age, at least according to some observers.

The 2003 Medicare Modernization Act is a classic case of modern-day rent seeking, and the story of the law's passage highlights some of the key elements of how rent seeking works today: legally, through campaign contributions, lobbying, and the revolving door—with the occasional heavy-handed tactic thrown in. The law added a prescription drug benefit to Medicare, but blocked the federal government from negotiating the prices it pays for covered drugs. This forced the program to overpay for drugs, transferring money from taxpayers to pharmaceutical companies and harmed the economy mainly because the money could have been used more efficiently. An article in the *Journal of General Internal Medicine* estimated that the inability to negotiate drug prices costs taxpayers over $20 billion per year.[164] The House Oversight Committee estimated that a separate provision that forces the government to pay the higher, unnegotiated price for drugs for people eligible for both Medicare and Medicaid cost an additional $3.7 billion in the first two years alone.[165]

The bill likely came out this way because pharmaceutical companies spent $100 million per year lobbying and $20 million per election cycle on campaign contributions in the early 2000s and, according to a *60 Minutes* investigation, at least 15 high-level government officials who were instrumental in the bill's passage soon went to work for pharmaceutical companies.[166] Congressman Billy Tauzin of Louisiana, who wrote the bill and steered it through the House, began negotiating to become president and CEO of PhRMA, a pharmaceutical company lobby group, the same month President Bush signed it into law. Working for the pharmaceutical industry, he earned $2 million a year, roughly 10 times his congressional salary.[167]

Republican Representative Walter Jones from North Carolina told *60 Minutes,* "The pharmaceutical lobbyists wrote the bill," and Democratic Representative John Dingell of Michigan said the same thing, noting that the bill "was written by their lobbyists."[168] Further, Jones stated that the bill and the process for its passage were worse than he had seen in his long political career, noting the vote was held at 3 AM, instead of during normal working hours: "I've been in politics for 22 years, and it was the ugliest night I have ever seen in 22 years."

The bill may have so favored the drug companies for other reasons—proponents claimed "small government" ideological opposition to government negotiating prices. Yet that very ideological opposition should have translated into opposition to expensive legislation, or at the very least into opposition to placing people who were eligible for two different government programs into the more expensive one.

Perhaps the ultimate case of rent seeking that has harmed the economy is the banking industry's use of its growing wealth to shift policy in its favor in ways that sparked the Great Recession. Indeed, this story would look familiar in the Gilded Age or a developing country. Over the past few decades, Wall Street influenced government so that it could engage in profitable, but quite risky lines of business. And when these risks proved too much for Wall Street to bear and threatened to take down the entire economy, the government bailed out well-connected Wall Street firms with virtually no strings attached as less politically connected businesses failed.

Banks, like other industries, used their money to gain political influence and access. And banks and their executives clearly had a lot of money to spend. Over the past several decades, banking roughly tripled as a share of the economy so that banking profits now represent 30 percent of all corporate profits.[169] At the same time, there was a dramatic increase in compensation for financial professionals. Bankers went from making up 11 percent of the top 0.1 percent of income earners in 1979 to 18 percent in 2005.[170]

With these extraordinary profits and salaries, bankers had money they could use to aid their cause. As MIT economist Simon Johnson and University of Connecticut law professor James Kwak write in their book about the banking crisis, the industry's influence was based on "the unprecedented amounts of money flowing through the financial sector, increasingly concentrated in a handful of megabanks."[171] FIRE—the term used for the broad financial, insurance, and real estate industry that many refer to as Wall Street—generally topped the list of industry contributors to political campaigns for the past several decades and ranked among the biggest spenders on lobbying. FIRE went from contributing just $108 million in the 1990 election cycle to $330 million in the 2006 election cycle, right before the crisis.[172] Lobbying spending enjoyed a similar trajectory, rising from $292 million in 1998 (when data first became available) to $432 million in 2006 (all in 2012 dollars).[173] In 2006, it employed a total of 2,848 lobbyists—half of whom had previously served in government.[174] That's more than five banking lobbyists for every member of Congress.

With its money, Wall Street dramatically altered policy.[175] For example, Atif Mian, Amir Sufi, and Francesco Trebbi, economists at Princeton, Chicago, and the University of British Columbia, studied the fate of a number of bills with the potential to affect subprime lending and concluded that "special interests, measured with campaign contributions from the mortgage industry, ... helped to shape government policies that encouraged the rapid growth of subprime mortgage credit."[176]

Certainly, a large degree of Wall Street's influence came not directly from contributions and lobbying, but from the prestige its riches provided and larger cultural shifts that its wealth helped engender. As Simon Johnson and James Kwak write: "Campaign contributions and the revolving door between private sector and government service gave Wall Street banks influence in Washington, but their ultimate victory lay in shifting the conventional wisdom in their favor, to the point where their lobbyists' talking points seemed self-evident to congressmen and administration officials."[177] The bottom line, however, is that Wall Street had a relatively strong influence on the political process, though its money was not the only factor at work.

Over a period of several decades, Wall Street pushed a host of legal and regulatory changes that helped boost bank profits but increased risks to the economy. Among the most significant changes Wall Street benefited from was the repeal of the Glass-Steagall Act, a law enacted after the Great Depression that reduced the risk of a financial crisis by separating investment banking from traditional bank lending, but that banks saw as an obstacle to entering profitable lines of business.[178] Another policy change allowed subprime lending to go virtually unregulated.[179] Former Federal Reserve board member Edward Gramlich wrote of the change: "In the subprime market, where we badly need supervision, a majority of loans are made with very little supervision."[180]

Still another rule change allowed banks to keep the riskiest mortgage-backed securities on their books with very little capital to back them up if they failed. This "turned banking rules upside down," the *National Journal* explained, because it meant that "risky pieces required less capital than safe ones."[181] A different decision allowed major investment banks to use internal models—instead of government regulators' models—to calculate the amount of capital they needed to hold, which allowed them the "flexibility" to increase leverage, and thus increase profits, not to mention risk.[182]

Several of the policy changes that benefited banks did not even have a plausible public policy justification. James Kwak has highlighted some of the most indefensible policy changes: "The Federal Reserve's decision not to undertake consumer protection examinations of nonbank mortgage lenders seems to contradict the intent of the Home Ownership and Equity Protection Act of 1994 ... [and] allowing IndyMac Bancorp to backdate its capital infusions to appear better capitalized than it actually was and avoid additional FDIC restrictions are also hard to defend as being in the public interest."[183]

Banks also worked to prevent new regulations on complex financial transactions called "derivatives," since these financial products were very profitable.[184] A derivative is a financial product that derives its value from an underlying asset—such as a stock—but does not involve the actual sale of the asset. Derivatives allow for greater trading and speculation since they allow an underlying asset to be divided up in many different ways. Investor Warren Buffett called derivatives "financial weapons of mass destruction," because they create significant risks for the economy as their value has significant uncertainty.[185]

One of the more infamous kinds of derivatives is the synthetic collateralized debt obligation, which helped banks make even more money during the housing bubble while increasing systemic risk. Wall Street maintained that these derivatives were low-risk, but they ended up carrying far more risk than bankers expected, a fact that became obvious as they imploded in value.[186]

The large risks created by all the policy changes favorable to Wall Street were a key spark of the Great Recession. To be sure, these policy changes that increased financial risks were not the only cause of the financial crisis, but they were a significant contributor. As University of Chicago finance professor Luigi Zingales explains: "The roots of this crisis have to be found in bad regulation, lack of transparency, and market complacency brought about by several years of positive returns."[187]

Not only did Wall Street money help cause the Great Recession, but once the financial crisis hit, Wall Street money helped influence Congress to bail out large banks on very generous terms. According to Atif Mian, Amir Sufi, and Francesco Trebbi: "Special interests in the form of higher campaign contributions from the financial industry increase the likelihood of supporting the Emergency Economic Stabilization Act," the bill commonly known as the bank bailout.[188] Estimates indicate that since the bailout, the six biggest banks were for years able to get an $82 billion "too big to fail" subsidy because markets accept lower returns from these banks, knowing the government will bail them out if trouble arises again.[189] In fact, some research suggests that a substantial reason for such high Wall Street profits and salaries is due to changes in government policy over recent decades.[190]

The very generous treatment of large Wall Street banks stands in stark contrast to how the government treated smaller banks, or how the United States encouraged other countries to deal with financial crises. Bailing out the banks may have been justified to help protect the economy from further harm, but the way they were bailed out is hard to defend. Johnson and Kwak explain: "Not only did the government choose to rescue the financial system—a decision few would question—but it chose to do so by extending a blank check to the largest, most powerful banks in the moment of greatest need. The government chose *not* to impose conditions that could reform the industry or even to replace the management of large failed banks.... This strategy ran counter to the approach the US Treasury Department had honed during the emerging market financial crises in the 1990s, when leading officials urged crisis-stricken countries to address structural problems quickly and directly."[191]

With the vast sweep of governmental decisions benefiting Wall Street, it is hard not to see deep and troubling trends. As its wealth increased, Wall Street used its money to influence government policy for its benefit, at the expense of the public. "Through campaign finance and political donations," as John Plender, a senior editorial writer for the *Financial Times,* explains, Wall Street "bought themselves protection from proper societal accountability."[192] Indeed, Wall Street's influence is so pervasive that, as Johnson and Kwak conclude, "The Wall Street banks are the new American oligarchy—a group that gains political power because of its economic power, and then uses that political power for its own benefit."[193]

The story of Wall Street's influence makes a strong case that the wealthy have been able to extract greater rents from government in recent decades. But a few more anecdotes can help show just how pervasive rent seeking has become. The 2005 Energy Bill—decried as a "piñata of perks for energy industries" by the *Washington Post* for its billions of dollars in subsidies for oil and gas, coal, and nuclear industries—provides yet another example where the substance of the law and the process that created it were particularly shameful.[194] Vice President Cheney was reported to have privately worked with lobbyists to formulate an early draft of the bill.[195] According to an *ABCNews* article, companies run and represented by at least 37 "Pioneer" and "Ranger" families—individuals who helped raise over $100,000 and $200,000 respectively for President Bush's reelection campaign—"stand to make billions from the energy bill."[196] Republican Senator John McCain of Arizona called a draft of the bill the "no-lobbyist-left-behind act."[197]

Not only did the energy bill waste money that could have been put to better use, but it provided significant advantages to wealthy existing industries, such as coal, that are unlikely to grow in the future, while continuing to put the energy competitors of the future, such as wind and solar, at a disadvantage.[198]

Rent seeking isn't just about government giveaways—as shameful as they may be. Rent seeking also includes the government limiting competition to benefit only a few well-connected companies at the expense of society and the economy. Take our slow, expensive Internet, for example. Being at the cutting edge of the Internet will drive future economic growth. As former Federal Communications Commission chair Julius Genachowski explains: "We are in a global bandwidth race. A nation's future economic security is tied to frictionless and speedy access to information. The faster we can connect our citizens the faster our economy can grow.... Much like the space race in the 20th century, success in this race will unleash waves of innovation that will go a long way toward determining who leads our global economy in the 21st century."[199]

The United States invented and pioneered the Internet, spreading connections far and wide so that citizens and businesses could take advantage of what it offered. Yet we have let our lead slip away—with slower, fewer, and more costly connections. As a New America Foundation report put it: "The U.S. has fallen from 1st to between 15th and 21st in the world in terms of broadband access, adoption, speeds and prices."[200]

Congress and regulatory agencies have handed monopolies to cable companies—the providers of most Internet service—and let them escape government regulations commonly placed on other kinds of monopoly providers like electric utilities that, for example, require a level of service and set conditions for price increases. As Edward Luce of the *Financial Times* explains: "Through brilliantly effective lobbying, US cable companies have escaped the universal access and affordability clauses that were imposed on telecoms and electricity companies in earlier eras."[201] Not only have cable companies blocked regulation, but they have also defeated efforts to provide public competition. Susan Crawford, a professor at the Benjamin N. Cardozo School of Law, and the author of *Captive Audience: The Telecom Industry and Monopoly Power in the New Gilded Age,* explains how "six Time Warner lobbyists persuaded the North Carolina legislature to pass a 'level playing field' bill making it impossible for cities in that state to create their own high-speed Internet access networks."[202]

Many more cases of rent seeking could be described—from the lengthening of the time that a copyright is protected so that companies could keep profitable product lines out of the public domain to a "bankruptcy reform" bill that "profited credit card companies at consumers' expense."[203] Similarly, additional quotations from longtime political observers could be mounted: from David Stockman, a former Congressman and budget director to President Ronald Reagan, saying that "crony capitalism ...

[has] gotten much worse," to Thomas Patterson, professor of government at Harvard University, arguing that "the robber barons of the late 19th century were pikers compared with today's moneyed interests," to Noble Prize–winning economist Joseph Stiglitz writing that today "rent seeking is pervasive in the American economy."[204]

For those who want more quantitative data on the trend, a review of the number of tax expenditures in the tax code provides additional evidence that the wealthy have been able to capture increasingly large rents over recent decades. Tax expenditures are special tax breaks for select groups or specific activities.[205] A few emblematic examples include the "carried interest loophole," which allows hedge fund managers to pay a lower tax rate on their income than most workers, and the numerous tax breaks for oil and gas companies, such as "expensing of intangible drilling costs."[206]

Since the federal government began keeping track of tax expenditures in the early 1970s, their numbers have grown steadily.[207] According to the Government Accountability Office, "Between 1974 and 2004, tax expenditures doubled in number from 67 to 146."[208] The number has continued to climb, so that by 2013 there were 173 tax expenditures, according to Pew Charitable Trusts.[209] Despite the fact that there have been several "tax reform" bills over this period, the number of special carve outs has continued to grow steadily, strongly suggesting that wealthy special interests have increasingly used their power to secure government benefits.[210]

To be fair, not all tax expenditures are clearly rent seeking. Some expenditures serve a broader purpose and do benefit the middle class. But they often contain some element of rent seeking since attempts to provide the same benefit to the middle class, but in a more efficient manner, often meet with industry opposition.[211] Further, the vast majority of tax expenditure dollars are directed to those with higher incomes. According to the Congressional Budget Office, about half of tax expenditure dollars go to those in the top income quintile, with most benefits going to the very top.[212] The top 1 percent of income earners get roughly one-sixth of all tax expenditures.

And then there is the most brazen form of rent seeking: corruption, which occurs when a government employee or elected official engages in illegal activity for personal benefit. All evidence indicates that corruption has increased as the middle class has declined. Rich individuals and firms appear to be bribing politicians more frequently.

While paper bags stuffed with cash being delivered surreptitiously to an elected official in exchange for a favor may seem the stuff of movies or the plague of other countries, such activities do happen in the United States. Indeed, in 2013 a former Washington, DC, city council member pleaded guilty to "accepting tens of thousands of dollars in cash stuffed in duffel bags and coffee cups while in office," and in 2009 a Louisiana congressman was convicted of corruption after FBI agents found $90,000 of cash stashed in a freezer that they traced back to a briefcase the Congressman received.[213] All five commissioners from Jefferson County, Alabama, were convicted of taking bribes to engage in activities that ultimately led to the bankruptcy of the county.[214] The bribery was so egregious that the judge who upheld the corruption convictions wrote: "'Kleptocracy' is a term used to describe '(a) government characterized by rampant greed and corruption.'... To that definition dictionaries might add, as a helpful illustration: 'See, for example, Alabama's Jefferson County Commission in the period from 1998 to 2008.'"[215]

Studies of official corruption find that it occurs more frequently in US states with higher levels of income inequality, such as Louisiana and Alabama, even after controlling for other factors that affect a region's corruption such as its average income and education levels.[216] Harvard's Edward Glaeser and Raven Saks, for example, examined corruption in US states between 1976 and 2002 and found that "income inequality ... increases corruption."[217]

While cross-state studies are helpful at showing that inequality is linked to corruption, they do not show whether overall levels of corruption have risen in recent decades. But the US Department of Justice has been keeping track of conviction statistics for official corruption since the 1970s and their statistics indicate that the number of government officials convicted of corruption as a share of the total population nearly quadrupled from 1972 to 2012.[218] It is important to note that these official government statistics have some flaws for measuring corruption over time because they measure convictions, not corruption.[219] A host of factors can influence conviction rates besides the corruption rate. But still, these time trend data are the best available, and they are consistent with other evidence.

The World Bank, for example, has maintained since 1996 the "Control of Corruption Index" based on international expert surveys that also indicates an increase in corruption.[220] Polls of the American public paint a similar picture. The American National Election Survey, a long-running academic poll, shows that, in 1972, 36 percent of Americans thought "quite a few" government officials were "crooked," and the percentage who felt similarly in 2012 rose to 60 percent.[221] While these surveys of the public corroborate the findings from official statistics, it is worth noting that they capture not only sentiments about strictly illegal corrupt activities, but also a broader assessment of rent seeking, the difference between illegal bribes and legal campaign contributions or a revolving door of lucrative job opportunities being lost on many.

A host of measures indicate that as inequality has increased in recent decades, government has increasingly been used to provide special favors to help wealthy and powerful interests. This has harmed the economy by wasting tax dollars, stifling competition and innovation, and contributing to the financial crisis of 2007 and 2008.

CONCLUSION

American government performs worse than it did several decades ago when the middle class was stronger. Over the past several decades as inequality has risen, the rich have used their growing wealth to gain influence over government policymaking, political conflict has intensified, and some of the basic elements of the civic community have weakened. And critically, these failures of government have hurt growth.

The disproportionate power of the wealthy to secure public policies to their liking—through lobbying, campaign expenditures, and other means of influence—has fundamentally harmed significant parts of the economy. Rent seeking has increased, as evidenced by the Wall Street bailout with no strings attached and the doubling of the number of tax breaks over the past few decades. Outright corruption has also risen sharply. Spending on higher education has stagnated and investments in infrastructure have fallen—even though the public strongly desires greater spending on these priorities.

Because of these perversions of government, we are no longer a leader in college attainment (having been passed by a host of competitors), our Internet is slow and costly, and our infrastructure is less reliable than in some developing countries. When these failures of government hinder other economies, they are easy to see. Though it is harder to admit that the same types of failures are happening in the United States, the evidence is clear that they are.

CHAPTER FOUR

Stable Consumer Demand

In 1914, Henry Ford took a bold action that changed the automobile industry and helped shape the American economy for decades to come. In that year, he more than doubled his workers' wages, paying them $5 per day—a big jump from the $2.34 he previously paid—and far above what the market required.[1] Newspapers ran headlines trumpeting the decision. As workers from around the country flocked to Detroit, eager to earn such a high wage, most took it for granted that Ford was acting based on some high ideal. Many supported Ford for what they presumed was an amazing act of kindness, though some business leaders condemned him for inserting moral values into the workplace where they felt they did not belong.[2] Indeed, the *Wall Street Journal* wrote a scathing editorial arguing that Ford's "Biblical" principles led him to commit "economic blunders, if not crimes."[3]

But Ford did not raise wages out of a noble principle or a fondness for workers. Indeed, Ford was notorious for running an organization that spied on employees at their homes and bloodied union organizers.[4] Rather, Ford's decision to raise wages was strictly business.[5]

Ford needed satisfied workers who would stay on the job and, as the owner of a big company churning out mass consumer products, he also benefited from a base of consumers with growing incomes who could afford his cars. As he explained: "The people who consume the bulk of goods are the people who make them.... That is a fact we must never forget—that is the secret of our prosperity."[6] Indeed, after raising wages, Ford nearly doubled car sales in just two years and significantly increased profits.[7]

The example of Henry Ford provides a good illustration of the key role middle-class demand plays in fostering economic growth and is also a fairly accurate description of how the US economy worked in the decades after World War II. During that period, workers were allowed to share more equally in the economy's gains, and because workers' incomes were rising, they could consume more. Because consumption was growing, companies had a strong incentive to invest in new factories, processes, and products, which helped make production more efficient and increased economic growth.

Unfortunately, this pattern no longer fits the US economy. In the years leading up to the Great Recession of 2007–2009, consumption was based heavily on rising debt instead of rising income. The debt that middle-class consumers shouldered made the economy more vulnerable to a crash, and has slowed the recovery.[8] Today, after the official end of the recession, the economy limps along because middle-class consumers have pulled back, as they struggle to reduce their debt load and adjust to declining incomes, which has made businesses reluctant to embark on new investments. As Nick Hanauer, an entrepreneur and venture capitalist who was the first nonfamily investor in Amazon, wrote in a 2011 column that echoed much of Henry Ford's thinking: "I can start a business based on a great idea, and initially hire dozens or hundreds of people. But if no one can afford to buy what I have to sell, my business will soon fail and all those jobs will evaporate."[9]

As a result, the American economy is likely to continue muddling along well below its potential output for many years costing the economy millions of potential jobs and trillions of dollars in lost growth. Adding insult to injury, during this period the long-term unemployed—of which there were 3.4 million in May 2014—have tended to lose skills, which makes it more difficult for them to reconnect to the labor force and reduces their productivity and earnings when they do.[10] And if interest rates rise significantly in the future, making debts more costly to repay, consumers could be forced to cut back to a greater degree than they already have. Thus the problem of constrained consumer demand will have a big impact on the long-run growth of the economy.[11]

THE ECONOMICS OF CONSUMER DEMAND
AND THE MIDDLE CLASS

The critical connection between demand and economic growth is central to a long and distinguished economic tradition. During the 1930s, as the Great Depression lingered on and on, the legendary British economist John Maynard Keynes explained how consumers and business could become trapped in a vicious cycle, where low levels of consumption and excess capacity lead to very little new investment or hiring. Under these conditions the economy would be unlikely to return itself to prior levels, and could instead become stuck for an extended period of time with very weak or even negative growth. Keynes argued that in order for the economy to grow there needed to be a proper balance between supply and demand.

Rising demand is necessary to spur the new investments that fuel growth.[12] Businesses make capital investments or hire more workers when they think there are enough consumers for their product to make the potential for profit worth the risks. Their expectations about consumer demand are critical. As Keynes argued, "New capital investment can only take place ... if *future* expenditure on consumption is expected to increase."[13] Business investment is highly sensitive to changes in consumer demand: when consumers pull back even slightly, businesses become quite reluctant to hire or invest.

This link between demand, investment, and growth means that when there is inadequate demand the economy can suffer through a long period where unemployment is high and growth slow or nonexistent. As Keynes wrote, "The mere existence of an insufficiency of effective demand may, and often will, bring the increase of employment to a standstill *before* a level of full employment has been reached."[14]

Unfortunately, in the 1970s Keynes fell somewhat out of favor in economics departments, though for many economists demand continued to play a key role in explaining how the economy works, especially during hard times. Even worse, for the past several decades, supply-side economics has dominated policymaking. As its name implies, supply side dismisses the importance of consumption and instead emphasizes the supply side, especially the cost of capital—affected largely by taxes and regulation—as the primary driver of investment. "Economists need give scant attention to the 'demand' side of their law of supply and demand," wrote Jude Wanniski, one of the early promoters of supply side.[15] The limits of consumers' "ability to demand rest entirely on the supply side of the equation."

Neglecting demand was, of course, pure folly. The importance of demand has always been apparent to those who cared to look, but since the Great Recession started, the value of consumer and investment demand has been painfully obvious. The US economy has been awash in supply—think of the crumbling housing market with foreclosed houses sitting vacant, for example. And the ability of the economy to supply even more didn't suddenly go away: carpenters didn't forget how to build houses, nor were factories destroyed so that businesses could no longer make things. The problem is that there just isn't enough demand. As John Williams, president and CEO of Federal Reserve Bank of San Francisco, explained in 2013: "The primary reason unemployment remains high is a lack of demand."[16]

Since the Great Recession, economists have come running back to Keynes. As Robert Lucas Jr., a University of Chicago economist critical of Keynes, quipped in 2008 as the economy was collapsing: "I guess everyone is a Keynesian in a foxhole."[17] Even some notable supply siders have had to acknowledge that the lack of aggregate demand has contributed to America's continued high unemployment and slow economic growth.[18] Bruce Bartlett, a former senior official in the Reagan and George H. W. Bush administrations, for example, wrote of the economy's recent struggles: "It's the aggregate demand, stupid."[19] Only a few die-hard supply siders still discount the importance of adequate demand growth and instead believe the misguided proposition that supply creates its own demand.[20] But of course, supply does not create its own demand—especially in recessions.

Though many academic economists understand the importance of demand, far too few recognized in the run-up to the

Great Recession that the weakened middle class was altering consumer demand in ways that threatened the economy. They simply didn't consider how rising inequality affected demand. As Nobel Prize–winning economist Joseph Stiglitz explained: "For years, the dominant paradigm in macroeconomics, which assumed that income distribution did not matter, at least for macroeconomic behavior, ignored inequality."[21] Indeed, a review of popular macroeconomics textbooks in 2004 found just one instance where income distribution was mentioned as affecting consumption.[22]

Economists ignored the weakness of the middle class because their main models of economic growth assumed that the economy could be thought about as if it were a single, "representative" person.[23] Even the more complicated versions of these models made similar assumptions.[24] These assumptions made the models relatively easy to work with, and for a time they seemed to produce useful results. But they were fundamentally flawed.

Because of their faulty models, many economists believed that rising debt levels among American consumers were nothing to worry about because, on average, American consumers were also becoming wealthier—the representative consumer was doing fine.[25] Never mind that most of the rise in wealth was concentrated among the very rich, or that any wealth gains for the middle class were based on a housing bubble. Though a few economists did warn in the run-up to the Great Recession that economic inequality was shaping consumer demand in ways that posed problems for the economy, they were generally outside the mainstream.[26]

Only since the Great Recession has the economics profession focused in earnest on the links between the middle class, demand, and economic growth. In part because of the newness of much of this research, there is still debate about exactly how the strength of the middle class affects economic growth through consumer demand. However, a few things are clear: First, the high levels of debt taken on by the middle class in the years prior to the Great Recession made the economy more susceptible to a crash and exacerbated the recession's severity. Second, the recovery has been very slow because the beleaguered middle class has reduced its consumption. These two facts provide powerful evidence that the weakening of the American middle class has profoundly harmed economic growth by affecting consumer demand.

DEBT AND THE LEAD-UP TO
THE GREAT RECESSION

In the decades leading up to the Great Recession, the middle class maintained high levels of consumption—despite stagnating incomes—by cutting back on their savings and taking on more and more debt. Indeed, the rise in debt for the middle class was staggering.

From 1960 to the mid-1980s, the total amount of household debt in the economy remained fairly steady as a percentage of disposable income.[27] But then debt began rising throughout the late 1980s and 1990s and skyrocketed in the 2000s, so that, by 2007, total household debt as a share of disposable income had roughly doubled over two decades.[28] Home mortgage debt accounted for most of the rise, but other forms of debt, such as credit card debt, also increased sharply.[29] Over the same time period, the national household savings rate plummeted from about 8 percent of disposable income to below 2 percent.[30]

The rising debt loads were heavily borne by the middle class.[31] For the rich, debt as a share of income grew very little.[32] But for everyone else—whose incomes were stagnating—the additional debt they took on translated into sharply rising debt burdens. In 2007, debt for the bottom 95 percent of income earners was well over 150 percent of income, while for the top 5 percent, debt reached only slightly above 60 percent of income.[33] Moreover, the middle class and the poor were highly leveraged—meaning that they had a lot of debt compared to their assets—while the rich had significant other assets to cover their debt if necessary.[34]

Because of debt-fueled consumption, demand remained quite strong—and actually increased.[35] In the decades leading up to the Great Recession, the American economy depended, to a shocking degree, on debt. According to one estimate, approximately 8 percent of aggregate demand before the economy collapsed was based on the extra borrowing of households in the bottom 95 percent of the income distribution.[36] For a while, this debt-based consumption helped prop up the economy. As Federal Reserve economist William Emmons wrote: "It is no exaggeration to say that consumer spending was the dominant source of economic growth" in the period before the crash.[37]

Why exactly middle-class demand was based so heavily on debt is debated, but there are likely a number of reasons rather than a single cause. To be sure, some people simply lacked impulse control and spent well beyond their means.[38] But the main story is that the weakness of the middle class combined together with increased availability of credit to fuel debt to record levels. Credit increased at least partially because the rich used their growing wealth to influence the political process and deregulate banking, as described in chapter 3, though technological changes, such as computer models that helped automate the loan process, were also very important.[39] With looser credit, more people could qualify for mortgages, home equity loans, and credit cards and take on higher levels of debt than they previously could. The fact that credit cards and especially mortgages—particularly for people with low credit scores, uneven income history, and little wealth—became more readily available was of critical importance to the rise of debt in America.[40] But if the middle class had been in better shape, it is unlikely that debt would have reached such high levels or been such a problem.

Many Americans took on additional debt because the cost of what are perceived as core middle-class goods—such as housing, education, and healthcare—increased more rapidly than their incomes, and they wanted to hang on to a middle-class lifestyle.[41] Indeed, between 1970 and 2009, the median home price increased at double the rate of inflation, as did the cost of college, while healthcare costs increased 50 percent faster than inflation.[42] With incomes stagnant, debt was the primary way to afford these middle-class basics.

The sharp increase in housing prices was critical because housing is typically the single biggest purchase that most households make, dwarfing other financial decisions. So when housing prices skyrocketed—most notably between 1998 and 2006—purchasing a home often necessitated going deep into debt, especially in areas where housing prices rose much more sharply than the national average.[43] And because a house is not just a place to live, but also a means of access to a school district, people were especially willing to stretch to afford a house in an area where their children would receive a good education.[44]

The role of rising house prices was important not just because it meant that the price of a necessity was increasing, but also because it temporarily boosted homeowners' net wealth. With home prices rising rapidly, homeowners were getting wealthier and they—and their lenders—could discount the amount of the debt they were accumulating. Because the middle class appeared wealthier, they felt justified in consuming more—even though their incomes weren't increasing. To a large degree, Americans used the value of their homes to maintain a middle-class lifestyle as their incomes stagnated. Atif Mian, a Princeton economist, and Amir Sufi, a finance professor at the University of Chicago, found that for every dollar increase in home equity during the housing boom, the average homeowner extracted 25 cents, much of which was likely used for additional consumption.[45]

Another part of the reason debt levels rose so much was that the consumption patterns of the very rich—whose incomes were growing rapidly—shifted the frame of reference for what the middle class felt they should consume.[46] A house or other product that once seemed more than adequate for a middle-class person felt inferior compared to the growing size and luxury of the purchases of those at the very top. A second bathroom so parents wouldn't have to share with their children or a third bedroom so children could have their own room no longer seemed excessive when the wealthy were adding on guest quarters to their already large homes. As a number of researchers have found, when people are exposed to how the wealthy consume, their consumption increases.[47]

But, no matter why Americans took on so much debt, such high levels of middle-class debt posed a great risk to the economy. The American middle class did not have much saved—and most of their assets were in the value of their homes. If trouble hit—if they lost their jobs or the value of their home dropped—the middle class would need to pare back sharply on their consumption or even default on their loans, which would have ripple effects throughout the economy.

By late 2007, trouble was starting to brew. Housing prices had stopped their meteoric rise and stood well below their peak in mid-2006, unemployment had started to inch up, and credit markets began to tighten.[48] Because of the precarious state of the middle class, these were ominous signs. If any of these conditions worsened, a cycle of falling demand could easily drive the economy steeply downward. Thus, on the eve of the Great Recession, the economy was set up for a great crash—and inequality had a role in pushing it there.

THE GREAT RECESSION AND THE COLLAPSE OF MIDDLE-CLASS DEMAND

The Great Recession officially started in December 2007, but panic really hit in the fall of 2008. The Dow Jones stock index fell a record 777 points in a single day, 765,000 people lost their jobs in just one month, housing prices dropped precipitously, and credit froze up until the federal government stepped in with massive bailouts for the large financial institutions that financed the housing bubble.[49]

Declining home prices, falling stock prices, tightening credit, and rising unemployment all reinforced one another and made debt harder and harder to repay. Because so many households were unable to repay their mortgages, the value of housing continued to decline, which caused great damage not only to homeowners but also to banks and other financial institutions on Wall Street.[50] Because Wall Street was in trouble, credit dried up, harming businesses that depended upon loans to finance investments and households seeking to buy homes. Lots of workers lost their jobs. The stock market dropped significantly as more and more companies faced threats. All of which dried up

demand. The longer the recession carried on, the more consumer spending dropped.[51] Sarah Bloom Raskin, then a member
of the board of governors of the Federal Reserve, summarized
these links in a speech in 2013 where she explained that "because
of how hard these lower- and middle-income households were
hit, the recession was worse, and the recovery has been weaker."[52]

Housing—the main source of middle-class debt—was especially important to the pullback in consumption and the subsequent downfall of the economy.[53] Housing is a far more important
asset to the middle class and the poor than it is to the rich, who
typically have other sources of wealth such as stocks and bonds.
As a result, when housing prices dropped by 30 percent from 2006
to 2009, the middle class and the poor suffered much greater
declines in net worth than the rich.[54] The decline in home prices
wiped out the small amount of wealth many middle-class and
poor families had been able to accumulate, so much so that many
were left owing far more than their house was worth.[55] And
because many middle-class families had such large mortgages,
the hit to their net worth was often much greater than the drop in
housing prices. In 2010, about one-third of all home sales were
short sales or foreclosures.[56] Even after all these distress sales, in
2011 one-quarter of all properties with a mortgage had negative
equity, meaning more was owed on the mortgage than the home
was worth.[57] One estimate finds that between 2007 and 2011, one-
fourth of Americans lost at least 75 percent of their wealth.[58]

With high levels of debt, stagnant incomes, and net worth in
free fall, the middle class and the poor pulled back on their
spending, which sent shockwaves throughout the economy.
Amir Sufi and Atif Mian estimated that over half of the recession's job losses resulted from the reduction in consumption
caused by the drop in housing prices. They wrote that the

"decline in aggregate demand related to household balance sheet weakness is the primary explanation for high and persistent unemployment during the economic slump."[59]

Similarly, Karen Dynan, then a fellow at the Brookings Institution, found that housing debt played a key role in exacerbating the recession. Dynan's research shows that in states that had experienced particularly strong housing booms in the lead-up to the recession, consumption for households with high levels of debt fell by twice as much as it did for other households when the Great Recession hit.[60]

The high levels of debt taken on by middle-class households were not the only factor that drove the Great Recession—risky Wall Street practices were of course key—but the weakness of the middle class was, undeniably, an important contributor. And all told, the Great Recession imposed a massive toll. The unemployment rate doubled between December 2007 and October 2009.[61] Twenty-two percent of America's household wealth was destroyed in just one year alone—2008—as housing prices plummeted and the stock market crashed.[62] After reaching their peak in early 2006, inflation-adjusted housing prices fell for nearly six years before finally bottoming out at the beginning of 2012, by which point they were approximately 40 percent lower.[63]

THE AFTERMATH OF THE GREAT RECESSION

There is also little doubt that weak consumer demand has hampered the recovery. The Great Recession was a shock for middle-class households and caused them to increase savings, reduce debt, and trim their spending. As the Fed's Raskin explained, households "are curtailing their spending in an effort to rebuild their nest eggs and may also be trimming their budgets in order to bring their debt levels into alignment with their new economic realities."[64] As a host of evidence indicates, consumers have pulled back and are, as economists put it, "deleveraging."[65] At the end of 2012, household debt as a percentage of income was about one-fifth below peak levels.[66] Savings rates in 2012 had increased to almost the levels they were in the mid-1990s.[67]

Not surprisingly, it is the middle class—far more so than the affluent—that are reducing their spending the most. Barry Cynamon and Steven Fazzari of Washington University found that since the recession the middle class has been consuming much less than they previously did, while the consumption among the affluent has enjoyed a much more robust recovery.[68] "The consumption rate of the bottom 95 percent collapsed," they wrote.[69] In contrast, they found that the top 5 percent were able to maintain their consumption much more successfully through the recession thanks to their higher incomes and comparatively small debt burdens. Similarly, the *Wall Street Journal* has emphasized that the decline in consumption from the middle class has been the problem. The rich still have money to spend and so companies that cater to them have done fine, but most companies are more reliant on middle-class demand, and they have suffered most. "Spending on luxury goods has generally held up in the aftermath of the recession," the article explained.[70] "But companies whose fortunes are linked to the pocketbooks of average Americans aren't doing as well."

Reducing spending and increasing savings are good for individuals seeking to get out of debt and build a nest egg. But it reduced aggregate demand, which weakened the recovery.[71] For years, consumer spending was lower than prerecession trends, and rose more slowly than after prior recessions.[72] As University of Massachusetts's Christian Weller explains: "Too much household debt ... remains the scourge of the U.S. economy," because it "holds back consumer spending."[73]

Not only do academic economists find that lack of demand is hurting the recovery, but so too do surveys of businesses. For several years after the Great Recession, monthly polls of small businesses consistently said that the single most important problem in the economy was "poor sales"—meaning weak demand.[74] A survey of economic forecasters found that most agreed that the "main reason U.S. companies are reluctant to step up hiring is scant demand."[75] Most large retailers now tell their investors that weak consumer demand is a risk to their business.[76]

Without sufficient consumer demand, businesses are afraid to hire employees or invest in new factories. Instead of investing and creating jobs, businesses are sitting on "record-high amounts" of money.[77] According to the Federal Reserve, as of the third quarter of 2013, nonfinancial companies held nearly $1.8 trillion in cash or other liquid assets.[78] At least part of the reason companies are doing so is because of the lack of demand.[79] As the *Wall Street Journal* explained: "The cash buildup shows the deep caution many companies feel about investing in expansion while the economic recovery remains painfully slow and high unemployment and battered household finances continue to limit consumers' ability to spend."[80]

As a result of weak demand and the corresponding lack of investment, the recovery from the Great Recession has been sluggish. Though the economy is starting to improve, the average rate of job growth since the recession ended has been so slow that if trends continue, estimates indicate, it could take several more years to finally reach the employment levels the United States maintained prior to the crash.[81]

The evidence makes clear that the high debt levels of the middle class and their stagnant incomes have held back the recovery and mired the economy in a prolonged period of weakness.[82] As Princeton economist Alan Krueger stated in a speech he gave in 2012: "We are in a period with excess capacity ... the economy would be in better shape and aggregate demand would be stronger if the size of the middle class had not dwindled as a result of rising inequality."[83] Even conservatives, such as John Makin, a resident scholar at the American Enterprise Institute, give a similar explanation for the prolonged sluggishness of the economy, indicating just how obvious this point is. In a paper from 2013, Makin explained that "the large wealth losses during 2008 prompted American households to restrict consumption to help restore wealth losses through a higher savings rate. The byproduct of this, of course, has been a slow pace of GDP growth and a subpar recovery."[84]

CONCLUSION

Growing middle-class consumption helps fuel economic growth by providing an impetus for businesses to hire workers, make new investments, and produce new goods and services. As Henry Ford recognized 100 years ago when he doubled his workers' wages, the economy depends upon consumers being able to afford the goods that businesses produce. More recently, the businessman Nick Hanauer provocatively made this point: "Only consumers can set in motion a virtuous cycle that allows companies to survive and thrive and business owners to hire. An ordinary middle-class consumer is far more of a job creator than I ever have been or ever will be."[85]

But, during the supply-side era the critical importance of demand was discounted by too many politicians and the key role middle-class consumers play in supporting this demand was overlooked by too many economists. The Great Recession showed the errors of such ignorance.

In the years leading up to the crash, consumption was based not on rising incomes as is necessary for sustainable growth, but on the growing debt load of the middle class. This made the economy more fragile and the crash much sharper than it would have been otherwise. And since the financial collapse, the recovery has been weak because the middle class—buffeted by high levels of debt, declining wages, and an inability or unwillingness to borrow more—has reduced their consumption. As Joseph Stiglitz explains: "In some sense the entire shortfall in aggregate demand—and hence in the US economy—today can be blamed on the extremes of inequality."[86] As this chapter makes clear, to get the economy back on track will take strong and sustainable demand from a thriving middle class.

CHAPTER FIVE

Human Capital

When Steve Jobs—the founder of several of the most important companies in the world including Apple and Pixar Animation Studios—was six years old, his father gave him some small tools and set aside a corner of his workbench. "Steve, this is your workbench now," his father said, and he began showing his son how to take things apart and put them back together.[1] Jobs's father was not highly educated—he never graduated from high school—but he was able to share his mechanical skills as well as his rudimentary knowledge of electronics with his son.

Over the years, Jobs spent a lot of time playing on that workbench, and among the most important projects he worked on were do-it-yourself kits with detailed instructions for building electronic devices. The kits were valuable because they gave Jobs an understanding of what was inside a finished product, but especially because they gave him a sense that he could actually build something he'd never worked on before. When he looked at a television or other piece of advanced equipment, he would think, "I haven't built one of those but I could."[2]

Though Jobs's parents were not highly educated and didn't have family wealth, they were able to provide a stable and supportive middle-class environment. During Jobs's childhood, his confidence, curiosity, and electronics knowledge were nurtured. For helping Jobs develop his skills, he credits not only his family but his fourth grade teacher, who was able to "re-ignite" his desire to learn, as well as some of the classes he attended in college.[3] This "human capital" when combined with some financial capital—from a small bit of savings Jobs had been able to sock away, the sale of his Volkswagen microbus, and similar contributions from his cofounder—enabled Jobs to start Apple.[4] And throughout his career, these skills helped him create novel products, from the Macintosh computer to the iPhone and iPad.

While Jobs was a unique talent, his story illustrates some basics of human capital, showing why it is important, but also hinting at why, as the middle class has weakened, we have fallen behind other countries in producing it.

Human capital is the stock of knowledge and skills that enable a person to perform economically valuable work. It is a broad concept that encompasses not only a person's education level, but also their experience, creativity, and health—all of which improve a worker's productivity.[5] When the middle class was stronger, more people had a chance to be like Steve Jobs and take full economic advantage of their talents. But as the middle class has weakened, it has become more difficult for individuals to develop and make use of their capacities.

Across a number of measures of human capital, America was once a leader, but now fares quite poorly. The United States has fallen behind many other countries on a host of educational outcomes. We have much worse health outcomes than other rich countries. Entrepreneurship is down, and has fallen by nearly half as a share of the population over recent decades. And in the most comprehensive measure of wasted talent, the ability of American children to rise above the economic position of their parents is below most other advanced countries. Not surprisingly, in a global survey conducted in 2013 of a broad range of human capital measures, the United States ranked just sixteenth.[6]

The sad state of human capital in America goes against the predictions of supply-side economics. According to supply side, growing levels of inequality provide greater incentives for people to get more education so they can earn more money.[7] In a similar vein, George W. Bush's White House argued that his tax cuts—which disproportionately benefited the highest income earners—would unleash "the entrepreneurial spirit," because "the lower the marginal rate, the greater the incentive to … start a new business."[8] Supply-side logic clearly failed to pan out. Instead of helping people develop and utilize their talents, extreme levels of economic inequality have weakened human capital in America, directly refuting the mechanisms underpinning supply-side economics.

The weakness of human capital in the United States is also an indictment of the faulty logic employed by too many academic economists. Though many economists recognized that inequality could on occasion hinder the development of human capital, much of the profession felt that on balance inequality promoted human capital. According to the standard economic theory, inequality provides incentives for individuals to acquire additional knowledge and skills. Supposedly, the greater the differences in earnings between people with high and low levels of education, the greater the incentive to pursue higher levels of education.[9] While there is a body of economic research showing that the poor and even the middle class often cannot make the optimal level of investments in their education because they do not have enough money or the ability to borrow, little of this research made its way into economists' understanding of growth—and thus the standard theory that inequality helps foster human capital and economic growth prevailed.[10]

Because the modern economy depends upon human capital, the failure to take advantage of America's human talents is causing deep harm to our economy.[11] As Nobel Prize–winning economist Theodore Schultz explains, "Human capital ... is the key to economic progress."[12] Some studies find that human capital is the most important factor for growth in the modern economy, while others find that it is of equal importance to physical capital or just slightly less important.[13] But virtually all find that it is critical.

To be sure, the relationships between inequality, education, health, entrepreneurship, and mobility are complicated and there are important feedback loops with inequality both causing and being caused by, for example, poor educational outcomes. These caveats are critical to a proper understanding, but they should not take away from the basic story that America is failing to fully develop and take advantage of the human capital of its people in significant part because of the decline of the middle class.

EDUCATION

Though his dad hadn't even finished high school, Steve Jobs went to college, which made him fairly typical of his era, when roughly 65 percent of men were more highly educated than their fathers.[14] This continual advancement helped make the United States a world leader in educational performance, graduating students from high school and college at a higher rate than most every other country in the world.[15] But today, fewer American children receive more education than their parents, and it is becoming increasingly common for children to receive less education than their parents.[16]

Because the United States is not rapidly increasing its education levels, it is falling behind other countries that are. High school graduation rates have hardly budged since the 1970s, and are well below the level of countries like the United Kingdom and even Hungary.[17] Our college graduation rates have also hardly moved in decades. The United States now ranks fourteenth in the world in college graduation rates, down from being tied for first not so long ago.[18]

International tests of high school students that measure math, science, and reading knowledge show that the United States is in the middle of the pack of wealthy countries, well behind countries like Finland, Canada, Korea, and Australia.[19] The United States has lower average test scores than many of its competitors because it has more low scorers—who can't perform even basic skills—as well as fewer high performers, with advanced thinking and reasoning skills.[20] The top 10 percent of Canadians, for example, scored about 10 points higher on an international reading test than the top 10 percent of Americans, while the bottom 10 percent of Canadians scored 33 points higher than the bottom-scoring Americans.[21] Comparisons with, for example, Finland produce similar results.[22]

These differences in test scores are not just about a few points; they have great meaning in the real world. As Joseph Merry, a sociologist at Ohio State, finds, low-scoring Americans are two years behind their Canadian counterparts, while high-scoring Americans are outpaced by almost a year.[23]

Studies of workplace skills produce similar results. American adults lag well behind other rich countries in the skills needed in the modern workplace.[24] Even worse, young adults are further behind on workplace skills than older Americans.

To proponents of trickle-down economics, the fact that the United States is falling behind in education doesn't make much sense. The economic rewards of a good education in the United States have been increasing over recent decades and are higher here than in some of the other countries that have passed us in educational attainment.[25] This should provide an economic incentive for people to do well in school and graduate from college. But future earning potential isn't the only thing that drives educational achievement, as Heather Boushey, the executive director of the Washington Center for Equitable Growth, and John Schmitt, a senior economist with the Center for Economic and Policy Research, highlight in their research.[26] Other factors matter quite a bit, including teacher quality, school structure, curriculum, level of parental support, other opportunities for students, and peer pressure, to name just a few. And of course the amount of money a family has to devote to the education of its children affects many of the factors that shape the quality of education.

In the United States, it is clear that money has become more important than ever for academic achievement. Our education system reinforces inequality. As inequality has risen, the rich can more easily afford to buy houses in areas with good neighborhood schools or send their children to private schools.[27] The rich can also more easily afford skyrocketing college tuitions, while these costs present more of a barrier to the education of children from middle-class and poor families.[28]

The wealthy also have far more money than the middle class to pay for enrichment activities like art classes and summer camps that boost academic achievement.[29] The wealthy even increasingly pay for "educational consultants" to help prepare their children for admissions to selective schools, from preschool all the way through college.[30] While the middle class and the poor have been spending more than they previously did on these enrichment activities, they can't compete with the growing wealth of the affluent.[31] The middle class doesn't have the income—or the ability to borrow—to keep up.[32] The middle class and the poor also are less likely than the rich to have the kinds of stable and predictable jobs that facilitate long-term investments in children.[33]

Inequality also tends to result in people living in areas where others have very similar incomes, and this residential segregation may be harming the educational performance of the less affluent.[34] This is especially likely now that public schools have become increasingly reliant on donations from parents, which means that public schools in poorer areas can access smaller donations from parents, while those in more affluent areas can rely on higher levels of donations.[35] Further, economic inequality also leads to political inequality, which leads to less spending on public education than would otherwise occur, as the wealthy resist paying taxes to support education spending, as described at length in chapter 3. Political inequality also often leads to education dollars being unequally distributed, with greater resources frequently going to more affluent areas.[36] Finally, healthier students perform better academically.[37] But in unequal societies, citizens, especially those who aren't affluent, are less healthy, as will be explained at length later in this chapter.

All in all, as inequality has risen, the wealthy have been able to make much greater investments in their children's education than the middle class and the poor have. As a result, family income has overshadowed other factors that determine how well individual students perform, such as talent and hard work.[38] Certainly, the rich often have noneconomic advantages to pass on that can affect education, such as their connections, expectations, family structure, and behaviors, but their money matters greatly.[39]

These factors have led to large and growing gaps in America between the educational outcomes of children from middle-class backgrounds and those of their upper-class peers. In fact, on tests of math and reading achievement, children from wealthy families outscore children from middle-class backgrounds by about twice the amount they did in the 1970s.[40] For poorer children, the gap with wealthier students is now 30 to 40 percent larger than it was 25 years ago.[41] While poor and middle-class students have increased their test scores over time, the wealthy have increased scores much more rapidly, widening the gap.[42]

The size of these gaps is staggering. The difference in educational performance between children from middle-class families and those from wealthy families is roughly the size of the black-white achievement gap.[43] The gap between poor and rich children is now nearly twice as large as the achievement gap between white students and black students.[44] As Sean Reardon, an education professor at Stanford, explains, "The rich now outperform the middle class by as much as the middle class outperform the poor."[45]

These stark income-based differences show up not just on tests, but also on other measures such as college graduation rates.[46] The wealthy are much more likely to attend and complete college than the poor or middle class—and over the past two decades these differences have widened sharply.[47] Over the past few decades the college completion rates for children raised in affluent families rose by about 20 percentage points, but they were stagnant for poorer families.[48] US Department of Education statistics now indicate that a middle-class student with high standardized test scores is less likely to complete college than a wealthy student with average test scores.[49] And a child from a poor family with high test scores is less likely to complete college than a wealthy child with low scores. Even for high school valedictorians, economic class matters for their college attendance.[50] Income-based differences in graduation from elite colleges are especially glaring. Only one-quarter of all students at these selective schools come from middle-class or poor families.[51] According to one estimate, the average annual income for the parents of Harvard students is now $450,000.[52]

That money is helping drive differences in educational outcomes in America can be most easily seen in early childhood, a period when a lot of learning and brain development occur.[53] Tests of infants, for example, show that on average children from wealthy and nonwealthy families have relatively similar levels of cognitive abilities.[54] But as these babies grow into toddlers and then reach school age, clear income-based differences emerge.[55]

Before kindergarten starts, most American families need to pay for child care out of their own pocketbooks, especially now that the vast majority of women with children work.[56] High-quality daycare and preschool are expensive and these costs have been increasing sharply: the weekly child-care costs paid by families with employed mothers grew by roughly 70 percent between 1985 and 2011, while median income was stagnant over this period.[57] As a result of these rapidly rising costs, the average family in 2011 that made child-care payments with a mother who worked full-time and a child under the age of five spent over 10 percent of its monthly income on child-care arrangements.[58]

But even spending such a high percentage of income on child care, many families still can't afford quality preschool—in part because the United States provides far less help for families with young children than most other developed countries.[59] So poor and middle-class children often make due with less. Many middle-class and poor children stay with neighbors or in informal care settings that, though generally safe, are not particularly educational, while their wealthier peers enjoy an enriching preschool environment with highly trained teachers working through an engaging curriculum. Indeed, the United States ranks twenty-third in the world in the percentage of four-year-olds enrolled in early childhood education.[60]

The significant differences in preschool environment help explain why middle-class and poorer children are already well behind their more affluent peers by the time they reach school age.[61] As Sean Reardon explains: "The academic gap is widening because rich students are increasingly entering kindergarten much better prepared to succeed in school than middle-class students."[62] Not all of these early differences are due to things money can buy—the wealthy also read more to their children, for example—but the ability to afford high-quality preschool is key.[63]

With such large class-based differences, the country's overall performance suffers because so many children are unable to reach their potential. Indeed, four- and five-year-old Americans lag behind children in other countries, such as Canada, on standardized test scores.[64] In fact, America's youngest students are behind those in leading countries by almost as much as our high school students.[65]

More generally, a growing body of research finds that countries with higher levels of economic inequality do worse academically than more equal countries.[66] For example, Dennis Condron, a sociologist at Oakland University, studied test scores of 15-year-olds in economically advanced countries and found that countries with higher levels of economic inequality had lower math and science test scores, even when controlling for factors such as GDP per capita.[67]

Other studies come to similar conclusions, even when they use different groups of countries, different tests of student achievement, and different statistical methods, providing strong evidence that economically unequal countries have worse education outcomes.[68] As Ming Ming Chiu, an education professor at SUNY Buffalo, and Lawrence Khoo, an economist at the City University of Hong Kong, find, students in countries with higher inequality generally have worse test scores.[69] Research on US states also finds that those with weaker middle classes—as measured by the share of income going to the middle 60 percent of the population—have lower scores on standardized math tests.[70]

All told, educational performance in the United States has suffered as inequality has risen to extreme levels and the middle class and the poor have had far fewer resources than the rich to devote to the education of their children. Critically, America's educational failings have big economic consequences. A report by McKinsey and Company, a global consulting firm, argues that the gap in academic achievement between children from high-income families and those from more modest backgrounds imposes "the economic equivalent of a permanent national recession."[71] If the United States raised its average score on international tests to the level of Finland, the United States could increase its GDP growth by roughly 1 percentage point per year, according to estimates by Eric Hanushek, a senior fellow at Stanford's Hoover Institution, and Ludger Woessmann, an economist at the University of Munich—which is a big deal since GDP growth is usually around 3 percent per year.[72] If America just made sure every student scored at a proficient level, the boost to GDP growth would be nearly as big, according to Hanushek and Woessmann's calculations.[73]

HEALTH

Health is the often overlooked component of human capital. But if a person is not healthy enough to regularly go to school or work, or, like Steve Jobs, dies prematurely in the middle of their working years, their ability to contribute to the economy is clearly curtailed. And if enough of a country's population suffers from poor health, then a nation's economy suffers. As a UN report explains, "Health is a key component of human capital, which in turn is an important determinant of economic growth."[74] A number of studies find that health has significant economic benefits, with one study estimating that 30 percent of the economic growth in wealthy countries is due to improvements in health.[75]

Unfortunately, the weakening of the middle class is very likely harming America's health. Certainly, many other factors have a more important influence on health, but money—and who has it—has played an increasingly important role.

There have been hundreds of studies looking at the connections between economic inequality and health, studying outcomes such as life expectancy, infant mortality, and years of healthy living, as well as a number of other measures. From these studies, we know that in the United States wealthier people are typically healthier than the middle class and the poor and that these class-based differences are getting bigger.[76] We also know that countries and regions with lower levels of economic inequality generally have healthier populations.[77] Finally, we know that health outcomes in the United States have fallen behind those in other rich countries over the past few decades.

As a comprehensive review of the data and research on health outcomes by the National Academy of Sciences in 2011 put it, "Over the past 25 years, life expectancy has been rising in the United States at a slower pace than has been achieved in many other high-income countries. Consequently, the United States has been falling steadily in the world rankings for level of life expectancy, and the gap between the United States and countries with the highest achieved life expectancies has been widening."[78] Indeed, the probability that an American will live to at least age 50 is now far below that of any of the other high-income countries that the National Academy's study examined.[79] Three decades ago, life expectancy was about average compared to other advanced countries; now it is the worst.[80]

And, for at least some segments of the US population, health outcomes have not only fallen behind those of other countries, but have actually deteriorated. Life expectancy for white women with low levels of education, for example, fell over the past two decades.[81] Similarly, the life expectancy for older women whose incomes are below the fortieth percentile has dropped markedly.[82] Further, the average birth weight of a child born in the United States has fallen since 1990, indicating that future health outcomes may worsen because low birth weight is a key predictor of chronic diseases in adulthood.[83] The fact that health outcomes for some Americans have actually gotten worse over recent decades is an astonishing fact. Since the advent of modern medicine, so long as there was no war or other disaster that caused major disruptions, people's health has generally gotten better over time.[84]

While there is broad agreement that economic inequality is correlated with poor health outcomes, there is an ongoing debate about whether high levels of inequality are actually causing the poor outcomes.[85] Some maintain that inequality reduces health directly by causing stress and other hardships, and indirectly, for example, by reducing access to healthcare for some people. In contrast, skeptical researchers argue that another factor, such as poverty, is actually driving the relationship—and once these factors are controlled for—inequality doesn't affect health.

The debate is highly contentious and unresolved, in part because data problems have made this a particularly tough question to settle.[86] Still, explanations that focus on poverty and try to rule out inequality or economic conditions that impact the broader middle class don't seem likely to explain all of the basic facts. Poverty rates are higher in the United States than in most other advanced countries, and people in poverty here typically have greater levels of material depravation, so poverty is likely part of the explanation. But poverty rates have not increased over the past few decades, and by some definitions, they have actually decreased.[87] Further, health outcomes have declined for a number of different groups of women, many of whom are not poor. And, compared to residents in other advanced countries, health outcomes not only for the poor but also for the middle class and above aren't great either. As the National Academy of Sciences put it, "The poor ranking of U.S. life expectancy is not merely the result of high mortality among those of low socioeconomic status. U.S. women at both higher and lower levels of socioeconomic status rank poorly in mortality."[88] This suggests that not only is poverty not the sole answer, neither is access to healthcare. As a result, efforts like the Affordable Care Act, which will increase access to health insurance and improve health outcomes for many (especially for poorer Americans), are unlikely to change the trend of America having worse health outcomes than most other rich countries.

In contrast, there is at least some good evidence that high levels of inequality are causing America's poor health. The review by the National Academy of Sciences explained that though firm conclusions are premature, "studies suggest that economic inequality could explain some of the difference in life expectancy between the United States and other countries." As another review of the literature, by Karen Rowlingson, a professor of social policy at the University of Birmingham, argued: "This is a highly complex area both theoretically and methodologically and there is still some disagreement among academics on many related issues, but the main conclusion here is that there is some evidence that income inequality has negative effects" on health.[89]

So while there is still debate about whether the extremely high levels of economic inequality in the United States are harming American's heath, there is a good probability it is true.[90] Further, even if inequality per se isn't driving the trends, the underlying mechanisms at work almost certainly involve the growing economic weakness of the middle class and the poor. Money matters for so many things that are related to health outcomes, from access to care, to levels of pollution in a neighborhood, to food quality and job stresses. And over recent decades the middle class and the poor have had a far harder time than the rich. As the National Academy of Sciences explained, "Socioeconomic status can be considered a fundamental cause of differentials in health and mortality and one that works through many mechanisms."[91] The financial weakness of the middle class and the poor over recent decades seems most likely to explain why health outcomes for the poor and the middle class have worsened compared to the rich, and why the United States has fallen behind so many other countries, though only additional research will explain all the links.

ENTREPRENEURSHIP

Good ideas don't naturally and inevitably lead to the creation of new companies. Someone needs to do the work of transforming an idea into a new company that sells a marketable product, as Steve Jobs did with Apple and Pixar. Those people are called entrepreneurs, and they play a key role in fostering economic growth. Entrepreneurs help introduce innovations, especially breakthrough innovations that create an entirely new market, and are critical in the early evolution of new industries—from automobiles in the early 1900s to high tech much later in the twentieth century—transforming small shops into world leaders.[92] Entrepreneurs also increase competition, forcing existing firms to be more productive and innovative, or else go out of business as part of the creative destruction that makes capitalism so dynamic.[93] And the new firms they create boost employment.[94]

As a result, entrepreneurs are critical for the growth of advanced countries.[95] But, as inequality has risen, entrepreneurship in America has weakened. The United States may pride itself on its entrepreneurial spirit, but the facts point to deep troubles with this self-conception.

It is notoriously hard to measure entrepreneurship—and there is no single official government measure—but overwhelming evidence points in the same downward direction.[96] For example, in the mid-1970s, for every 10,000 Americans over

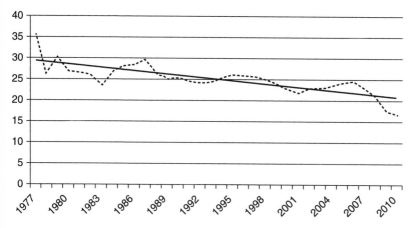

Figure 3. The decline of new firm creation (per 10,000 workers). Source: Barry C. Lynn and Lina Khan, "Out of Business: Measuring the Decline of American Entrepreneurship" (Washington, DC: New America Foundation, 2012).

age 16 there were more than 35 new businesses created each year with at least one employee.[97] Over recent decades, that number steadily declined so that there were just 17 new businesses per 10,000 Americans in 2010, a reduction of over half, as can be seen in figure 3.

Other measures show the same downward trend.[98] The share of the workforce that is self-employed has been declining since at least the early 1990s, a particularly troubling sign since many people counted in official government statistics as self-employed are not really entrepreneurs, but rather do contract work for their former employer.[99] Start-up firms represented almost 13 percent of all businesses in the early 1980s, but only 8 percent in recent years.[100] Similarly, young firms that have been in business for less than five years have also been in steep decline, falling from around 50 percent of all firms in 1980 to close to 35 percent by 2010.[101]

International comparisons are not particularly good either. An analysis of entrepreneurship in 22 rich countries, for example, found that the United States has among the lowest rate of self-employment and employment in small businesses.[102] It is true that on some measures of entrepreneurship—especially, for example, "nascent entrepreneurship" that is very early in the process of building a successful business—the United States fares well compared to other advanced countries, but on many critical measures, such as ownership and employment, America is in the middle or bottom of the pack.[103]

That the United States is producing fewer entrepreneurs is a sharp blow to trickle-down economics. Tax cuts for the rich and the chance to get astronomically rich should have increased entrepreneurship, according to the theory. Yet the more inequality has risen, the more entrepreneurship has declined.

People need many things to become entrepreneurs, including skills, risk tolerance, and a good idea, in addition to education and health.[104] But, of the factors that can be easily measured, perhaps the most important factor that leads a person to become an entrepreneur is whether or not they have the money to do so. Starting a business takes capital to buy supplies and equipment, rent space, advertise, and hire people. If would-be entrepreneurs don't have money of their own or from their family, they are often out of luck. Because new businesses are so risky and likely to fail, banks are often reluctant to lend to startup businesses—unless the entrepreneur has assets to back up the loan.[105] As economists put it, most would-be entrepreneurs are "credit-constrained," meaning they don't have enough money to fully fund their business.[106] So the amount of wealth a person has significantly influences whether or not they will be able to be an entrepreneur.

Critically, a sizeable, but not extravagant, level of wealth is most conducive to promoting entrepreneurship. A middle- to upper-middle-class level of wealth is the sweet spot for entrepreneurship.

The research indicates that there is a threshold level of wealth that entrepreneurs need, but beyond the threshold, additional wealth doesn't make a person much more likely to become an entrepreneur. In fact, very high wealth levels appear to make people less likely to become entrepreneurs, presumably because they have other alternatives for making significant sums of money, such as investing in hedge funds or other people's businesses, and don't need to take the risks inherent in entrepreneurship.[107]

As UCLA economist Francisco Buera explains, "For low wealth levels, entry into entrepreneurship increases with wealth because it relaxes the borrowing constraint.... For high wealth levels, however, entry into entrepreneurship and wealth become negatively related."[108] Similarly, Camilo Mondragón-Vélez, an economist for the World Bank, finds that wealth has a "hump-shaped" effect on entrepreneurship, rising up to a point, but then declining.[109] Not surprisingly, a Kauffman Foundation survey of American entrepreneurs found that 72 percent come from middle-class backgrounds—a vast overrepresentation since less than half of the public meets their measure of middle class.[110] The Kauffman Foundation also found that less than 1 percent of entrepreneurs came from very rich or very poor backgrounds.

As a result, the great wealth gains for those at the top in recent decades haven't produced a surge in entrepreneurship. Instead, the long-term financial stress on middle-class families is reducing the creation of new businesses in the US economy.[111] As Barry Lynn and Lina Khan argue, "With family balance sheets ravaged by stagnant wages and skyrocketing costs for healthcare and higher education, fewer and fewer average families have the savings needed to invest in a small business."[112] Though the net wealth increase experienced by many middle-class Americans during the housing boom in the early 2000s did briefly produce a small increase in entrepreneurship, the increase was not enough to change the overall trends of declining entrepreneurship.[113] This should not be surprising, given the long-term weakness of the middle class and the fact that much of the housing wealth was used to finance consumption that enabled people to maintain what they felt was a middle-class lifestyle.[114]

Other factors related to the weakness of the middle class also likely play a smaller, but still important, role in the decrease in entrepreneurship. Entrepreneurs generally have higher levels of education, but America's educational attainment has been stagnating, driven by wide economic inequities, as discussed above.[115] And the decline in trust in America has made starting a business more difficult because entrepreneurs depend heavily upon others being willing to trust their business plan and judgment.[116]

Also important is that the growing market power of a few large companies and banks—fueled by weak enforcement of antimonopoly laws—has squeezed out small businesses.[117] At least part of the reason more companies have been able to exert monopoly power and push out small competitors is their political influence, which has risen because of income inequality.[118] Finally, the weakness of the US social safety net—especially gaps in healthcare coverage—has made being an entrepreneur particularly risky here compared to most other advanced countries.[119]

All in all, the weakness of the middle class has contributed to the decline in entrepreneurship in recent decades.

ECONOMIC MOBILITY

The opportunity for a child to rise above the economic position of their parents is the essence of the American Dream. Being able to get ahead through hard work and talent is deeply revered in the American psyche.[120] Indeed, Steve Jobs, and his rise from a modest, middle-class beginning to become one of the richest men in the world, is part of the American Dream—though for most the dream is a more modest one, realizing their potential and doing a bit better than their parents.[121]

As James Truslow Adams, the historian who popularized the phrase "American Dream," explained in his book, published in 1931: "It is not a dream of motor cars and high wages merely, but a dream ... in which each man and each woman shall be able to attain to the fullest stature of which they are innately capable ... regardless of the fortuitous circumstances of birth or position."[122] Adams emphasized that the American Dream is about escaping social orders that prevent people from fully developing and using their human capital: "It has been a dream of being able to grow to fullest development as man and woman, unhampered by the barriers which had slowly been erected in the older civilizations."

But unfortunately, in America, whether a child's parents are rich, middle class, or poor makes a far bigger difference than it should. Family wealth—not just effort and ability—plays a large role in determining a person's economic future. Studies show that a child born to parents whose incomes put them in the top fifth of the economic distribution is, compared to a child born middle class, two and a half times more likely to end up in the top fifth as an adult.[123] The odds are even worse for a child born to poor parents.[124]

While it is difficult to measure intergenerational mobility—the technical term for how much a parent's level of income is passed on to their children—because doing so requires tracking families over time, the evidence indicates that mobility in the United States has either declined or remained constant over recent decades. Studies by Bhashkar Mazumder, an economist at the Federal Reserve Bank of Chicago, find, for example, that economic mobility in the United States increased in the middle part of twentieth century when economic inequality was low, but has decreased significantly since 1980.[125] However, Harvard's Raj Chetty and his coauthors find that, over a shorter time period of study, intergenerational mobility has remained unchanged in recent decades.[126]

That the United States has—at best—the same level of economic mobility as we did when Jim Crow, its vestiges and other practices enforced a segregated society is shocking. The country has made great strides to get rid of many of the legal and social barriers that kept minorities—especially blacks—poor for generations. Minorities are no longer forced to attend segregated schools, prevented from buying homes in "white" neighborhoods, or blocked from entering "white" professions. But, unfortunately, our extreme levels of economic inequality have created new kinds of barriers for economic mobility.

One way to think about how little mobility the United States has is that the correlation between a parent's income and the income of their children is just about the same as the correlation between parent's height and the height of their children. As Princeton economist Alan Krueger explains: "The chance of a person who was born to a family in the bottom 10 percent of the income distribution rising to the top 10 percent as an adult is about the same as the chance that a dad who is 5'6" tall having a son who grows up to be over 6'1" tall. It happens, but not often."[127]

What is so chilling about such a close relationship between the income of a parent and that of their children is that income is not inherited genetically from parents the way height is; the close relationship rather indicates that society is preventing some children from realizing their full potential. Certainly some factors that contribute to income—such as intelligence—are partially inherited, but the research suggests that this is true only to a relatively small degree. Isabel Sawhill, a senior fellow at the Brookings Institution, and her coauthors estimate that "not more than 4 percent of the variation in children's earnings can be associated with the genetic transmission of cognitive ability."[128]

That mobility in the United States doesn't fare well in comparison to other countries also provides compelling evidence that something in American society is to blame.[129] "It's becoming conventional wisdom that the U.S. does not have as much mobility as most other advanced countries," Isabel Sawhill has noted.[130] "I don't think you'll find too many people who will argue with that." In just the past few years, there have been five significant studies showing that the United States has less mobility than other wealthy nations.[131] And the differences are quite big—intergenerational economic mobility is three times higher in countries like Denmark and Finland than it is in the United States.[132]

International comparisons also show that countries with lower levels of economic inequality have much greater economic mobility.[133] As an Organisation for Economic Co-Operation and Development (OECD) report put it: "Intergenerational earnings mobility is low in countries with high inequality such

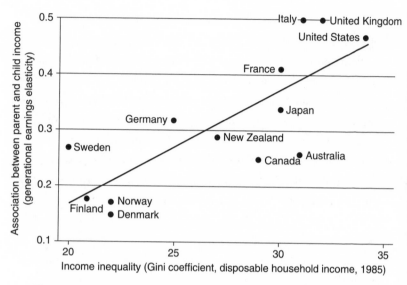

Figure 4. The Great Gatsby curve. More inequality is associated with less mobility across generations. Source: Miles Corak, "How to Slide Down the 'Great Gatsby Curve'" (Washington, DC: Center for American Progress, 2012).

as ... the United States, and much higher in the Nordic countries where income is distributed more evenly."[134] To highlight this relationship between inequality and mobility, Miles Corak, an economist at the University of Ottawa, created what has become known as the "Great Gatsby" curve by overlaying data from a number of countries on a simple graph. According to Corak's analysis, parents pass on more of their advantages or disadvantages in unequal countries, as can be seen in figure 4.[135]

Comparisons within the United States come to similar conclusions. Raj Chetty and his coauthors find that more middle-class regions in the United States have much higher levels of mobility than unequal regions.[136] Middle-class Salt Lake City, for example, has mobility levels that compare favorably with the most mobile countries in the world, while unequal regions such as Charlotte, North Carolina, have less mobility than any other rich country.

While the data clearly show that high levels of inequality and a weak middle class are correlated with lower levels of mobility, economists are still sorting out the reasons why.[137] Many factors undoubtedly contribute to this relationship, including the values, motivations, and aspirations that parents pass on to their children, as well as the high levels of poverty in the United States compared to other advanced countries.[138]

But the strength of the middle class matters quite a bit. Mobility is affected by education, health, and the ability to start a business, among other things. And these factors are shaped by the strength of the middle class, as described at length in this chapter. America's extreme level of income inequality and the lack of money for everyone but the very rich have led to worse education, health, and entrepreneurship outcomes than would otherwise have occurred.

Beyond the links between mobility and the middle class described in this chapter, other factors affected by inequality, such as government policy, help determine mobility levels.[139] Investments in preschool, such as Head Start, which provides early education for lower-income families, can help foster economic mobility.[140] But Pew's Economic Mobility Project found that the United States has spent less as a share of the economy on programs such as Head Start that promote mobility for low- and middle-income families since 1980.[141] Indeed, the US government now spends about two and a half times more money promoting mobility for higher-income households through things like tax breaks for retirement savings than it does for lower-income households.[142] As Miles Corak explains: "The United States stands out in the degree to which government programs are relatively more advantageous for the advantaged in society."[143]

The American public recognizes the connection between growing inequality and declining mobility. In a Pew poll, 71 percent of the public agreed that "greater economic inequality means that it is more difficult for those at the bottom of the income ladder to move up the ladder," while 27 percent disagreed.[144]

All of this means that as income inequality has risen, income increasingly affects a person's ability to take full advantage of their potential. When a child's station in life is determined solely by the status of their parents, it's often called a caste system. And caste systems are inherently economically inefficient because they waste human talent. As the noted Princeton sociologist Melvin Tumin wrote in 1953, such systems "tend to limit the chances available to maximize the efficiency of discovery, recruitment and training of 'functionally important talent.'"[145]

The United States is not a caste society: people still rise above the income level of their parents; we have far less racial segregation than we once did; and people from around the world continue to move here. But the United States is suffering from the waste of human potential endemic in a caste system. And this waste of human potential has clear economic consequences. As the OECD explains, "Inequality of opportunity will inevitably impact economic performance as a whole, even if the relationship is not straightforward."[146]

Several scholars have developed theoretical models to explain how low levels of mobility reduce economic growth by preventing resources from being efficiently allocated.[147] But perhaps the easiest way to think about how wasting human potential harms the economy is to take a case from America's past. Not so long ago, talented women and minorities were commonly blocked by a number of legal and social barriers from working as doctors and lawyers and in other professional jobs. In 1960, for example, 94 percent of doctors and lawyers were white men.[148]

But in recent decades, we have made significant progress in removing these barriers as women and minorities have been more able to fully use and develop their skills, so that, by 2008, 38 percent of doctors and lawyers were women or minorities. Society has reaped significant economic benefits from this greater use of human potential. Estimates from economists at the University of Chicago and Stanford indicate that 15 to 20 percent of productivity growth since 1960 has come from women and minorities being able to work in occupations that take full advantage of their talents.[149]

CONCLUSION

America is wasting the talents of too many of its citizens because of our extreme level of inequality. The United States has now fallen behind our international competitors on a host of measures of human capital. Education, health, entrepreneurship, and mobility have all suffered because of the weakness of the middle class. These are ominous signs for our future economic strength. Paul Krugman summed up the problem nicely when he wrote: "Do talented children in low-income American families have the same chance to make use of their talent—to get the right education, to pursue the right career path—as those born higher up the ladder? Of course not. Moreover, this isn't just unfair, it's expensive. Extreme inequality means a waste of human resources."[150]

According to trickle-down economics, these downward trends shouldn't be occurring. The fact that entrepreneurship has declined and education has stagnated, even as the rewards for both have risen sharply, presents a sharp challenge to conventional wisdom. Clearly, the potential to strike it rich is not the all-powerful incentive that its proponents make it out to be. Rather, a number of factors affect these outcomes, especially the strength of the middle class.

To get the economy back on track, we need to make sure everyone has a real opportunity to succeed. If the middle class were stronger, more Americans would be able to achieve their full economic potential. Americans would be better educated and healthier. They would also be more likely to become entrepreneurs and do better financially than their parents. And healthy, highly educated citizens who rise above their conditions of birth and become entrepreneurs would make the US economy much more dynamic.

CHAPTER SIX

Creating a Middle-Class Society

The goal of this book has been to explain how the hollowing out of the middle class and extreme levels of inequality have harmed America's economy by undermining trust, causing poor governmental performance, weakening and destabilizing demand, and blocking human capital development. In advancing this argument, the book aims to encourage economists to study inequality through a much broader lens than they have in recent decades and provide additional fuel for the ongoing introspection forced upon the discipline by its obvious failings in the lead-up to the Great Recession. Most importantly, the book aspires to help change how politicians think about economic policy. *Hollowed Out* aims to replace the trickle-down mindset that infects the thinking of too many elected officials with the more accurate understanding that the economy grows from the middle out. The economy needs to work for everyone or it doesn't work very well.

The entire economic debate will change and politics will operate much differently once politicians stop assuming that wealth will trickle down from the rich and instead understand that the middle class is a critical input into a thriving economy, not merely an output of a healthy economy. Instead of giving lip service to the middle class, a critical mass of policymakers will really get behind policies to reduce inequality and strengthen and grow the middle class. When this shift happens, the numerous policy agendas that academics, think tanks, and advocacy groups have developed in recent years to help rebuild the middle class will have a much better chance of becoming reality.[1] And many more new and creative policies will be developed. Public policy will once again be geared to help the public. The key is for politicians to make a mental change and recognize that strengthening and growing the middle class is critical to the economy's future.

Some argue that in the modern global economy there is little that government can do to create a middle-class society. Changes in technology and globalization have allowed the top 1 percent to command extraordinary incomes in ways that were not possible a generation ago and inevitably left the middle class facing greater downward pressure on their wages, the argument goes.[2] While technological change and globalization are important contributors to inequality and make the challenges facing government tougher, the claim that policy is helpless against these forces is clearly wrong.

Government policy matters quite a bit. For over three decades, too much of government policymaking has helped the rich at the expense of the middle class. We've had bailouts for big banks but not small businesses, lower tax rates for hedge fund managers than for their secretaries, and protections for well-connected monopoly companies but few safeguards for consumers subject to their predatory practices. The government has spent lavishly on overpriced prescription drugs, but failed to make adequate investments in public infrastructure. Politicians have created tax incentives for CEO "performance" pay that has no relationship to actual performance, but allowed the minimum wage to lose value so that it is worth less in inflation-adjusted dollars now than in the 1960s. With rules like these, it is not surprising that the middle class is in trouble.

To drive home the point that policy matters: other wealthy countries also face similar challenges from globalization and technology, but not all have seen their middle class wither to the same degree as the United States. Thirty years ago the United States had the highest median income of any big country, but because incomes have grown much faster in other countries this may no longer be true.[3] Indeed, over the past two and a half decades, most rich countries had higher income growth for the middle class than the United States.[4] And in the United States far more workers are in jobs with very low wages than in countries such as Germany, Japan, Denmark, and Finland.[5] Similarly, compared to the United States, the share of income going to the top 1 percent hasn't changed very much over the past several decades in countries such as Germany, the Netherlands, and Australia.[6] In continental Europe between 1975 and 2008, the top 1 percent received about 10 percent of the total income growth in these countries, while in the United States over this period the top 1 percent received over 50 percent of the income growth.[7] As Emmanuel Saez, an economics professor at UC Berkeley, and his coauthors write: "The fact that high-income countries with similar technological and productivity developments have gone through different patterns of income inequality at the very top supports the view that institutional and policy differences play a key role in these transformations."[8] Compared to many other countries, we have had much greater increases in inequality, weaker wage growth for the middle class, and more poverty-level jobs, indicating that the policy choices America has made have had a strong influence on the strength of the middle class.

The American public understands that government choices matter. Indeed, far more so than anything else, they hold policy failures responsible for weakening the middle class. In a *National Journal* poll from 2013, 54 percent of Americans blamed "elected officials making the wrong policy decisions" for wages not keeping up with costs over the past few decades, while just 17 percent blamed technology and globalization.[9] Twenty-three percent of Americans blamed business leaders, and 6 percent didn't know who to blame. Further, Americans think government policies can make a big difference in rebuilding the middle class. According to a *USA Today* poll from 2014, 67 percent of Americans believe the government can play a role in reducing the gap between the wealthy and everyone else.[10] Even during the trickle-down era, when most policies have favored the wealthy and those that benefit the poor and the middle class have generally been relatively modest, different policy choices have led to different outcomes for the middle class: both President Ronald Reagan and President Bill Clinton presided over relatively long periods of economic growth, and the rich did extremely well under both, yet income gains for the middle class and the poor were much higher under Clinton.[11]

THE OUTLINES OF AN AGENDA

Government policy clearly matters, so the natural question to ask is, what should be done? The point of this book is not to describe a policy agenda, but rather to explain why a middle-class agenda is needed and to help make its success more likely.

Still, this book can help inform a reform agenda. Several of the ways that a strong middle class and low levels of inequality make the economy work lead directly to policy solutions.

Perhaps the most important reforms that are needed are those that help equalize political power between the wealthy and everyone else, as made clear in chapter 3. We need to reduce the influence of money in politics and boost the civic engagement of nonwealthy Americans to help make our democracy and economy function properly again. Not only will these democratic reforms help shrink the rent seeking that is endemic in US government, they will also enable the public's desire for greater spending on education and infrastructure to be more clearly heard.

To ensure that the middle class stands on more equal footing with the wealthy in our democracy, we should limit the amount of money that can be spent on elections, provide true transparency about the money that is allowed to be spent, introduce innovative solutions that amplify the impact of small-dollar contributions from average citizens, and progressively tax lobbying activities.[12] These reforms would help reduce the advantages the rich have in American democracy. They would not only shrink money down to size, but also increase civic engagement because they would make middle-class citizens feel that their voice has more equal weight in the process. We can also more directly encourage citizens to participate in politics by automatically registering citizens in advance of an election, encouraging early voting, putting election days on a weekend or a new holiday, getting rid of so many different election dates by consolidating elections, and beating back new voter ID laws that will prevent American citizens from being able to vote.[13]

This book also highlighted the need to improve early childhood education so that the children of the poor and the middle class have similar developmental opportunities as the wealthy early in life. Increasing the learning opportunities for children in their earliest years will take an investment in quality universal preschool, so that all four-year-olds can develop their talents under the direction of skilled teachers.[14] It will also require efforts to improve access, affordability, and quality of child care for the years before preschool begins.[15] Finally, parents will need the ability to take time off from their jobs—without fear of being fired—to take care of their children when they get sick and are not allowed to participate in these group care settings.[16]

Because the huge debt loads of the middle class helped drive the Great Recession to great depths and continue to hold back the economy, we need to take steps to minimize the problems of debt, especially housing debt. We can start by reducing the principal on mortgages that the government controls from inflated precrash prices to the actual value of the home.[17] To help minimize future debt problems, mortgages can be structured so that the risks, as well as the benefits, of sudden changes in home prices are shared between bankers and homeowners, and banks should be better supervised so they internalize more of the risks of the debt they create.[18] Student loan debt threatens to become the next debt crisis, so policymakers should take steps to reduce the burden of this debt, such as by allowing borrowers to refinance at much lower rates, as well as reducing the cost of college for students so that debt levels don't get so high again.[19]

Other necessary reforms may not have been called out as specifically in the previous pages, but still follow directly from the middle-out logic. Ensuring that ordinary Americans have a fair shot and that their hard work is rewarded not only would benefit workers and the middle class, but would spill over to provide big boosts to the economy. Throughout America's history, the combination of fair rules for everyone and the American belief in working hard to get ahead has been a powerful economic force. From the Homestead Act of 1862, which gave ordinary Americans free land in exchange for their sweat equity, to the GI Bill, which enabled a generation to go to college in return for their service to the country, to laws creating a minimum wage and guaranteeing workers the right to join unions, America's economy and our middle class have been built through policies that take advantage of everyone's contributions.

But we need to update these kinds of policies for modern America. We don't have free land to give away to farmers, but we can still promote a kind of sweat equity by encouraging companies to adopt broad-based sharing programs such as granting workers an ownership stake or a share of profits based on workers' collective performance.[20] When a company does well, so should all of its workers—not just executives at the very top. Research indicates that these policies not only raise worker incomes significantly, but also boost productivity.[21]

The GI Bill was for veterans returning from World War II, but we don't need or want a massive military mobilization. So we should broaden the definition of national service and provide significant college assistance for young people who help our country meet its many needs.[22] Similarly, a modern approach to the minimum wage is needed. During the middle part of the twentieth century, the minimum wage ensured more of a middle-class lifestyle because it was regularly increased to keep it at about half of the country's average wage.[23] Unfortunately, the value of the minimum wage has been allowed to erode so that it is now a poverty wage. Just as bad, coverage and enforcement of minimum wage laws are inadequate so that many people are paid less than the minimum, which causes standards for all workers to be in jeopardy.[24] A contemporary approach to the minimum wage would raise it appreciably and formally link it to half the average worker's wage so that it would continue to rise as standards of living increase, as well as make sure it covers all workers and is adequately enforced.[25]

In a similar vein, our laws enabling workers to join together in unions to negotiate with their employer for higher wages have been weakened significantly over recent decades and no longer ensure that workers can freely choose to join a union. To take just one example, if a company breaks the law and fires or illegally punishes a worker for wanting to join a union—which estimates indicate happens about once every 18 minutes—there are no fines for the company and the best a worker can hope for after years of legal battles is to be reinstated and receive their back pay, minus any money they made in the meantime.[26] In large part because our current laws make it unnecessarily difficult for a worker to join a union, the labor movement has weakened sharply over the past few decades.[27]

Modernizing union law so that all workers can freely choose whether to join a union, as well as updating the responsibilities of unions so that they are more oriented toward promoting the success of the firm, such as through work councils that give workers input on day-to-day operations, is essential to rebuilding the middle class and ensuring that work is rewarded.[28] When workers join together in unions, they have greater power in the workplace, which enables them to negotiate for higher wages and benefits, and the standards that union workers set often spill over and help nonmembers in other workplaces.[29] More fundamentally, unions help ordinary citizens participate in democracy, giving voice and power to the concerns of the middle class.[30] Unions and their active membership are one of the few countervailing forces in our democracy to balance the power of the wealthy and of corporations. While unions—like any democratic organization—sometimes support policies that are in their narrow interest, they make democracy work for the middle class by getting citizens involved in politics and working daily in the political trenches.[31] As critical as other citizen groups are, parent-teacher associations, for example, generally do not challenge the political power of the wealthy and corporations in the same way as unions can. Indeed, it is hard to imagine how America can have a strong middle class without workers having strong organizations to represent their interests.

Because rebuilding the union movement is so essential to rebuilding the middle class, the strength of these links is worth elaborating on. Across the globe, the countries with the strongest middle classes have strong union movements.[32] Similarly, US states with higher concentrations of union members have stronger middle classes.[33] And over much of American history, the strength of the middle class has moved up and down in tandem with the strength of unions.[34] According to Bruce Western and Jake Rosenfeld, sociologists at Harvard and the University of Washington: "Union decline explains one-third of the growth in inequality" over recent decades.[35] The close correlation between the share of Americans who are members of unions and the share of income going to the middle 60 percent of Americans can be seen in figure 5.

It is important to note that some people will argue that these policies, particularly raising the minimum wage and boosting unionization, will harm the economy. But this opposition is based on a trickle-down mindset, not a middle-out one. This opposition also highlights the need to update arguments for these sorts of policies to better explain how they make the

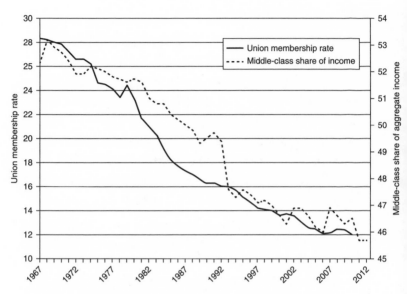

Figure 5. Middle-class incomes shrinking as union membership rates decrease. Source: David Madland, Karla Walter, and Nick Bunker, "Unions Make the Middle Class; Without Unions, the Middle Class Withers" (Washington, DC: Center for American Progress, 2011).

economy stronger by building up the middle class. These policies need to be understood as critical steps to help balance political power and ensure that hard work is rewarded, which will have significant economic benefits.

Much of the time, arguments against policies to help the middle class are based on research that ignores the key role the middle class plays in making democracy and the economy work. As Daron Acemoglu, an MIT economist, and James Robinson, a Harvard political scientist, who study the importance of good governance on economic growth, write: "The standard approach to policy-making and advice in economics implicitly or explicitly ignores politics and political economy."[36] Union policy provides a good example of this phenomenon at work, as Acemoglu and Robinson note. Virtually all of the research on the economic impact of unions agrees that they help workers raise their wages, but some of the research finds that unions can reduce employment at organized firms.[37] As a result, many economists are skeptical about unions. But unions have a much broader and more beneficial impact on the economy than economists commonly understand. As Acemoglu and Robinson argue, "Unions do not just influence the way the labor market functions; they also have important implications for the political system ... balancing the political power of established business interests and political elites."[38] Thus unions have a far more positive economic impact than they are often given credit for.

Similarly, many economists are skeptical of a higher minimum wage because some research shows that it might reduce employment, though much of the recent research shows it has no effect on employment.[39] Increasing the minimum wage would have relatively little direct impact on the balance of political power, but it would have a more significant impact on the paychecks of workers and would thus increase consumer demand.[40] It can also encourage the development of human capital by incentivizing firms to adopt a high-road business model and by reducing turnover, which enables workers to stay on the job longer and acquire more firm-specific skills.[41] As part of a suite of policies necessary to rebuild the middle class, the minimum wage is good for the economy.

The same kinds of arguments can be made for a host of other policies necessary to reduce inequality. Wall Street clearly needs to be better regulated to prevent companies from taking excessive risks that boost company profits and CEO pay but undermine the stability of the economy. Not every policy necessary to reregulate

Wall Street will pass muster under a standard economic cost-benefit analysis, but such reforms would serve the larger purpose of balancing power in the economy and democracy and reducing the risk of financial collapse.[42] In a similar vein, most research indicates that making the rich pay higher rates of taxes than the middle class and poor has very little impact—positive or negative—on economic growth.[43] But in the long run, more progressive taxation is good for the economy because it is necessary to pay for critical investments in preschool, for example, and to help reduce America's extreme levels of inequality.[44]

This is why IMF economists Jonathan Ostry, Andrew Berg, and Charalambos Tsangarides found in their study of growth around the world that government policies to reduce inequality are generally beneficial. Their research showed that while some government policies to reduce inequality can have a direct impact that is slightly negative, the overall effect on the economy of these policies was largely positive because the economic benefits of reducing inequality dramatically outweighed any harm done. As the authors explained: "On average, across countries and over time, the things that governments have typically done to redistribute do not seem to have led to bad growth outcomes . . . and the resulting narrowing of inequality helped support faster and more durable growth."[45] Certainly radical redistribution schemes can harm growth, but the kinds of inequality-reducing policies that are within the norm of American experience are good for the economy.

GOING FORWARD

Many other reforms are needed to give the middle class a fighting chance, including a commitment to maintaining full employment, greater investments in infrastructure, trade policies that support American workers, and effective antitrust enforcement so that large companies can't bully small businesses and middle-class customers.[46] The policies laid out in this chapter are only a start toward helping rebuild the middle class because the goal of this book is not to specify a policy agenda but to show how strengthening the middle class would improve the American economy.

Replacing the trickle-down mindset with a middle-out perspective will take time and work. Yet it is starting to happen. Indeed, in August 2014, Standard & Poor's, an economic analysis company, reduced its projections for future US growth because they have come to see "extreme income inequality as a drag on long-run economic growth."[47] That nonpartisan analysts have begun to incorporate the consequences of a hollowed-out middle class into their economic analysis is an important change. But to get to a place where rebuilding the middle class is seen by most everyone in power as an essential input for the economy and where it thus becomes a guiding tenant of policymaking will take the continued efforts of scholars to highlight the connections between the middle class and growth, of the public to demand their politicians listen, and of a few elected officials to lead their peers. Hopefully this book can play a role in sparking the transformation to an era where the economy no longer stagnates from the top down but grows from the middle out.

ACKNOWLEDGMENTS

I am thankful for the help and support of many people who helped make this book possible.

E.J. Dionne, Michael Tomasky, and Elbert Ventura deserve thanks for their help in publishing the essay that eventually became this book. I also want to thank Peter Richardson for having the vision to see the potential in turning that essay into this book, as well as Naomi Schneider, Ally Power, and Robert Demke for helping this book across the finish line.

I am particularly grateful for the help of readers of drafts, including Christian Weller, Ulrich Boser, Ruy Teixeira, Nick Hanauer, Adam Hersh, Nick Bunker, and a number of anonymous reviewers. Their thoughts significantly improved this book.

At the Center for American Progress, I have been fortunate to have such supportive colleagues, including Neera Tanden, John Podesta, Lori Lodes, Tara McGuinness, Marc Jarsulic, John Halpin, Heather Boushey, Michael Ettlinger, Greg Kaufmann, and Sarah Miller, who have encouraged me and helped shape my thinking on this topic. I owe a significant debt to Keith Miller, Ethan Gurwitz, Karla Walter, Danielle Corley and Brendan Duke for all their help. I could not have done this without their efforts. I also want to thank Milan Kumar, Will

Hamilton, Ashesh Rambachan, Robbie Williamson, Karina Hernandez, Marc Priester, Mason Miller, and Myat Su for their assistance.

I am indebted to the countless scholars in academia, think tanks, and elsewhere whose work has influenced this book. Their papers and books, and, on occasion, conversations, were invaluable. I am also thankful for all the people who have helped me in my career and gotten me to the place where I could write this book.

I am of course grateful for the support and inspiration my parents, siblings, extended family, and friends have given throughout this process.

Most importantly, I want to thank Karin, Charlie, and Jasper for allowing me the time to write this book and supporting me and putting up with me while I was doing so.

NOTES

CHAPTER ONE

1. Edward Conard, interview with Jon Stewart, *The Daily Show,* April 30, 2012, www .edwardconard.com/ed-conard-on-the-daily-show-with-jon-stewart-discussing-his-book-and-why-risk-taking-isnt-the-enemy-of-a-properly-functioning-economy/.

2. Adam Davidson, "The Purpose of Spectacular Wealth, According to a Spectacularly Wealthy Guy," *New York Times Magazine,* May 1, 2012.

3. Jude Wanniski, *The Way the World Works* (Washington, DC: Regnery, 1978).

4. George Gilder, *Wealth and Poverty* (New York: Bantam, 1982).

5. For information on Reagan's quoting of Gilder, see Larissa MacFarquhar, "The Gilder Effect," *New Yorker,* May 29, 2000; Bruce Chapman, "Gilder and Wealth: Why Reagan Agreed," *Discovery News,* August 14, 2012, www.discoverynews.org/2012/08/_george_ gilders_bestselling_eco63251.php; John Tamny, "The Essential George Gilder Explains How Economies Work," *Forbes,* June 16, 2013, www.forbes.com/sites/johntamny/2013/06/16 /the-essential-george-gilder-explains-how-economies-work/. For Reagan's quotation, see Steven R. Weisman, "Reagan Criticizes Democrats in Speech at a GOP Dinner," *New York Times,* May 5, 1982, www.nytimes.com/1982/05/05/us/reagan-criticizes-democrats-in-speech-at-a-gop-dinner.html. Note that Representative Jack Kemp was probably the first political leader to champion trickle-down, but Reagan was clearly the most powerful early voice for trickle-down.

6. For a description of how most economists rejected the idea that tax cuts pay for themselves, see, for example, Jonathan Chait, *The Big Con: Crackpot Economics and the Fleecing of America* (New York: Houghton Mifflin, 2007). For additional examples of economists rejecting this notion, see Richard Kogan and Aviva Aron-Dine, "Claim That Tax Cuts 'Pay for Themselves' Is Too Good to Be True" (Washington, DC: Center on Budget and Policy Priorities, 2006).

7. Arthur M. Okun, *Equality and Efficiency: The Big Tradeoff* (Washington, DC: Brookings Institution, 1975).

8. Finis Welch, "In Defense of Inequality," *American Economic Review* 89, no. 2 (1999): 1–17.

9. American Economic Association, "Proceedings of the One Hundred Fourteenth Annual Meeting," *American Economic Review* 92, no. 2 (2002): 479–530; American Economic Association, "Richard T. Ely Lecturers," www.aeaweb.org/honors_awards/ely_lecturers .php.

10. Note that there is some research that suggests unequal monetary rewards may not even provide much of a positive incentive. See, for example, Alain Cohn and others, "Social Comparison in the Workplace: Evidence from a Field Experiment," Discussion Paper 5550 (Institute for the Study of Labor, 2011); Alain Cohn, Ernst Fehr, and Lorenz Goette, "Fair Wages and Effort Provision: Combining Evidence from the Lab and the Field," Working Paper 107 (University of Zurich, Department of Economics, 2013); David Card and others, "Inequality at Work: The Effect of Peer Salaries on Job Satisfaction," *American Economic Review* 102, no. 6 (2012): 2981–3003; Daniel H. Pink, *Drive: The Surprising Truth about What Motivates Us* (London: Penguin, 2009).

11. See, for example, Joseph E. Stiglitz, "Macroeconomic Fluctuations, Inequality, and Human Development," *Journal of Human Development and Capabilities: A Multi-Disciplinary Journal for People-Centered Development* 13, no. 1 (2012): 31–58. In this piece Stiglitz writes: "For years, the dominant paradigm in macroeconomics, which assumed that income distribution did not matter, at least for macroeconomic behavior, ignored inequality." See also Joseph E. Stiglitz, "Rethinking Macroeconomics: What Failed, and How to Repair It," *Journal of the European Economic Association* 9, no. 4 (2011): 591–645. Robert Solow, "Building a Science of Economics for the Real World," testimony before the House Committee on Science and Technology Subcommittee on Investigations and Oversight, US House of Representatives, July 20, 2010, https://web.archive.org/web/20110204034313 /http://democrats.science.house.gov/Media/file/Commdocs/hearings/2010/Oversight /20july/Solow_Testimony.pdf.

12. See, for example, Welch, "In Defense of Inequality"; Gary S. Becker, "How Can Inequality be Good?," *Hoover Digest* 3 (2011), www.hoover.org/publications/hoover-digest /article/83976; Gary S. Becker and Kevin M. Murphy, "The Upside of Income Inequality," *American*, May/June 2007, www.american.com/archive/2007/may-june-magazine-contents /the-upside-of-income-inequality/#FN2. Note that these authors recognize that inequality can sometimes hinder the development of human capital, but still feel that inequality promotes human capital development.

13. Note that while some economists paid attention to broader influences on the economy and considered the potential harm from inequality, including Michal Kalecki in the 1930s, Nikolas Kaldor and Gunnar Myrdal in the 1950s and 1960s, and some heterodox economists in the United States, these economists were generally outside the mainstream.

14. Nicholas Phillipson, *Adam Smith: An Enlightened Life* (New Haven, CT: Yale University Press, 2010). See also arguments from John Stuart Mill, another early economist, who argued that "a person is not likely to be a good economist who is nothing else." Quoted in Dimitris Milonakis and Ben Fine, *From Political Economy to Economics: Method, the Social and the Historical in the Evolution of Economics Theory* (New York: Routledge, 2009). Also note Irving Fisher's presidential address to the American Economic Association in 1919 where he encouraged the discipline to study inequality and broader social questions from a more holistic perspective. See Irving Fisher, "Economists in Public Service: Annual Address of the President," *American Economic Review* 9, no. 1 (1919): 5–21.

15. Sjoerd Beugelsdijk and Robbert Maseland, *Culture in Economics: History, Methodological Reflections and Contemporary Applications* (New York: Cambridge University Press, 2011).

See also Oliver Williamson, "Transaction Cost Economics: How It Works; Where It Is Headed," *De Economist* 146, no. 1 (1998): 25–58, for a description of the narrow nature of most economic inquiry.

16. Milonakis and Fine, *From Political Economy to Economics*.

17. For noneconomist criticism, see, for example, Jonathan Rowe, "Why Economists Are So Often Wrong," *On the Commons*, February 25, 2009, http://jonathanrowe.org /why-economists-are-so-often-wrong. For an outsider economist perspective, see Samuel Bowles, *Microeconomics: Behavior, Institutions, and Evolution* (Princeton, NJ: Princeton University Press, 2004). For insider criticism, see, for example, Williamson, "Transaction Cost Economics"; Douglass C. North, *Structure and Change in Economic History* (New York: W.W. Norton, 1981). Behavioral economists have also worked to point out some of the short-comings of traditional economic theory, with among the more noted examples being Daniel Kahneman and Amos Tversky, who first proposed prospect theory in 1979 and illustrated some of the issues with expected utility theory. See Daniel Kahneman and Amos Tversky, "Prospect Theory: An Analysis of Decision Under Risk," *Econometrica* 47, no. 2 (1979): 263–291.

18. Paul Krugman, "How Did Economists Get It So Wrong?," *New York Times*, September 2, 2009, www.nytimes.com/2009/09/06/magazine/06Economic-t.html?pagewanted = all; Stiglitz, "Rethinking Macroeconomics." For more on the criticism of economics, see, for example, John Quiggin, *Zombie Economics: How Dead Ideas Still Walk among Us* (Princeton, NJ: Princeton University Press, 2010); Robert Skidelsky, *Keynes: The Return of the Master* (New York: Public Affairs, 2009); John Cassidy, *How Markets Fail: The Logic of Economic Calamities* (Princeton, NJ: Princeton University Press, 2009); Justin Fox, *The Myth of the Rational Market: A History of Risk, Reward, and Delusion on Wall Street* (New York: Harper-Collins, 2009).

19. Ronald Coase, "Saving Economics from the Economists," *Harvard Business Review*, December 2012.

20. Lawrence Summers argued that Piketty's empirical work is a "Nobel Prize–worthy contribution." See Lawrence Summers, "The Inequality Puzzle," *Democracy Journal*, Summer 2014. Thomas Piketty quoted in Thomas Piketty, *Capital in the Twenty-First Century* (Cambridge, Mass.: Harvard University Press, 2014).

21. Peter H. Lindert and Jeffrey G. Williamson, "American Incomes before and after the Revolution," *Journal of Economic History* 73, no. 3 (2013): 725–765. In this source the authors state, "There was no documented place on the planet that had a more egalitarian distribution in the late eighteenth century." See also Jordan Weissmann, "Income Inequality: It's Worse Today Than It Was in 1774," *Atlantic*, September 19, 2012, www.theatlantic.com /business/archive/2012/09/us-income-inequality-its-worse-today-than-it-was-in-1774 /262537/; Chrystia Freeland, "America, Land of the Equals," *New York Times*, May 3, 2012, www.nytimes.com/2012/05/04/us/04iht-letter04.html; Kevin Phillips, *Wealth and Democracy* (New York: Broadway, 2002).

22. Chrystia Freeland, "Colonial America: How Swede It Was," *Reuters*, May 3, 2012, http://blogs.reuters.com/chrystia-freeland/tag/peter-lindert/.

23. This quotation is taken from a letter written by Thomas Jefferson to Dr. Thomas Cooper on September 10, 1814. The full letter can be found at National Archives, "Thomas Jefferson to Thomas Cooper, 10 September 1814," http://founders.archives.gov /documents/Jefferson/03-07-02-0471.

24. For the history of US inequality over time, see Jeffrey G. Williamson and Peter H. Lindert, *American Inequality: A Macroeconomic History* (Waltham, MA: Academic Press, 1980). For a different interpretation of changes in inequality based on wage differentials, see

Robert A. Margo, "The History of Wage Inequality in America, 1820 to 1970," Working Paper 286 (Jerome Levy Economics Institute of Bard College, 1999). See also Emmanuel Saez and Thomas Piketty, "The Evolution of Top Incomes: A Historical and International Perspective," *AEA Paper and Proceedings: Measuring and Interpreting Trends in Economic Inequality* 96, no. 2 (2006): 200–205.

25. For more on the history of US inequality over time, see note 24. See also Sam Pizzigati, *The Rich Don't Always Win: The Forgotten Triumph over Plutocracy That Created the American Middle Class, 1900–1970* (New York: Seven Stories Press, 2012). When looking at income growth over time, between the late 1940s and early 1970s incomes of Americans at all socioeconomic levels grew rapidly compared to the growth witnessed by the majority of Americans in recent decades. See, for example, Chad Stone and others, "A Guide to Statistics on Historical Trends in Income Inequality" (Washington, DC: Center on Budget and Policy Priorities, 2013). For additional descriptions of how Americans' incomes and standard of living improved in the postwar period compared to the past several decades, see Edward N. Wolff, *What Has Happened to the Quality of Life in the Advanced Industrialized Nations?* (Northampton, MA: Edward Elgar, 2004); Robert Reich, *Supercapitalism: The Transformation of Business, Democracy, and Everyday Life* (New York: Vintage, 2008).

26. Paul Krugman, "Introducing This Blog," *Conscience of a Liberal Blog,* September 18, 2007, http://krugman.blogs.nytimes.com/2007/09/18/introducing-this-blog/.

27. According to the US Census Bureau, the median household income in 2013 was $51,939 dollars, while in 1989 it was $52,432 (figures in 2013 dollars). See US Census Bureau "Table H-6. Regions—All Races by Median and Mean Income: 1975 to 2013," www.census.gov/hhes/www/income/data/historical/household/. Note that figures produced by the Congressional Budget Office that incorporate the effect of government taxes and transfers produce similar, but less pessimistic trends as those discussed in this section. Congressional Budget Office, "Trends in the Distribution of Household Income Between 1979 and 2007," www.cbo.gov/sites/default/files/10-25-HouseholdIncome_0.pdf.

28. Between 1989 and 2013 the average incomes of the bottom three quintiles all declined in inflation-adjusted terms, while the average income of the fourth quintile increased by only 5 percent. By comparison, the average income of the top quintile grew by nearly 20 percent, and the average income of the top 5 percent grew by 29 percent. See US Census Bureau "Table H-3. Mean Household Income Received by Each Fifth and Top 5 Percent," www.census.gov/hhes/www/income/data/historical/household/.

29. The measure of hourly compensation referenced here is real median hourly compensation (including both wages and benefits) of production/nonsupervisory workers. According to the Economic Policy Institute, while this measure of median hourly compensation grew by only 0.27 percent per year from 1973 to 2011, worker productivity grew by 1.56 percent per year during that same time period. See Lawrence Mishel and others, "The State of Working America: 12th Edition" (Washington, DC: Economic Policy Institute, 2012), table 4.23. By comparison, real GDP grew at a rate of approximately 2.8 percent year, based on author's calculations using data from the Bureau of Economic Analysis. For data, see Bureau of Economic Analysis, "National Economic Accounts: Gross Domestic Product (GDP)," www.bea.gov/national/index.htm#gdp. Other research from the Economic Policy Institute further illustrates these trends and shows that between 1979 and 2013 average hourly compensation of production and nonsupervisory workers grew by a total of only 8 percent while productivity grew by 65 percent. See Elise Gould, "Why America's Workers Need Faster Wage Growth—and What We Can Do About It" (Washington, DC: Economic Policy Institute, 2014).

30. Michael Greenstone and Adam Looney, "The Great Recession May Be Over, but American Families Are Working Harder Than Ever," *Brookings on Job Numbers Blog*, July 8, 2011, www.brookings.edu/blogs/jobs/posts/2011/07/08-jobs-greenstone-looney.

31. This statement refers to hourly wages as of 2012. See Lawrence Mishel and Colin Gordon, "Real Hourly Wage Growth: The Last Generation," *Economic Policy Institute Blog*, October 10, 2012, www.epi.org/blog/real-hourly-wage-growth-last-generation/: this shows that real median hourly wages earned by males declined by 5.8 percent between 1973 and 2012. These figures represent an update of the figures presented in the Economic Policy Institute's State of Working America report, which analyzed these trends through 2011. See Mishel and others, "The State of Working America: 12th Edition."

32. The median age of the US labor force increased from 34.6 years old in 1980 to 41.9 years old in 2012, and is projected by the Bureau of Labor Statistics to continue rising to 42.6 by 2022. See Mitra Toossi, "Labor Force Projections to 2020: A More Slowly Growing Workforce," *Monthly Labor Review*, January 2012; Mitra Toossi, "Labor Force Projections to 2022: The Labor Force Participation Rate Continues to Fall," *Monthly Labor Review*, December 2013. That older workers generally make more than younger workers is illustrated by looking at weekly and hourly earnings as well as household incomes. For weekly and hourly earnings by age from 1979 through 2012, see US Bureau of Labor Statistics, "Highlights of Women's Earnings in 2012" (2013), table 17. Note that in 2012 earnings steadily increased with age until falling slightly after age 65. When looking at median household income, households headed by workers between age 45 and 54 had the highest median incomes in 2013. See US Census Bureau, "Table H-10. Age of Head of Householder: All Races by Median and Mean Income: 1967 to 2013," www.census.gov/hhes /www/income/data/historical/household/.

33. Isabel V. Sawhill and John E. Morton, "Economic Mobility: Is the American Dream Alive and Well?" (Washington, DC: Economic Mobility Project, 2007). See also US Census Bureau, "Historical Income Tables: People," www.census.gov/hhes/www /income/data/historical/people/. These figures from the Census Bureau show that between 1973 and 2013 males' median income fell by 27.7 percent for those age 25 to 34 years old and by 18.5 percent for those age 35 to 44 years old.

34. US Senate Health, Education, Labor, and Pensions Committee, "Saving the American Dream: The Past, Present, and Uncertain Future of America's Middle Class" (2011); David Madland and Nick Bunker, "5 Charts on the State of the Middle Class" (Washington, DC: Center for American Progress, 2012). See also Center for American Progress, "The Middle-Class Squeeze" (2014), which shows that between 2000 and 2012 the costs of many key elements of middle-class security increased at a faster rate than middle-class incomes grew.

35. This refers to mean debt held by households in the middle 60 percent of the wealth distribution. Edward Wolff, "Household Wealth Trends in the United States, 1962–2013: What Happened over the Great Recession?" Working Paper 20733 (National Bureau of Economic Research, 2014). See also Aldo Barba and Massimo Pivetti, "Rising Household Debt: Its Causes and Macroeconomic Implications—a Long-Period Analysis," *Cambridge Journal of Economics* 33 (2008): 113–137; Neil Bhutta, "Mortgage Debt and Household Deleveraging: Accounting for the Decline in Mortgage Debt Using Consumer Credit Record Data," Working Paper 14 (Federal Reserve Board, 2012); Karen Dynan and Donald Kohn, "The Rise in U.S. Household Indebtedness: Causes and Consequences," Working Paper 37 (Federal Reserve Board, 2007).

36. These figures are taken from table A6, "Top Fractiles Income Levels (Including Capital Gains) in the United States Adjusted for Price Inflation," in Emmanuel Saez's

updated income distribution tables, found at Emmanuel Saez, "Emmanuel Saez," http://
elsa.berkeley.edu/~saez/. Note that the income measure used here is the sum of all
income components reported on tax returns (wages and salaries, pensions received, profits
from businesses, capital income such as dividends, interest, or rents, and realized capital
gains). Government transfers are excluded, as are nontaxable fringe benefits from employers such as employer-provided health insurance.

37. For example, in 1979, someone in the top 1 percent of income earners made roughly
10 times more than someone in the middle. By 2007, someone in the top 1 percent earned
over 28 times what someone in the middle earned. Author's calculations using data from
the Congressional Budget Office. Numbers refer to changes in average before-tax incomes
of the top 1 percent and the middle 20 percent. Average income figures are available in the
supplemental tables in table 3 of Congressional Budget Office, "Number of Households,
Average Income, and Shares of Income for All Households, by Before-Tax Income Group,
1979 to 2010," www.cbo.gov/publication/44604. The original report they were presented
in is Congressional Budget Office, "The Distribution of Household Income and Federal
Taxes, 2010" (2013). Note that work by Emmanuel Saez has shown very similar trends. For
example, see Emmanuel Saez, "Striking It Richer: The Evolution of Top Incomes in the
United States (Updated with 2012 Preliminary Estimates)" (Berkeley: University of California, Berkeley, 2013). For a review of different data sources available for comparisons
between the rich and the middle class, see Stone and others, "A Guide to Statistics on Historical Trends in Income Inequality."

38. Lawrence Mishel and Alyssa Davis, "CEO Pay Continues to Rise as Typical
Workers are Paid Less" (Washington, DC: Economic Policy Institute, 2014).

39. Saez, "Striking it Richer."

40. For information on the share of income going to the middle class, see Keith Miller
and David Madland, "What the New Census Data Show about the Continuing Struggles
of the Middle Class" (Washington, DC: Center for American Progress Action Fund, 2014).
Trends in the share of income going to the top 1 percent are a product of the author's calculations based on figures in table A3, "Top Fractiles Income Shares (Including Capital
Gains) in the United States," in Emmanuel Saez's updated income distribution tables,
found at Emmanuel Saez, "Emmanuel Saez." Numbers reflect the change in the top 1 percent's share of income from 1982 to 2012. These figures were reported in graphical form in
Saez, "Striking It Richer." See note 36 on measures of income used by Saez. It should also
be noted that the 2012 estimate is a preliminary estimate. Note that work by the Congressional Budget Office has shown similar trends. Their figures show that the share of total
before-tax income taken home by the top 1 percent of households increased from 8.9 percent in 1979 to 13.4 percent in 2009. Figures are available in the supplemental tables found
at Congressional Budget Office, "The Distribution of Household Income and Federal
Taxes, 2008 and 2009," www.cbo.gov/publication/43373. The original report they were
presented in is Congressional Budget Office, "The Distribution of Household Income and
Federal Taxes, 2008 and 2009" (2012).

41. Alan B. Krueger, "Consequences of Inequality in the United States," speech,
Washington, DC, January 12, 2012.

42. This refers to the income gains between 2009 and 2012. See Saez, "Striking It
Richer."

43. The bottom 90 percent of families held 22.8 percent of all wealth in 2012, according
to calculations by Emmanuel Saez and Gabriel Zucman. See Emmanuel Saez and Gabriel
Zucman, "Wealth Inequality in the United States Since 1913: Evidence from Capitalized

Income Tax Data," Working Paper 20625 (National Bureau of Economic Research, 2014). Other estimates of these figures produce very similar results, for example, a report by Linda Levine for the Congressional Research Service found that in 2010 the bottom 90 percent of households held 25.4 percent of total net worth. See Linda Levine, "An Analysis of the Distribution of Wealth Across Households, 1989–2010" (Washington, DC: Congressional Research Service, 2012). Calculations by Edward Wolff presented in the Economic Policy Institute's State of Working American report also found that in 2010 the bottom 90 percent of households controlled just 23.3 percent of national wealth. See Mishel and others, "The State of Working America: 12th Edition." Furthermore, a 2014 report from the Center for Economic Policy Research using data from the Survey of Consumer Finances shows that most households saw their wealth decline between 1989 and 2013 and found that redistribution of wealth to those higher up in the income distribution continued between 2010 and 2013. See David Rosnick and Dean Baker, "The Wealth of Households: An Analysis of the 2013 Survey of Consumer Finances" (Washington, DC: Center for Economic and Policy Research, 2014).

44. Saez and Zucman, "Wealth Inequality in the United States Since 1913: Evidence from Capitalized Income Tax Data."

45. Kerry A. Dolan and Luisa Kroll, "Inside The 2014 Forbes 400: Facts and Figures About American's Wealthiest," *Forbes*, September 29, 2014, www.forbes.com/sites/kerryadolan/2014/09/29/inside-the-2014-forbes-400-facts-and-figures-about-americas-wealthiest/.

46. Central Intelligence Agency, "The World Factbook—Country Comparison: Distribution of Family Income," www.cia.gov/library/publications/the-world-factbook/rankorder/2172rank.html. Note that these comparisons are based on estimates from different years.

47. Anthony B. Atkinson, Thomas Piketty, and Emmanuel Saez, "Top Incomes in the Long Run of History," *Journal of Economic Literature* 49, no. 1 (2011): 3–71. See also Facundo Alvaredo and others, "The Top 1 Percent in International and Historical Perspective," *Journal of Economic Perspectives* 27, no. 3 (2013): 3–20.

48. From the mid-1940s to the late 1970s, the economy grew about 3.7 percent per year. That was about 1 percentage point higher per year than subsequent growth—and the difference doesn't change much if the Great Recession is included or excluded. Note also that Piketty argues productivity growth was twice as high in the earlier period: see Piketty, *Capital in the Twenty-First Century*. For more on inequality and growth research about the United States and its regions, see, for example, Manuell Pastor Jr. and Chris Benner, "Been Down So Long: Weak-Market Cities and Regional Equity," in *Retooling for Growth: Building a 21st Century Economy in America's Older Industrial Areas*, ed. Richard M. McGahey and Jennifer S. Vey (Washington, DC: American Assembly, 2008); Ugo Panizza, "Income Inequality and Economic Growth: Evidence from American Data," *Journal of Economic Growth* 7, no. 1 (2002): 25–41; Manuel Pastor Jr. and others, *Regions That Work: How Cities and Suburbs Can Grow Together* (Minneapolis: University of Minnesota Press, 2000); Anil Rupasingha, Stephan J. Goetz, and David Freshwater, "Social and Institutional Factors as Determinants of Economic Growth: Evidence from the United States Counties," *Papers in Regional Science* 81, no. 2 (2002): 139–155; Barry Bluestone and Bennett Harrison, *Growing Prosperity: The Battle for Growth with Equity in the Twenty-First Century* (Berkeley: University of California Press, 2001); Peter H. Lindert and Jeffery G. Williamson, "Growth, Equality and History," *Explorations in Economic History* 22, no. 4 (1985): 341–377; Randall Eberts, George Erickcek, and Jack Kleinhenz, "Dashboard Indicators for the

Northeast Ohio Economy: Prepared for the Fund for Our Economic Future," Working Paper 0605 (Federal Reserve Bank of Cleveland, 2006).

49. For data on per capita growth rates of advanced countries over the past several decades, see Piketty, *Capital in the Twenty-First Century*, 511; and Thomas Piketty, Emmanuel Saez, and Stefanie Stantcheva, "Optimal Taxation of Top Labor Incomes: A Tale of Three Elasticities," Working Paper 17616 (National Bureau of Economic Research, 2011), figure 4.

50. See, for example, Torsten Persson and Guido Tabellini, "Is Inequality Harmful for Growth?," *American Economic Review* 84, no. 3 (1994): 600–621; George R.G. Clarke, "More Evidence on Income Distribution and Growth," *Journal of Development Economics* 47, no. 2 (1995): 403–427; Klaus Deininger, "New Ways of Looking at Old Issues: Inequality and Growth," *Journal of Development Economics* 57, no. 2 (1998): 259–287; Roberto Perotti, "Growth, Income Distribution, and Democracy: What the Data Say," *Journal of Economic Growth* 1, no. 2 (1996): 149–187; Alberto Alesina and Dani Rodrik, "Distributive Politics and Economic Growth," *Quarterly Journal of Economics* 109, no. 2 (1994): 465–490; Dierk Herzer and Sebastian Vollmer, "Inequality and Growth: Evidence from Panel Cointegration," *Journal of Economic Inequality* 10, no. 4 (2012): 489–503; Erwan Quintin and Jason L. Saving, "Inequality and Growth: Challenges to the Old Orthodoxy," *Economic Letter* 3, no. 1 (2008): 1–8; Simon Sturn and Till van Treeck, "Income Inequality as a Cause of the Great Recession? A Survey of Current Debates" (Switzerland: International Labour Office, 2012); Roland Bénabou, "Inequality and Growth," *NBER Macroeconomics Annual* 11 (1996): 11–74.

51. William Easterly, "The Middle Class Consensus and Economic Development" (Washington, DC: World Bank, 2001).

52. Andrew G. Berg and Jonathan D. Ostry, "Inequality and Unsustainable Growth: Two Sides of the Same Coin" (Washington, DC: International Monetary Fund, 2011). See also their more recent paper: Jonathan D. Ostry, Andrew Berg, and Charalambos G. Tsangarides, "Redistribution, Inequality and Growth" (International Monetary Fund, 2014).

53. The debate about this cross-country research includes questions such as what countries should be compared, over what time period, and with what data and statistical techniques. For examples of studies that have not found significant negative impacts of inequality on growth or have arrived at more mixed conclusions, see the following list. Note that these studies generally analyze growth over a relatively short period of time, which can give an incomplete picture of the relationships between inequality and growth, especially because many impacts take a long period of time to develop. As Heather Boushey and Carter C. Price find: "Most research shows that, in the long term, inequality is negatively related to economic growth and that countries with less disparity and a larger middle class boast stronger and more stable growth." Heather Boushey and Carter C. Price, "How Are Economic Inequality and Growth Connected?" (Washington, DC: Washington Center for Equitable Growth, 2014). Also note that these more skeptical studies typically occurred before the Great Recession. Adequate study of events like the Great Recession is necessary to properly understand the relationship between inequality and growth since the financial crash was caused to a significant degree by extreme levels of inequality. Further, events like the Great Recession indicate some of the limitations of cross-country regression analysis, especially because of the significant spillover effects of a recession starting in one country infecting others. Robert J. Barro, "Inequality and Growth in a Panel of Countries," *Journal of Economic Growth* 5, no. 1 (2000): 5–32; Kristin J. Forbes, "A Reassessment of the Relationship between Inequality and Growth," *American Economic Review* 90, no. 4 (2000): 869–887; Stephen Knowles, "Inequality and Economic

Growth: The Empirical Relationship Reconsidered in the Light of Comparable Data," *Journal of Developmental Studies* 41, no. 1 (2005): 135–159; Dan Andrews, Christopher Jencks, and Andrew Leigh, "Do Rising Top Incomes Lift All Boats?," *B.E. Journal of Economic Analysis and Policy* 11, no. 1 (2011): 1–43.

54. Heather Boushey and Adam S. Hersh, "American Middle Class, Income Inequality, and the Strength of Our Economy" (Washington, DC: Center for American Progress, 2012). Note that David Moss, Anant Thaker, and Howard Rudnick, "Inequality and Decision Making: Imaging a New Line of Inquiry," Working Paper 13–099 (Harvard Business School, 2013), makes a similar point.

55. For information on how the relationship between economic inequality and financial collapse is not as simple or direct as some have tried to claim, see, for example, Anthony B. Atkinson and Salvatore Morelli, "Economic Crises and Inequality," Research Paper 2011/06 (United Nations Development Programme, 2011); Paul Krugman, "Inequality and Crises: Coincidence or Causation?," slides prepared for Luxembourg Income Study, June 28, 2010. See also Arjun Jayadev, "Distribution and Crisis: Reviewing Some of the Linkages," in *The Handbook of the Political Economy of Financial Crises*, ed. Martin H. Wolfson and Gerald A. Epstein (Oxford: Oxford University Press, 2013).

56. For support that the recession began in the United States, see Kristin Forbes, Jeffrey Frankel, and Charles Engel, "Introduction to Special Issue on the Global Financial Crisis," *Journal of International Economics* 88, no. 2 (2012): 215–218; Steven B. Kamin and Laurie Pounder DeMarco, "How Did a Domestic Housing Slump Turn into a Global Financial Crisis?," International Finance Discussion Paper 994 (Board of Governors of the Federal Reserve System, 2010); United Nations Department of Economic and Social Affairs, "The Global Social Crisis: Report on the World Social Situation 2011" (2011); Justin Yifu Lin and Volker Treichel, "Unexpected Global Financial Crisis: Researching Its Root Cause," Policy Research Working Paper 5937 (World Bank, 2012); Fabio C. Bagliano and Claudio Morana, "The Great Recession," *Journal of Banking & Finance* 36, no. 1 (2012): 1–13; Neil Fligstein and Jacob Habinek, "Sucker Punched by the Invisible Hand: The World Financial Markets and the Globalization of the US Mortgage Crisis," *Socio Economic Review*, March 14, 2014, doi:10.1093/ser/mwu004.

57. Stiglitz, "Macroeconomic Fluctuations, Inequality, and Human Development." See also Arjun Jayadev, "Distribution and Crisis."

58. Similar claims have also been made in more political environments, including by William Jennings Bryan, who argued that "the Democratic idea, however, has been that if you legislate to make the masses prosperous, their prosperity will find its way up through every class which rests upon them." William Jennings Bryan, "Cross of Gold," speech, Chicago, IL, July 9, 1896. See also the Swedish model developed by Gösta Rehn and Rudolf Meidner and in Gunnar Myrdal's advocacy for land reform in underdeveloped countries. See Gunnar Myrdal, "The Equality Issue in World Development," *American Economic Review* 79, no. 6 (1989): 8–17.

59. See chapter 2 for full details.

60. Congressional Budget Office, "Public Spending on Transportation and Water Infrastructure" (2010). The Congressional Budget Office reports that federal, state, and local spending on infrastructure totaled 2.4 percent of GDP in 2007, the most recent year for which data was available. If we had spent a similar amount to what we spent in the mid-1960s (3 percent) in 2007 that would have come to $89 billion in additional infrastructure spending per year.

61. See chapter 5 for additional details.

62. See chapter 5 for additional details.

63. Though this book is focused on the United States, I think these same basic effects apply elsewhere; however, the actual impacts are contingent on the institutions and culture of each country. Put another way, inequality and a weak middle class can undermine trust, government, demand, and human capital in all settings. But the level at which inequality and a weak middle class start to have severe negative consequences differs by society, as do the exact ways these harms manifest themselves.

64. Robert Solow, interview with Alexandra Mitukiewicz, *Washington Center For Equitable Growth*, December 9, 2013, www.youtube.com/watch?v = 20NXQ470nSM.

65. For job loss figures, see Center on Budget and Policy Priorities, "Chart Book: The Legacy of the Great Recession" (2013); Michael Greenstone and Adam Looney, "The Lasting Effects of the Great Recession: Six Million Missing Workers and a New Economic Normal," *Brookings on Job Numbers Blog*, September 12, 2013, www.brookings.edu /blogs/jobs/posts/2013/09/12-jobs-gap-greenstone-looney. Estimates of lost economic growth in dollar terms vary. The Dallas Federal Reserve has conservatively estimated that between $6 trillion and $14 trillion worth of output was forgone due to the recession of 2007–2009, but also notes that costs could be much greater if factors such as changes to US total wealth, nonfinancial consequences of the recession, and the costs of the government's response are properly factored in. A Government Accountability Office report from 2013 noted that depending on the methodology and assumptions used to estimate lost growth, the figure could range from a few trillion dollars to well over $10 trillion. A report from 2012 by Better Markets estimated that GDP loss between 2008 and 2018 would total approximately $7.6 trillion, but that an additional loss of $5.2 trillion would have occurred if not for government intervention, bringing the total potential loss to $12.8 trillion. See Tyler Atkinson, David Luttrell, and Harvey Rosenblum, "How Bad Was It? The Costs and Consequences of the 2007–09 Financial Crisis" (Dallas, TX: Federal Reserve Bank of Dallas, 2013); Government Accountability Office, "Financial Regulatory Reform: Financial Crisis Losses and Potential Impacts of the Dodd-Frank Act" (2013); Dennis Kelleher, Stephen Hall, and Katelynn Bradley, "The Cost of the Wall Street-Caused Financial Collapse and Ongoing Economic Crisis Is More Than $12.8 Trillion" (Washington, DC: Better Market, 2012).

66. The averages of the annualized GDP growth rates for the 1980s, 1990s, 2000s, and first three years of the 2010s are all lower than the averages of the annual growth rates seen in the 1950s, 1960s, and 1970s based on data from the Bureau of Economic Analysis. This is true even if the negative GDP growth rates for 2008 and 2009 are removed from the calculation. This is according to author's calculations based on Bureau of Economic Analysis data available in table 1.1.1 of Bureau of Economic Analysis, "National Income and Product Accounts Tables," www.bea.gov/iTable/iTable.cfm?ReqID = 9&step = 1#reqid = 9&step = 1&isuri = 1&903 = 1. See also J.T. Young, "The Worst Four Years of GDP Growth in History: Yes, We Should Be Worried," *Forbes*, April 12, 2013, www.forbes.com/sites /realspin/2013/04/12/the-worst-four-years-of-gdp-growth-in-history-yes-we-should-be-worried/.

67. Michael Ettlinger and Michael Linden, "The Failure of Supply-Side Economics" (Washington, DC: Center for American Progress, 2012); Mark Thoma, "Did the Bush Tax Cuts Lead to Economic Growth?," *CBS News*, November 30, 2010, www.cbsnews.com /8301-505123_162-39741024/did-the-bush-tax-cuts-lead-to-economic-growth/; Chye-Ching Huang, "Recent Studies Find Raising Taxes on High-Income Households Would Not Harm the Economy" (Washington, DC: Center on Budget and Policy Priorities, 2012).

68. For a review of academic studies, see Andrew Fieldhouse, "A Review on the Economic Research on the Effects of Raising Ordinary Tax Rates" (Washington, DC: Eco-

nomic Policy Institute, 2013). See also Michael Ettlinger and John S. Irons, "Take a Walk on the Supply Side" (Washington, DC: Center for American Progress, 2008); Aviva Aron-Dine, Richard Kogan, and Chad Stone, "How Robust Was the 2001–2007 Economic Expansion?" (Washington, DC: Center on Budget and Policy Priorities, 2008).

69. Ettlinger and Irons, "Take a Walk on the Supply Side." See also Chait, *The Big Con.*

70. President Barack Obama, "Remarks by the President at a Campaign Event," speech, Los Angeles, CA, October 8, 2012. See also David Madland and Gadi Dechter, "The Evolution of Obama's Middle-Out Economics" (Washington, DC: Center for American Progress Action Fund, 2012); and speeches from President Obama's second term, including President Barack Obama, "Remarks by the President at the 'Let Freedom Ring' Ceremony Commemorating the 50th Anniversary of the March on Washington," speech, Washington, DC, August 28, 2013; President Barack Obama, "Remarks by the President on the Economy," Galesburg, IL, July 24, 2013; President Barack Obama, "Remarks by the President on Economic Mobility," speech, Washington, DC, December 4, 2013.

71. Obama, "Remarks by the President on Economic Mobility."

72. See, for example, "When the middle class is doing well … they're spending more money, businesses have more customers, businesses make more profits, and then hire more workers." President Barack Obama, debate with Governor Mitt Romney, Denver, CO, October 3, 2012.

73. See, for example, Governor Martin O'Malley's speech where he said, "Trickle-down economics has been an abject failure for 99 percent of Americans. If we want to deliver better results—if we want to strengthen our middle class and expand middle class opportunity—then we have to be willing to make better choices." Martin O'Malley, "Better Choices for a Stronger Middle Class," speech, Washington, DC, May 30, 2013. See also Madland and Dechter, "The Evolution of Obama's Middle-Out Economics"; Martin O'Malley, "What Maryland Does Better than Texas," *Washington Post,* September 17, 2013, www.washingtonpost.com/opinions/gov-omalley-what-maryland-does-better-than-texas /2013/09/17/0c6b00f2-1faf-11e3-94a2-6c66b668ea55_story.html; Mark Peters, "States' Rift on Taxes Widen," *Wall Street Journal,* May 23, 2013, http://online.wsj.com/news/articles /SB10001424127887323648304578497411113160332.

74. The top marginal tax rate fell from 90 percent in the 1960s and is less than 40 percent today, and was even lower for much of the George W. Bush presidency. See, for example, Council of Economic Advisors, "Economic Report of the President" (Government Printing Office, 2013). Note the average tax rate paid by the rich fell significantly over this period too. For example, the average tax rate paid by the 0.01 percent was roughly cut in half from the mid-1970s to the mid-2000s. The rate fell from around 70 percent in 1960 to around 35 percent in 2004. See Mishel and others, "The State of Working America: 12th Edition," figure 2Q. For similar trends, see also Council of Economic Advisors, "Economic Report of the President"; Thomas Hungerford, "Taxes and the Economy: An Economic Analysis of the Top Tax Rates since 1945 (Updated)" (Washington, DC: Congressional Research Service, 2012); National Economic Council, "The Buffett Rule: A Basic Principle of Tax Fairness" (White House, 2012). For estimates of changes in average tax rates that do not attempt to control for the impact of income growth among the very wealthy, see Congressional Budget Office, "The Distribution of Household Income and Federal Taxes, 2008 and 2009"; Binyamin Appelbaum, "Tax Burden for Most Americans Is Lower Than in the 1980s," *New York Times,* November 29, 2012, www.nytimes.com/2012/11/30/us/most-americans-face-lower-tax-burden-than-in-the-80s.html?pagewanted = 1&_r = 1. In addition, Pizzigati, *The Rich Don't Always Win*—based on Janet McCubbin and Fritz Scheuren, "Individual Income Tax Shares and Average Tax Rates, Tax Years 1951–1986," *Statistics*

of Income Bulletin 8, no. 4 (1989): 39–74—reports that the average tax rate paid by the 400 individuals reporting the highest adjusted gross income each year fell by half from the 1960s to 2009.

75. For example, in 1997 a majority of both House and Senate Democrats voted for the Taxpayer Relief Act of 1997, which, among other things, lowered capital gains tax rates. This bill was then signed into law by Democratic president Bill Clinton. See Govtrack, "H.R. 2014 (105th): Taxpayer Relief Act of 1997," www.govtrack.us/congress/bills/105/hr2014. Additionally, in 2001 a total of 12 Senate Democrats voted to pass the first round of tax cuts under President Bush, which passed the Senate by a margin of only 58–33. See Govtrack, "H.R. 1836 (107th): Economic Growth and the Tax Payer Reconciliation Act of 2001 (on the Conference Report)," www.govtrack.us/congress/votes/107–2001/s170. In 2003, the second round of Bush tax cuts received extremely little Democratic support in either the House or the Senate, but if it were not for the two Democrats who voted in favor of the bill it likely would have failed to pass the Senate. See "H.R. 2 (108th): Jobs and Growth Tax Relief Reconciliation of 2003 (On the Conference Report)," www.govtrack.us/congress/votes/108–2003/s196.

76. For more information on Clinton tax policies, see Michael Linden, "Fact versus Fiction in Latest Supply-Side Debate" (Washington, DC: Center for American Progress, 2011); Linden, "The Middle Class Series: Federal Tax Code and Income Inequality" (Washington, DC: Center for American Progress, 2012).

77. Karen Dewitt, "Cuomo Looks to Former Rivals to Head Tax Cutting Commission," *WXXI News*, October 2, 2013, http://wxxinews.org/post/cuomo-looks-former-rivals-head-tax-cutting-commission.

78. Michael Howard Saul, "Mayor Says More Billionaires Would Ease City's Economic Situations," *Wall Street Journal*, September 20, 2013, http://online.wsj.com/news/articles/SB10001424127887323808204579087582341293444.

79. John Wagner, "Democrat Douglas F. Gansler Calls for Cut in Md. Corporate Income Tax Rate," *Washington Post*, August 29, 2013, http://articles.washingtonpost.com/2013–08–29/local/41578236_1_gansler-democrat-douglas-f-corporate-income-tax-rate.

80. Peter Dreier and Christopher Martin, "'Job Killers' in the News: Allegations without Verification" (Cedar Falls: University of Northern Iowa, 2012).

81. The projected tax cut offered to millionaires under the most recently assessed iteration of the Romney tax plan was approximately $390,000 if current law was used as the baseline in the estimation. This is compared to a tax cut for millionaires of roughly $141,000 provided by the Bush tax cuts. For the most recent projection based on Romney's plan, see Tax Policy Center, "T12–0038—Romney Tax Plan without Unspecified Base Broadeners; Baseline: Current Law; Distribution of Federal Tax Change by Cash Income Level, 2015," www.taxpolicycenter.org/numbers/displayatab.cfm?Docid = 3296. For tax cut provided by Bush, see Michael Linden and Seth Hanlon, "Mitt Romney's Tax Plan in 5 Charts" (Washington, DC: Center for American Progress Action Fund, 2012).

82. The budget proposal put forward by Chairman Paul Ryan seeks to cut the top marginal tax rate from 39.6 percent to 25 percent, while Romney's proposed plan only sought to cut it from 35 percent to 28 percent. According to the Center on Budget and Policy Priorities, "The tax cuts for high-income filers would necessarily be larger under Ryan's Plan than under Romney's." See Chuck Marr, Chye-Ching Huang, and Nathaniel Frentz, "The Ryan Budget's Tax Cuts: Nearly $6 Trillion in Cost and No Plausible Way to Pay for It" (Washington, DC: Center on Budget and Policy Priorities, 2013).

83. Analysis of these proposals shows that, to meet proponents' stated goal of not increasing the deficit, tax increases on the middle class would have been required. For details of the tax increases required to accommodate the Romney proposal, see Samuel Brown, William Gale, and Adam Looney, "On the Distributional Effects of Base-Broadening Income Tax Reform" (Washington, DC: Tax Policy Center, 2012). For details of the increases required to accommodate the Ryan proposal, see Marr, Huang, and Frentz, "The Ryan Budget's Tax Cuts."

84. For example, North Carolina recently passed a set of tax code changes that have been projected to increase taxes on the middle class and poor, in part due to the elimination of the state's earned income tax credit. See Citizens for Tax Justice, "North Carolina Faces Disastrous New Tax Laws," www.ctj.org/taxjusticedigest/archive/2013/07/north_carolina_facing_disastro.php#.UnpXOuKp3oZ. Note also that a tax bill signed into law by Governor Brownback in Kansas in 2012 increased taxes on those with the lowest incomes while providing tax cuts for the very wealthy. See Institute on Taxation and Economic Policy, "Tax Bill Signed by Governor Brownback Makes Kansas an Outlier" (2012). For more on regressive tax reform proposals, see David Madland, "The Not-So-Secret Conservative Plot to Raise Taxes on the Middle Class" (Washington, DC: Center for American Progress, 2011), www.americanprogress.org/issues/budget/news/2011/04/27/9409/the-not-so-secret-conservative-plot-to-raise-taxes-on-the-middle-class/; Paul Breer and Kevin Donohoe, "REPORT: In 12 States, GOP Plans to Slash Corporate Taxes While Increasing Burden on Working Families," *ThinkProgress,* March 16, 2011, http://thinkprogress.org/politics/2011/03/16/151008/gop-state-corporate-tax-cuts/.

85. The Bush tax cuts, for example, disproportionately benefited the wealthy. See Joel Friedman and Isaac Shaprio, "Tax Returns: A Comprehensive Assessment of the Bush Administration's Record on Cutting Taxes" (Washington, DC: Center on Budget and Policy Priorities, 2004); Citizens for Tax Justice, "The Bush Tax Cuts Cost Two and a Half Times as Much as the House Democrats' Health Care Proposal" (2009). But they still did provide some benefit to the middle class as charts 3 and 4 in this column make clear: Zachary A. Goldfarb, "The Legacy of the Bush tax Cuts, in Four Charts," *Washington Post Wonkblog* January 2, 2013, www.washingtonpost.com/blogs/wonkblog/wp/2013/01/02/the-legacy-of-the-bush-tax-cuts-in-four-charts/.

86. Phillips, *Wealth and Democracy*; Norton Garfinkle, *The American Dream vs. the Gospel of Wealth: The Fight for a Productive Middle Class Economy* (New Haven, CT: Yale University Press, 2006). See also the introduction to Pizzigati, *The Rich Don't Always Win,* especially the quotation from 1925 from the chair of the Republican National Congressional Committee: "Heavy taxes upon the man of wealth and upon corporations ... strangle business, act as a deadweight on commerce, and slow down the wheels of industry."

87. During this period, thinkers such as Herbert Spencer and William Graham Sumner espoused variations of Social Darwinist thinking that generally called for less government intervention and regulation and for the elimination of forced redistribution from the wealthy to the poor. See, for example, William Graham Sumner, *What Social Classes Owe One Another* (New York: Harper & Brothers, 1883). For more on how Social Darwinism influenced thought and policy throughout the late nineteenth and early twentieth centuries, see Phillips, *Wealth and Democracy.*

88. Andrew W. Mellon, *Taxation: The People's Business* (New York: Macmillan, 1924).

89. For quotes from Mellon, see ibid.

90. John Maynard Keynes, *The General Theory of Employment, Interest, and Money* (London: Macmillan, 1936); Skidelsky, *Keynes.*

91. See, for example, President Richard Nixon's statement that he was "now a Keynesian in economics." Reuters, "Nixon Reportedly Says He Is Now a Keynesian," *New York Times,* January 7, 1971, http://query.nytimes.com/gst/abstract.html?res=9505E4DA123DE53 BBC4F53DFB766838A669EDE.

92. See, for example, Skidelsky, *Keynes.* See also Bruce Bartlett, *The New American Economy: The Failure of Reaganomics and a New Way Forward* (New York: Palgrave Macmillan, 2009), which argues, "Just as Keynesian economics went off the wrong track and became discredited, I think supply-side economics has also reached the end of its useful life."

93. See, for example, Mark Blyth, *Great Transformations: Economic Ideas and Institutional Change in the Twentieth Century* (New York: Cambridge University Press, 2002), for the conscious use of the problem of inflation to promote an alternative theory.

94. Keynes, *General Theory of Employment, Interest and Money.*

95. Paraphrased from ibid.

96. For books that have highlighted elements of middle out, see Robert Reich, *Aftershock: The Next Economy & America's Future* (New York: Vintage, 2010); Raghuram G. Rajan, *Fault Lines: How Hidden Fractures Still Threaten the World Economy* (Princeton, NJ: Princeton University Press, 2010); Joseph E. Stiglitz, *The Price of Inequality: How Today's Divided Society Endangers Our Future* (New York: W.W. Norton, 2012).

97. Paul Ryan, "Saving the American Idea: Rejecting Fear, Envy and the Politics of Division," speech, Washington, DC, October 26, 2011.

98. N. Gregory Mankiw, "Defending the One Percent," *Journal of Economic Perspectives* 27, no. 3 (2013): 21–34.

CHAPTER TWO

1. Edward C. Banfield, *The Moral Basis of a Backward Society* (Glencoe, IL: Free Press, 1958).

2. In 2012, 32 percent of Americans thought that most people could be trusted, down from 47 percent in 1973. Numbers from author's analysis of 2012 General Social Survey data, which can be found at "General Social Survey," www3.norc.org/gss+website/. See also Eric M. Uslaner, *Divided Citizens: How Inequality Undermines Trust in America* (New York: Demos, 2002).

3. Uslaner, *Divided Citizens;* Eric M. Uslaner, *Moral Foundations of Trust* (Cambridge: Cambridge University Press, 2002); Eric M. Uslaner and Oguzhan C. Dincer, "Trust and Growth," *Public Choice* 142, no. 1 (2010): 59–67.

4. Philip Keefer and Stephen Knack, "Social Capital, Social Norms and the New Institutional Economics" (Washington, DC: World Bank, 2004).

5. Oliver E. Williamson, "Transaction Cost Economics: How It Works, Where It Is Headed," *De Economist* 146 (1998): 23–58.

6. Note that as an alternative means of protection, market participants could focus on very short-term exchanges, where the chance of exploitation is less. But that means missing out on, for example, loans, investments in fixed assets like buildings, and many employment contracts that are necessarily longer-term commitments. See, for example, Keefer and Knack, "Social Capital, Social Norms and the New Institutional Economics," for a discussion of spot markets. Marc Sangnier argues that "shorter contracts will be privileged by low-trust principals as they want to keep control over the business relation by leaving open the possibility of renegotiation during subsequent periods." Marc Sangnier,

"Does Trust Favor Macroeconomic Stability?," Working Paper 2009–40 (Paris-Jourdan Sciences Economiques, 2009).

7. Oliver E. Williamson, "Transaction-Cost Economics: The Governance of Contractual Relations," *Journal of Law and Economics* 22, no. 2 (1979): 233–261; Oliver E. Williamson, "Transaction-Cost Economics: How it Works, Where It Is Headed"; John R. Commons, "Institutional Economics: The Problem of Social Cost," *American Economic Review* 21, no. 193 (1960): 648–657; Douglass C. North, *Structure and Change in Economic History* (New York: W. W. Norton, 1982); Samuel Bowles, *Microeconomics: Behavior, Institutions, and Evolution* (Princeton, NJ: Princeton University Press, 2006).

8. Jon Hilsenrath, "How a Trust Deficit Is Hurting the Economy," *Wall Street Journal*, January 27, 2013, http://online.wsj.com/article/SB10001424127887323854904578264161278400462.html.

9. Francis Fukuyama, *Trust: The Social Virtues and the Creation of Prosperity* (New York: Free Press, 1996).

10. Ernst Fehr and Simon Gächter, "Fairness and Retaliation: The Economics of Reciprocity," *Journal of Economic Perspectives*, 40, no. 14 (2000): 159–181.

11. Robert Boyd, Peter J. Richerson, and Joseph Henrich, "The Cultural Niche: Why Social Learning Is Essential for Human Adaptation," *Proceedings of the National Academy of Sciences of the United States of America* 108, supplement 2 (2011); Peter J. Richerson and Robert Boyd, "The Evolution of Free Enterprise Values," in *Moral Markets: The Critical Role of Values in the Economy*, ed. Paul J. Zak (Princeton, NJ: Princeton University Press, 2008); Samuel Bowles, *The New Economics of Inequality and Redistribution* (Cambridge: Cambridge University Press, 2012); Samuel Bowles and Herbert Gintis, *A Cooperative Species: Human Reciprocity and Its Evolution* (Princeton, NJ: Princeton University Press, 2011); Robert L. Trivers, "The Evolution of Reciprocal Altruism," *Quarterly Review of Biology* 46, no. 1 (1971): 35–57; John M. Gowdy and others, "Economic Cosmology and the Evolutionary Challenge," *Journal of Economic Behavior and Organization* 90 (2013): 11–20.

12. Richerson and Boyd, "The Evolution of Free Enterprise Values." Italics in original.

13. Uslaner, *The Moral Foundations of Trust.*

14. Fehr and Gächter, "Fairness and Retaliation"; Robert Cialdini and others, "Reinterpreting the Empathy—Altruism Relationship: When One into One Equals Oneness," *Journal of Personality and Social Psychology* 73, no. 3 (1997): 481–494.

15. Fehr and Gächter, "Fairness and Retaliation."

16. For an introduction to this literature, see Joyce Berg, John Dickhaut, and Kevin McCabe, "Trust, Reciprocity, and Social History," *Games and Economic Behavior* 10 (1995): 122–142.

17. Eric M. Uslaner, "Trust and the Economic Crisis of 2008," *Corporate Reputation Review* 13, no. 2 (2010): 110–123.

18. Uslaner, *Divided Citizens*; Uslaner, *Moral Foundations of Trust*; Uslaner and Dincer, "Trust and Growth"; Christian Larsen, *The Rise and Fall of Social Cohesion* (Oxford: Oxford University Press, 2013). Note that Larsen emphasizes that inequality works indirectly by fueling perceptions of others.

19. Paul J. Zak and Stephen Knack, "Trust and Growth," *Economic Journal* 111, no. 470 (2001): 295–321; Keefer and Knack, "Social Capital, Social Norms and the New Institutional Economics"; George Akerlof, "Distance and Social Decisions," *Econometrica* 65, no. 5 (1997): 1005–1027.

20. Paul K. Piff and others, "Higher Social Class Predicts Increased Unethical Behavior," *Proceedings of the National Academy of Sciences of the United States* 109, no. 11 (2012): 4086–4091.

21. Shaun P. Hargreaves Heap, Jonathan H.W. Tan, and Daniel John Zizzo, "Trust, Inequality, and the Market," *Theory and Decision* 74, no. 3 (2013): 311–333. Note that this study is an important advance over prior experiments that attempted to study the effects of inequality by showing the distribution of incomes but did not reveal the income level of partners.

22. Study was conducted by *Reader's Digest*, reported in *The Economist* on June 22, 1996, and later evaluated by Stephen Knack. See Stephen Knack, "Trust, Associational Life and Economic Performance" (Washington, DC: World Bank, 2001).

23. Knack, "Trust, Associational Life and Economic Performance."

24. Lukas Neville, "Do Economic Equality and Generalized Trust Inhibit Academic Dishonesty? Evidence from State-Level Search-Engine Queries," *Psychological Science* 23, no. 4 (2012): 339–345. As University of Manitoba business professor Lukas Neville explains: "When there is higher economic inequality, people are less likely to view one another as trustworthy. This lower generalized trust, in turn, is associated with a greater prevalence of academic dishonesty."

25. Stephen Knack and Philip Keefer, "Does Social Capital Have an Economic Payoff? A Cross-Country Investigation," *Quarterly Journal of Economics*, 112, no. 4 (1997): 1251–1288; Zak and Knack, "Trust and Growth"; Keefer and Knack, "Social Capital, Social Norms and the New Institutional Economics"; Christian Bjornskov, "Determinants of Generalized Trust: A Cross-Country Comparison," *Public Choice* 130, nos. 1–2 (2007): 1–21; Alberto Alesina and Eliana La Ferrara, "Who Trusts Others?," *Journal of Public Economics* 85, no. 2 (2002): 207–234; Uslaner, "Trust and the Economic Crisis of 2008"; Eric M. Uslaner "Trust as a Moral Value" (College Park: University of Maryland, 2001). Note that there is a debate about whether survey questions are a better measure of trust or trustworthiness. See Edward L. Glaeser and others, "Measuring Trust," *Quarterly Journal of Economics* 115, no. 3 (2000): 811–846; and Olof Johannson-Stenman, Minjah Mahmud, and Peter Martinsson, "Trust, Trust Games and Stated Trust: Evidence from Rural Bangladesh," *Journal of Economic Behavior and Organization* 95 (2011): 286–298: they argue that survey questions better measure trustworthiness. But some argue that different measures of trust and trustworthiness are highly correlated and thus survey questions are good measures: for example, Knack, "Trust, Associational Life and Economic Performance"; and Keefer and Knack, "Social Capital, Social Norms and the New Institutional Economics." Noel D. Johnson and Alexandra Mislin, "How Much Should We Trust the World Values Survey Trust Question?," *Economics Letters* 116, no. 2 (2012): 210–212, finds that survey question measures of trust are highly correlated with experimentally measured trust.

26. The 14 state-level measures of social capital, along with the Comprehensive Social Capital Index, are described in Robert D. Putnam, *Bowling Alone: The Collapse and Revival of American Community* (New York: Simon & Schuster, 2000), 290–291 and table 4. The underlying sources of these data are given in the endnotes to those pages.

27. For measures of trust and measures of the relative equality of each nation's economy including their calculated Gini coefficient estimates, see Organization for Economic Co-Operation and Development, "Society at a Glance 2011—OECD Social Indicators" (2011). See also Larsen, *The Rise and Fall of Social Cohesion*, table 1.1. For estimates of the share of wealth going to the top 1 percent of earners—which can be viewed as another measure of relative equality—see Facundo Alvaredo and others, "The Top 1 Percent in International and Historical Perspective," *Journal of Economic Perspectives* 27, no. 3 (2013): 3–20.

28. Jean M. Twenge, W. Keith Campbell, and Nathan T. Carter, "Declines in Trust in Others and Confidence in Institutions among American Adults and Late Adolescents, 1972–2012," *Psychological Science* 25, no. 10 (2014): 1914–1923. But for a criticism of the over-

time relationship, see Javier Olivera, "On Changes in General Trust in Europe," Discussion Paper 80 (Gini Project, 2013). But note that the study only analyzes changes from 2002 to 2010, which is a very short time period and thus likely to understate the relationship.

29. Author's analysis of 2012 General Social Survey data, which can be found at "General Social Survey," www3.norc.org/gss+website/. See also Uslaner, *Divided Citizens*.

30. See Larsen, *The Rise and Fall of Social Cohesion*, table 1.1.

31. Gabriel Almond and Sidney Verba, *Civic Culture: Political Attitudes and Democracy in Five Nations* (Newbury Park, CA: Sage, 1989), found that in 1960, Americans believed most people could be trusted (United States 55%; United Kingdom 49%; Germany 19%; Italy 7%; Mexico 30%). Note that this polling suggests that trust may have started to decline in the United States before inequality began rising—but it is hard to know how much weight to place on this one poll without other supporting surveys from this time period. Still, even if considerable weight is placed on this one poll, the drop of 7 percentage points over almost a decade and a half is not particularly large, but it does suggest that other factors besides inequality likely explain at least some of the drop in trust over the past several decades. I discuss these other factors at greater length in the text.

32. Alexis de Tocqueville, *Democracy in America* (Washington, DC: Library of America, 2004).

33. Larsen, *The Rise and Fall of Social Cohesion*.

34. See, among others, Alesina and La Ferrara, "Who Trusts Others?"; Uslaner, *Moral Foundations of Trust*; Uslaner and Dincer, "Trust and Growth."

35. Larsen, *The Rise and Fall of Social Cohesion*.

36. For information on US levels of diversity from this time period, see Philip Roeder, "Ethnolinguistic Fractionalization (ELF) Indices, 1961 and 1985," updated September 18, 2001, http://pages.ucsd.edu/~proeder/elf.htm. Using data from the Atlas Narodov Mira, a dataset constructed by researchers in the Soviet Union, as well as data from *The World Handbook of Political and Social Indicators*, 2nd ed., Roeder finds that the United States is one of the most diverse developed countries, behind only Canada, Belgium, and Switzerland in 1961. For more, see Alberto Alesina, Arnaud Devleeschauwer, William Easterly, Sergio Kurlat, and Romain Wacziarg, "Fractionalization," *Journal of Economic Growth* 8, no. 2 (2003): 155–194; James Fearon, "Ethnic and Cultural Diversity by Country," *Journal of Economic Growth* 8, no. 2 (2003): 195–222; Natalka Patsiurko, John Campbell, and John Hall, "Measuring Cultural Diversity: Ethnic, Linguistic and Religious Fractionalization in the OECD," *Ethnic and Racial Studies* 35, no. 2 (2012): 195–217.

37. See the discussion in Larsen, *The Rise and Fall of Social Cohesion*, 17. In 1980 in Denmark, immigrants and their children made up only 3.1 percent of the population, and most came from neighboring countries. But by 2009, immigrants and their children made up 10.6 percent of the population, and two-thirds came from non-Western countries.

38. According to the OECD, the percentage of Sweden's population that was foreign-born in 2012—the most recent year for which OECD figures are available—was 15.5 percent while the percentage of the United States's population that was foreign-born that year was 13.0 percent. See Organisation for Economic Co-Operation and Development, "International Migration Outlook 2014" (2014), www.oecd.org/migration/integrationindicators/keyindicatorsbycountry/name,218350,en.htm.

39. See ibid., 17 and table 2.9

40. John Stuart Mill, *Principles of Political Economy with Some of Their Applications to Social Philosophy* (London: Longmans, Green, 1909).

41. Kenneth J. Arrow, "Gifts and Exchanges," *Philosophy and Public Affairs* 1, no. 4 (1972): 343–362.

42. Sjoerd Beugelsdijk and Robbert Maseland, *Culture in Economics: History, Methodological Reflections and Contemporary Applications* (New York: Cambridge University Press, 2011).

43. Dimitris Georgarakos and Sven Fürth, "Household Repayment Behavior: The Role of Social Capital, Institutional, Political, and Religious Beliefs," Working Paper (University of Frankfurt and Goethe University of Frankfurt, 2012). Luigi Guiso, Paola Sapienza, and Luigi Zingales, "The Role of Social Capital in Financial Development," *American Economic Review* 94, no. 3 (2004): 526–556.

44. Sven Oskarsson, PerOla Öberg, and Torsten Svensson, "Making Capitalism Work: Fair Institutions and Trust," *Economic and Industrial Democracy* 30, no. 2 (2009): 294–320.

45. See, for example, Alex Edmans, "Does the Stock Market Fully Value Intangibles? Employee Satisfaction and Equity Prices," *Journal of Financial Economics* 101, no. 4 (2011): 621–640; Olubunmi Faleye and Emery A. Trahan, "Labor-Friendly Corporate Practices: Is What Is Good for Employees Good for Shareholders?," *Journal of Business Ethics* 101, no. 1 (2011): 1–27; Greg Filbeck and Dianna Preece, "Fortune's Best 100 Companies to Work for in America: Do They Work for Shareholders?," *Journal of Business Finance and Accounting* 30, nos. 5–6 (2003): 771–797; Douglas L. Kruse, Joseph R. Blasi, and Richard B. Freeman, "Does Linking Worker Pay to Firm Performance Help the Best Firms Do Even Better?," Working Paper 17745 (National Bureau of Economic Research, 2012); Andrea Moro, Devendra Kodwani, and Mike Lucas, "Trust and the Demand for Personal Collateral in SME—Bank Relationships," *Journal of Entrepreneurial Finance* 16, no. 1 (2012): 87–108; Brian Uzzi, "The Source and Consequences of Embeddedness for the Economic Performance of Organizations: The Network Effect," *American Sociological Review* 61, no. 4 (1996): 674–698.

46. Hans Westlund and Frane Adam, "Social Capital and Economic Performance: A Meta-Analysis of 65 Studies," *European Planning Studies* 18, no. 6 (2010): 893–919. Note that the analysis included studies that focused on trust and related concepts such as social capital.

47. Keefer and Knack, "Social Capital, Social Norms and the New Institutional Economics." See also Keefer and Knack, "Does Social Capital Have an Economic Payoff?"; Zak and Knack, "Trust and Growth." For further evidence, see Roman Horvath, "Does Trust Promote Growth?," *Journal of Comparative Economics* 41, no. 3 (2012): 777–788; Olivier Coibion, Yuriy Gorodnichenko, and Dmitri Koustas, "Amerisclerosis? The Puzzle of Rising U.S. Unemployment Persistence," *Brookings Papers on Economic Activity* (Fall 2011): 353–384.

48. Note that other studies similarly find that trust is as important as education to economic growth. See, for example, Paul Whitely, "Economic Growth and Social Capital," *Political Studies* 48, no. 3 (2000): 443–466.

49. See, for example, Sjoerd Beugelsdijk, Henri de Groot, and Anton van Schaik, "Trust and Economic Growth a Robustness Analysis," *Oxford Economic Papers* 56, no. 1 (2004): 118–134; Uslaner and Dincer, "Trust and Growth"; Westlund and Adam, "Social Capital and Economic Performance." Other reviews of the literature are even more positive, such as Keefer and Knack, "Social Capital, Social Norms and the New Institutional Economics"; and Stephen Knack, "Social Capital, Growth, and Poverty: A Survey of Cross-Country Evidence," in *The Role of Social Capital in Development: An Empirical Assessment,* ed. Christiaan Grootaert and Thierry van Bastelaer (Cambridge: Cambridge University Press, 2002).

50. For examples of such studies analyzing economically advanced areas, see Guido Tabellini, "Culture and Institutions: Economic Development in the Regions of Europe,"

Journal of the European Economic Association 8, no. 4 (2010): 677–716; Semith Akcomakl and Bas tal Weel, "Social Capital, Innovation and Growth: Evidence from Europe," *European Economic Review*, 53, no. 5 (2009): 544–567; Sjoerd Beugelsdijk and Ton Van Schaik, "Differences in Social Capital between 54 Western European Regions," *Regional Studies* 39, no. 8 (2005): 1053–1064; Semih Akcomak and Bas ter Weel, "How Do Social Capital and Government Support Affect Innovation and Growth? Evidence from the EU Regional Support Programmes," in *Innovation Policy in Europe: Measurement and Strategy*, ed. Claire Nauwelaers and Rene Wintjes (Northampton, MA: Edward Elgar, 2008).

51. Uslaner and Dincer, "Trust and Growth." For county-level evidence, see Anil Rupasingha, Stephan J. Goetz, and David Freshwater, "Social and Institutional Factors as Determinants of Economic Growth: Evidence from the United States Counties," *Papers in Regional Science* 81, no. 2 (2002): 139–155.

52. Yann Algan and Pierre Cahuc, "Inherited Trust and Growth," *American Economic Review* 100, no. 5 (2010): 2060–2092. It is important to note that they use an advanced statistical technique—historically based instrumental variables—to argue that trust causes economic growth, providing confirming evidence for the results of other kinds of research.

53. See, for example, Orley C. Ashenfelter, David E. Bloom, and Gordon B. Dahl, "Lawyers as Agents of the Devil in a Prisoner's Dilemma Game," *Journal of Empirical Legal Studies* 10, no. 3 (2013): 399–423. But for a claim that lawyers are more than a transaction cost, see Ronald Gilson, "Value Creation by Business Lawyers: Legal Skills and Asset Pricing," *Yale Law Journal* 94, no. 2 (1984): 239–313.

54. Stewart Macaulay, "Non-Contractual Relations in Business: A Preliminary Study," *American Sociological Review* 28, no. 1 (1963): 55–70.

55. Ashenfelter, Bloom, and Dahl, "Lawyers as Agents of the Devil in a Prisoner's Dilemma Game."

56. Author's calculation based on figures provided by the American Bar Association, which collects data on the numbers of resident and active lawyers in each state from state bar associations or licensing agencies. To calculate the percentage of the workforce that is lawyers, this number was divided by the Bureau of Labor Statistic's estimates of the total number of seasonally adjusted nonfarm employees in December of the given year. These figures will not line up exactly with those provided by the ABA because the figure listed by the ABA as "2012" was actually measured on December 31, 2011, and consequently the author has chosen to label this as the figure for 2011. ABA-provided figures may also include the number of lawyers working in Puerto Rico while the BLS employee estimates do not include estimates for Puerto Rico's total workforce. However, due to the extremely low number of lawyers operating in Puerto Rico as a percentage of all lawyers, this factor should not significantly impact these estimates. See American Bar Association, "Legal Profession Statistics" (2011), www.americanbar.org/resources_for_lawyers/profession_statistics.html. Note that Census Bureau figures show a trend very similar to the ABA data, but are not used because the decennial census stopped collecting data on the number of lawyers in 2000. Similarly, IPUMS occupational data that include both decennial census numbers and American Community Survey numbers show a similar trend between 1970 and 2012, with the percentage of employed persons that were lawyers increasing from 0.35 percent to 0.75 percent. While these figures are lower, the percentage change they illustrate over time is actually higher. Note that in 1970 occupational questions were asked of all workers over the age of 14, while in later years these questions were only asked of workers age 16 and over. Data can be found at Steven Ruggles and others, *Integrated Public Use Microdata Series: Version 5.0* [machine-readable database] (Minneapolis: University of Minnesota, 2010).

57. Ian Wyatt and Daniel Hecker, "Occupational Changes during the 20th Century" (Washington: *Monthly Labor Review*, March 2006).

58. See Robert Putman, "Social Capital: Measurement and Consequences" (Cambridge, MA: Harvard University, 2013).

59. Author's analysis of *Integrated Public Use Microdata Series* occupational data. Note that in 1970 occupational questions were asked of all workers over the age of 14, while in later years these questions were only asked of workers age 16 and over. Note also that figures from 1970 were taken from decennial census data, while figures for 2012 were taken from American Community Survey data. For data, see Steven Ruggles and others, *Integrated Public Use Microdata Series: Version 5.0.*

60. For a review of some other theories of why lawyers increased, see, for example, Robert C. Clark, "Why So Many Lawyers? Are They Good or Bad?" *Fordham Law Review* 61, no. 2 (1992): 275–302.

61. Ibid.

62. In addition to the ABA lawyer data in note 55, note that Putnam argues that between 1900 and 1970 the share of lawyers in the workforce was remarkably stable. See Putman, "Social Capital." For a more thorough rejection of the government regulation hypothesis, see B. Peter Pashigian, "The Market for Lawyers: The Determinants of the Demand for and Supply of Lawyers," *Journal of Law and Economics* 20, no. 1 (1977): 53–86.

63. For a review of some theories of why lawyers increased, see, for example, Clark, "Why So Many Lawyers?"

64. Data for 2000s comes from Stephen P. Magee, "The Optimum Number of Lawyers and a Radical Proposal for Legal Change" (Austin: University of Texas, 2010), while data from the 1980s comes from Ray August, "The Mythical Kingdom of Lawyers: America Doesn't Have 70 Percent of Earth's Lawyers," *ABA Journal* 78, no. 4 (1992): 72–74. But for the difficulty with international comparisons of lawyers, see J. Mark Ramseyer and Eric Rasumusen, "Comparative Litigation Rates," Discussion Paper 681 (John M. Olin Center for Law, Economics and Business at Harvard University, 2010). Note that table 1 shows that the United States has more lawyers and lawsuits than other advanced countries.

65. Author's analysis of 2012 Occupational Employment Statistics data from the Bureau of Labor Statistics and 2012 American Community Survey data from the US Census Bureau. When looking at the top 50 most populous metro areas, the top 10 most unequal cities as measured by their Gini coefficients had a slightly higher percentage of their workforce that were lawyers (0.58 percent) than did the bottom 10 (0.54 percent). Note that the Gini coefficients being used are ACS one-year estimates. Data can be found at Bureau of Labor Statistics, "Occupational Employment Statistics," www.bls.gov/oes/tables.htm; US Census Bureau, "American Fact Finder," http://factfinder2.census.gov/faces/nav/jsf/pages/index.xhtml#none.

66. Author's analysis of 2012 Occupational Employment Statistics data from the Bureau of Labor Statistics and 2012 American Community Survey data from the US Census Bureau. In 2012 the Miami-Fort Lauderdale-Pompano Beach metro area had a Gini coefficient of 0.50, and lawyers comprised 0.80 percent of employed workers. The New Orleans-Metairie-Kenner metro area had a Gini coefficient of 0.50, and lawyers comprised 0.61 percent of employed workers. The Indianapolis-Carmel metro area had a Gini coefficient of 0.45, and lawyers comprised 0.43 percent of employed workers. The Portland-Vancouver-Hillsboro metro area had a Gini coefficient of 0.44, and lawyers comprised 0.33 percent of employed workers.

67. Author's analysis of 2012 Occupational Employment Statistics data from the Bureau of Labor Statistics, 1970 decennial census data from the US Census Bureau, and

2012 American Community Survey from the US Census Bureau. The average percentage of the workforce among all states in 2012 that were lawyers was 0.38 percent. Despite all three states ranking in the top eight states in terms of the percentage increase in the share of their populations that are non-White between 1970 and 2012, Hawaii (0.31 percent), New Mexico (0.38 percent), and Arizona (0.38 percent) all had average or below average shares of their workforce that were lawyers in 2012. Data can be found at Bureau of Labor Statistics, "Occupational Employment Statistics," www.bls.gov/oes/tables.htm; US Census Bureau, "American Fact Finder," http://factfinder2.census.gov/faces/nav/jsf/pages/index.xhtml#none; US Census Bureau, "Census of Population and Housing," www.census.gov/prod/www/decennial.html.

68. Clark, "Why So Many Lawyers?"

69. Author's calculation. Lawyers' mean salary figure taken from Bureau of Labor Statistics, "Occupational Employment and Wages: Lawyers," www.bls.gov/oes/current/oes231011.htm.

70. US industry spends about $300 billion on R & D annually according to Battelle, "2014 Global R&D Funding Forecast," December 2013.

71. See, for example, Kevin M. Murphy, Andrei Shleifer, and Robert W. Vishny, "The Allocation of Talent: Implications for Growth," Working Paper 3530 (National Bureau of Economic Research, 1990); Stephen P. Magee, William A. Brock, and Leslie Young, *Black Hole Tariffs and Endogenous Policy Theory: Political Economy in General Equilibrium* (New York: Cambridge University Press, 1989). For a different perspective, see George L. Priest, "Lawyers, Liability and Law Reform," *Denver University Law Review* 71, no. 1 (1993): 115–149.

72. For research on the trends, see James E. Bessen and Michael J. Meurer, "The Direct Costs from NPE Disputes," Working Paper 12–34 (Boston University School of Law, 2012). For research on the economic costs of patent trolling, see, for example, Catherine Tucker, "Patent Trolls and Technology Diffusion" (Boston: Massachusetts Institute of Technology, 2013); James Bessen, Jennifer Ford, and Michael J. Meurer, "The Private and Social Costs of Patent Trolls," *Regulation* 34, no. 4 (2012): 26–35.

73. For a review of the increase in security guards, see W.C. Cunningham, J.J. Strauchs, and C.W. Van Meter, "Private Security Trends, 1970–2000: The Hallcrest Report II" (Woburn, MA: Hallcrest Systems, 1990), www.ncjrs.gov/App/publications/Abstract.aspx?id = 127147; Kevin Strom and others, "The Private Security Industry: A Review of the Definitions, Available Data Sources, and Paths Moving Forward" (Research Triangle Park, NC: RTI International, 2010).

74. Author's analysis of *Integrated Public Use Microdata Series* occupational data. Note that in 1970 occupational questions were asked of all workers over the age of 14, while in later years these questions were only asked of workers age 16 and over. Note also that figures from 1970 were taken from decennial census data, while figures for 2012 were taken from American Community Survey data. For data, see Steven Ruggles and others, *Integrated Public Use Microdata Series: Version 5.0*. Note also that author's analysis of original decennial census summary reports yields similar results. In 1970, approximately 0.43 percent of the employed workforce were security guards according to the decennial census. Over the next several decades, the share of security guards grew steadily, so that by 2002—the last year for which comparable data are available—roughly 0.68 percent of the workforce were security guards, an increase of nearly 60 percent. These figures were calculated using the estimate of employed individuals labeled "Guards and Police, Except Public Service" for 1970 as printed in table 276 of Bureau of the Census, "1980 Census of Population: Detailed Population Characteristics: United States Summary" (1983). This figure was then divided by the estimate of total nonfarm employment for 1970 derived from

the Current Employment Statistics survey. These figures can be found at Bureau of Labor Statistics, "Current Employment Statistics—CES (National)," www.bls.gov/ces/. Estimates since 2002 suggest that the trend continues to get worse. Author's analysis of statistical abstracts of the United States. This figure was calculated using the estimate of employed individuals labeled "Guards and Police, Except Public Service" for 2002 as printed in table 615 of United States Census Bureau, "Statistical Abstract of the United States: 2003" (2003). This figure was then divided by the estimate of total nonfarm employment for 2002, derived from the Current Employment Statistics survey. These figures can be found at Bureau of Labor Statistics, "Current Employment Statistics—CES (National)," www.bls.gov/ces/. It should be noted that this estimate is derived from Current Population Survey data and not decennial census data, as the estimate for 1970 was, meaning that different survey methodologies were employed, which may impact the comparability of estimates. However, in both cases the same category of guard labor was used and CPS estimates are frequently compared to decennial census estimates for benchmarking purposes. The year 2002 was selected because this is the last year the category "Guards and Police, Except Public Service" was used to measure guard employment. Though the security guard definition changed, the trends after 2002 indicate continued high levels of guard employment.

75. Author's analysis of *Integrated Public Use Microdata Series* occupational data. Note that in 1970 occupational questions were asked of all workers over the age of 14, while in later years these questions were only asked of workers age 16 and over. Note also that figures from 1970 were taken from decennial census data, while figures for 2012 were taken from American Community Survey data. For data, see Steven Ruggles and others, *Integrated Public Use Microdata Series: Version 5.0*.

76. Author's analysis of Current Employment Statistics survey data from the Bureau of Labor statistics and *Integrated Public Use Microdata Series* occupational data. While census data show the share of all employed persons that are security guards increasing from roughly 0.40 percent to 0.69 percent between 1970 and 2012—an increase of roughly 73 percent—Bureau of Labor Statistics data show the share of all private employment that was considered "services-providing" rising from roughly 61.97 percent to 83.67 percent over that same span, an increase of approximately 35 percent. Data can be found at Bureau of Labor Statistics, "Current Employment Statistics—CES (National)," www.bls.gov/ces/.

77. Author's calculation using measures of security guard employment described above and an estimate of mean annual security guard earnings in 2002 taken from the Bureau of Labor Statistics's Occupational and Employment Statistics program. The mean annual earnings of "Security Guards" in 2002 were $21,060 (in 2002 dollars). While this BLS occupational category will not align perfectly with the "Guards and Police, Except Public Service" category used for the employment totals, the annual wage estimate is used here only to provide an approximation of the savings that might have been realized were the proportion of security guards to all employed workers to have remained the same in 2002 as it was in 1970. The total savings were adjusted for inflation using the CPI-W values for 2002 and 2013. For annual wage estimates, see Bureau of Labor Statistics, "2002 National Occupational Employment and Wage Estimates: Protective Service Occupations," www.bls.gov/oes/2002/oes_33Pr.htm#%282%29.

78. "Uniform Crime Report Statistics—Property Crime Rates," www.ucrdatatool. gov/Search/Crime/State/RunCrimeStatebyState.cfm.

79. Author's analysis of 2012 Occupational Employment Statistics data from the Bureau of Labor Statistics and 2012 American Community Survey from the US Census Bureau. The average percentage of the workforce among all states in 2012 that was security was

0.71 percent. While West Virginia and Pennsylvania ranked above average in the percentages of their populations that were white in 2012, they both had above average percentages of their workforces that were security guards: 0.83 percent and 0.74 percent. North Carolina and Alaska ranked below average in the percentages of their populations that were white in 2012, and both had slightly below average percentages of their workforces that were security guards: 0.70 percent and 0.66 percent. Data can be found at Bureau of Labor Statistics, "Occupational Employment Statistics," www.bls.gov/oes/tables.htm; US Census Bureau, "American Fact Finder," http://factfinder2.census.gov/faces/nav/jsf/pages/index.xhtml#none.

80. Stewart D'Alessio, David Eitle, and Lisa Stolzenberg, "The Impact of Serious Crime, Racial Threat, and Economic Inequality on Private Police Size," *Social Science Research* 34, no. 2 (2005): 267–282; Jason Carmichael and Stephanie Kent, "The Persistent Significance of Racial and Economic Inequality on the Size of Municipal Police Forces in the United States, 1980–2010," *Social Problems* 61, no. 2 (2014): 259–282; David Jacobs and Ronald Helm, "Testing Coercive Explanations of Order: The Determinants of Law Enforcement Strength over Time," *Social Forces* 75, no. 4 (1997): 1361–1392; Jonathan Dirlam, "Economic Inequality or Racial Threat? The Determinants of Police Strength," PhD diss., Ohio State University, 2013.

81. Stephanie Kent and David Jacobs, "Social Divisions and Coercive Control in Advanced Societies: Law Enforcement Strength in Eleven Advanced Nations from 1975–1994," *Social Problems* 51, no. 3 (2004): 343–361.

82. Note that studies test the impact of inequality—and thus only indirectly the role of trust—but their results that inequality is a key contributor to the use of guard labor, even when controlling for racial diversity and crime, are supportive of the argument that trust is shaping these trends. I did not find studies that directly test the role of trust in comparison with these other variables.

83. Alfred Rappaport, *Saving Capitalism from Short-Termism: How to Build Long-Term Value and Take Back Our Financial Future* (New York: McGraw-Hill, 2011).

84. Steven Shavell, "Risk Sharing and Incentives in the Principal and Agent Relationship," *Bell Journal of Economics* 10, no. 1 (1979): 55–73; Eugene F. Fama, "Agency Problems and the Theory of the Firm," *Journal of Political Economy* 88, no. 2 (1980): 288–307; Michael C. Jensen and William H. Meckling, "Theory of Firms: Managerial Behavior, Agency Cost and Ownership Structure," *Journal of Financial Economics* 3, no 4 (1976): 305–360; James A. Mirrlees, "The Optimal Structure of Incentives and Authority within an Organization," *Bell Journal of Economics* 7, no. 1 (1976): 105–131; Adolph A. Berle and Gardiner C. Means, *The Modern Corporation and Private Property* (New York: Macmillan, 1932).

85. See, for example, Gary Miller and Andrew Whitford, "Trust and Incentives in Principal-Agent Negotiations: The 'Insurance/Incentive Trade-Off,'" *Journal of Theoretical Politics* 14, no. 2 (2002): 231–267.

86. See, for example, Miller and Whitford, "Trust and Incentives in Principal-Agent Negotiations."

87. Total incentive-based pay figure is the percentage of total compensation provided in the form of bonuses, payouts from long-term incentive plans, option grants, and stocks as illustrated in Carola Frydam and Dirk Jenter, "CEO Compensation," *Annual Review of Financial Economics* 2, no. 1 (2010): 75–102, figure 2, panel B. Note that some of the other categories also include payments that could be considered incentive pay, and so this estimate likely understates incentive pay. Other studies have different estimates, but similar trends. See, for example, Martin J. Conyon and others, "The Executive Compensation Controversy: A Transatlantic Analysis" (Milan, Italy: Fondazione Rodolfo de Benedetti, 2011); Carola Frydman and Raven Saks, "Executive Compensation: A New View from a Long-

Term Perspective, 1936–2005," *Review of Financial Studies* 23, no. 5 (2010): 2099–2138; Additionally, estimates indicate that incentive pay has increased since then. See Christina Rexrode, "Median CEO Pay Rises to $9.7 Million in 2012," *Associated Press*, May 22, 2013, http://bigstory.ap.org/article/median-ceo-pay-rises-97-million-2012.

88. Steven Kaplan, "CEO Pay and Corporate Governance in the U.S.: Perceptions, Facts, and Challenges," *Journal of Applied Corporate Finance* 25, no. 2 (2013): 8–25. See also Kevin Murphy and Jan Zabojnik, "Managerial Capital and the Market for CEOs," Working Paper 1110 (Queen's University Department of Economics, 2006).

89. Peggy Hsieh, Timothy Koller, and S. R. Rajan, "Weighing the Pros and Cons of Earnings Guidance: A McKinsey Survey" (New York: McKinsey, 2006). Note that CEOs in Europe—which generally has higher levels of trust than the United States—receive substantially less incentive pay than do their US counterparts. See Conyon and others, "The Executive Compensation Controversy"; Kevin Murphy, "Executive Compensation: Where We Are, and How We Got There," *Handbook of the Economics of Finance* (2013): 211–356.

90. William Baber, Patricia Fairfield, and James Haggard, "The Effect of Concern about Reported Income on Discretionary Spending Decisions: The Case of Research and Development," *Accounting Review* 66, no. 4 (1991): 819–829; Mary M. Bange and Werner F. M De Bondt, "R & D Budgets and Corporate Earnings Targets," *Journal of Corporate Finance* 4, no. 2 (1998) 153–184; Susan Perry and Robert Grinaker, "The Relationship between Earnings Goals and Expenditures for Repairs and Maintenance," *Journal of Applied Business Research* 11, no. 4 (1995): 58–63.

91. Thomas D. Fields, Thomas Z. Lys, and Linda Vincent, "Empirical Research on Accounting Choice," *Journal of Accounting and Economics* 31 (2001): 255–307.

92. Michael C. Jensen, "Agency Costs of Overvalued Equity," *Financial Management* 34, no. 1 (2005): 6–19. Jensen argues that when company stocks become significantly overvalued, this creates impossible-to-maintain expectations that are too often met by illegal actions.

93. John R. Graham, Campbell R. Harvey, and Shiva Rajgopal, "The Economic Implications of Corporate Financial Reporting," *Journal of Accounting & Economics* 40, nos. 1–3 (2005): 3–73.

94. Rappaport, *Saving Capitalism from Short-Termism.*

95. Christian Weller and Amanda Logan, "Ignoring Productivity at Our Own Peril" (Washington, DC: Center for American Progress, 2007). Note also other studies that focus just on stock price performance, such as Michael Cooper, Huseyin Gulen, and P. Raghavendra Rau, "Performance for Pay? The Relation between CEO Incentive Compensation and Future Stock Price Performance," Working Paper (Social Science Research Network, 2013), who find that high incentive pay for CEOS leads to worse stock performance.

96. For a review of the causes of short-termism, see Rappaport, *Saving Capitalism from Short-Termism.* For additional discussion of the role of trust, see John Kay, *The Kay Review of UK Equity Markets and Long-Term Decision Making: Final Report* (London: UK Department for Business Innovation & Skills, 2012).

97. See, for example, ibid.; Pavlos E. Masouros and Mark Roe, *Corporate Law and Economic Stagnation: How Shareholder Value and Short-Termism Contribute to the Decline of the Western Economies* (The Hague: Eleven International, 2013).

98. Jensen and Meckling, "Theory of Firms."

99. Rappaport, *Saving Capitalism from Short-Termism.*

100. A number of studies have shown investors' monetary allocations to be sensitive to short-term institutional performance, including Erik R. Sirri and Peter Tufano, "Costly Search and Mutual Fund Flows," *Journal of Finance* 53, no. 5 (1998): 1589–1622; Richard A.

Ippolito, "Consumer Reaction to Measures of Poor Quality: Evidence from the Mutual Fund Industry," *Journal of Law and Economics* 35, no. 1 (1992): 45–79; Judith Chevalier and Glenn Ellison, "Risk Taking by Mutual Funds as a Response to Incentives," *Journal of Political Economy* 105, no. 6 (1997): 1167–1200. For more information on how investors' desire for liquidity and immediate gains can incentivize investment managers to pursue short-term investment strategies, see Jeremy C. Stein, "Why Are Most Funds Open-End? Competition and the Limits of Arbitrage," *Quarterly Journal of Economics* 120, no. 1 (2005): 247–272; Li Jin and Leonid Kogan, "Managerial Career Concern and Mutual Fund Short-Termism," Working Paper (Harvard Business School, 2007).

101. Natasha Burns, Simi Kedia, and Marc Lipson "Institutional Ownership and Monitoring: Evidence from Financial Misreporting," *Journal of Corporate Finance* 16, no. 4 (2010): 443–455.

102. Banfield, *The Moral Basis of a Backward Society.*

CHAPTER THREE

1. Thomas Jefferson, *Notes on the State of Virginia* (Richmond, VA: J. W. Randolph, 1853). For more about Jefferson's concerns about inequality, see Letter from Thomas Jefferson to James Madison, October 28, 1785. For the text of this letter, see "Equality," http://press-pubs.uchicago.edu/founders/documents/v1ch15s32.html.

2. James Madison, "Federalist #10," in *The Federalist Papers* (1787).

3. United States Constitution, art. 1, sec. 9, cl. 8.

4. Ellen Holmes Pearson, *Remaking Custom: Law and Identity in the Early American Republic* (Charlottesville: University of Virginia Press, 2011).

5. Michael J. Thompson, *The Politics of Inequality: A Political History of the Idea of Economic Inequality in America* (New York: Columbia University Press, 2012).

6. Andrew Jackson opposed the bank because "the rich and powerful too often bend the acts of government to their selfish purposes." For text of his veto message dated July 10, 1832, see "Andrew Jackson, Veto Message," http://press-pubs.uchicago.edu/founders/documents/a1_8_18s20.html. Lincoln understood that slavery threatened the economic security of white farmers and laborers, and thus democracy: "Slavery is wrong in its effect upon white people and free labor; it is the only thing that threatens the Union." When talking specifically about the rights of workers to strike, Lincoln stated, "If you give up your convictions and call slavery right as they do, you let slavery in upon you—instead of white laborers who can strike, you'll soon have black laborers who can't strike." See the evening press printing of Abraham Lincoln, "Speech at Hartford Connecticut," speech, Hartford, CT, March 5, 1860, in Roy P. Basler and others, eds., *The Collected Works of Abraham Lincoln,* vol. 4 (New Brunswick, NJ: Rutgers University Press, 1953). Theodore Roosevelt feared that our democracy was being undone by a "small class of enormously wealthy and economically powerful men, whose chief object is to hold and increase their power." Theodore Roosevelt, "New Nationalism Speech," speech, Osawatomie, KS, August 31, 1910; Franklin D. Roosevelt, "Speech before the 1936 Democratic National Convention," speech, Philadelphia, PA, June 27, 1936. In that speech Roosevelt also argued that inequality was a problem for democracy: "For too many of us the political equality we once had won was meaningless in the face of economic inequality."

7. Note that institutions can be used to refer to broader social norms, as well as government, but in this chapter I focus on the use of institutions to refer to government institutions, laws, and norms.

8. Douglass C. North, *Structure and Change in Economic History* (New York: W. W. Norton, 1981). The full quotation is as follows: "When economists talk about their discipline as a theory of choice and about the menu of choices being determined by opportunities and preferences, they simply have left out that it is the institutional framework which constrains people's choice sets."

9. For critiques of the efficient market hypothesis, see, for example, John Quiggin, *Zombie Economics: How Dead Ideas Still Walk among Us* (Princeton, NJ: Princeton University Press, 2010); John Cassidy, *How Markets Fail: The Logic of Economic Calamities* (Princeton, NJ: Princeton University Press, 2009); Justin Fox, *The Myth of the Rational Market: A History of Risk, Reward, and Delusion on Wall Street* (New York: HarperCollins, 2009; Joseph Stiglitz, "Needed: A New Economic Paradigm," *Financial Times*, August 19, 2010.

10. Ronald Reagan, "Inaugural Address," speech, Washington, DC, January 20, 1981.

11. Lisa Mascaro, "GOP's State of the Union Message: Obama Made It Worse," *Los Angeles Times*, January 24, 2012, http://articles.latimes.com/2012/jan/24/news/la-pn-gop-chorus-obama-made-worse-20120124.

12. North, *Structure and Change in Economic History*.

13. See, among many others, Stephen Knack and Philip Keefer, "Institutions and Economic Performance: Cross-Country Tests Using Alternative Institutional Measures," *Economics and Politics* 7, no. 3 (1995): 207–227; Stephen Knack and Philip Keefer, "Why Don't Poor Countries Catch Up? A Cross-National Test of an Institutional Explanation," *Economic Inquiry* 35, no. 2 (2007): 590–602; Alberto Chong and Cesar Calderon, "Causality and Feedback between Institutional Measures and Economic Growth," *Economics and Politics* 12, no. 1 (2000): 69–81; Andrei Shleifer and Robert W. Vishny, "Corruption," *Quarterly Journal of Economics* 108, no. 3 (1993): 599–617; Daniel Kaufmann and Aart Kray, "Growth without Governance," *Economia* 3, no. 1 (2002): 169–229.

14. Stephen Knack, "Governance and Growth: Measurement and Evidence," Discussion Paper 02/05 (University of Maryland Center for Institutional Reform and the Informal Sector, 2002); Dani Rodrik, Arvind Subramanian, and Francesco Trebbi, "Institutions Rule: The Primacy of Institutions over Geography and Integration in Economic Development," *Journal of Economic Growth* 9, no. 2 (2004): 131–165. Note that in another paper Rodrik argues that low levels of economic inequality helped Korea's and Taiwan's government reduce rent seeking, which was critical to these countries' growth. See Dani Rodrick, "Getting Interventions Right: How South Korea and Taiwan Grew Rich," *Economic Policy: A European Forum* 20, no. 20 (1995): 53–97. Further, according to several academics, the point that good government is a prerequisite for strong growth has now reached the level of consensus. Christian Bjørnskov, a Danish economist at Aarhus University, and Pierre-Guillaume Méon, an economist at the Free University of Brussels, have written, "The notion that the quality of a country's institutional framework is a key determinant of development has reached the status of a consensus." Christian Bjørnskov and Pierre-Guillaume Méon, "Is Trust the Missing Root of Institutions, Education, and Development?" *Public Choice* 157, no. 3 (2013): 641–669. Similarly, Stephen Knack has written, "An emerging consensus among development and growth economists views good governance as a prerequisite to sustained increases in living standards." Knack, "Governance and Growth."

15. Josh Bivens, "Public Investment: The Next New Big Thing for Powering Economic Growth" (Washington, DC: Economic Policy Institute, 2012).

16. David Aschauer, "Is Public Expenditure Productive?," *Journal of Monetary Economics* 23 (1989): 177–200; Alicia Munnell, "How Does Public Infrastructure Affect Regional Economic Performance?," *New England Economic Review* (1990): 11–33; Luis Serven and Cesar

Calderon, "The Effects of Infrastructure Development on Growth and Income Distribution," Working Paper 3400 (World Bank Policy Research, 2004).

17. For additional discussion of the economic benefits of education, see chapter 5. And for a critical take, see Edward Wolff, *Does Education Really Help? Skill, Work and Inequality* (Oxford: Oxford University Press, 2006).

18. Anna Bernasek, "What's the Return on Education," *New York Times,* December 11, 2005, www.nytimes.com/2005/12/11/business/yourmoney/11view.html?_r = 0.

19. And some even take a very negative view of government spending, fearing that any kind of "redistributive" spending harms the economy. But see Philip Keefer and Stephen Knack, "Polarization, Politics, and Property Rights: Links between Inequality and Growth," *Public Choice* 111, nos. 1–2 (2002): 127–154, which posits that redistributive policies may actually be good for growth because of their effect on equality; and Jonathan D. Ostry, Andrew Berg, and Charalambos G. Tsangarides, "Redistribution, Inequality and Growth" (International Monetary Fund, 2014), for similar findings. See also Daron Acemoglu and James Robinson, "Economics versus Politics: Pitfalls of Policy Advice," *Journal of Economic Perspectives* 27, no. 2 (2013): 173–192, who argue that a narrow view about the inefficiency of certain redistributive policies is often wrong because it ignores the larger sociopolitical framework. They note that getting rid of such redistributive policies "rather than promoting economic efficiency can significantly reduce it." For a more broad view on why public investment matters for stimulating growth and why giving too much attention to addressing short-term budget deficits may endanger long-term economic development, see William Easterly, Timothy Irwin, and Luis Serven, "Walking Up the Down Escalator: Public Investment and Fiscal Stability," *World Bank Research Observer* 23, no. 1 (2008): 37–56.

20. For a review of the economic literature on the harm of rent seeking, see John Craig and David Madland, "How Campaign Contributions and Lobbying Can Lead to Inefficient Economic Policy" (Washington, DC: Center for American Progress, 2014).

21. Joseph E. Stiglitz and Linda J. Bilmes, "The 1 Percent's Problem," *Vanity Fair,* May 31, 2012.

22. Johann Graf Lambsdorff, "Corruption and Rent-Seeking," *Public Choice* 113, nos. 1–2 (2002): 97–125.

23. Paolo Mauro, "Why Worry about Corruption?," *International Monetary Fund Economic Issues* 6 (1997): 1–13.

24. Sergey Anokhin and William Schultz, "Entrepreneurship, Innovation, and Corruption," *Journal of Business Venturing* 24, no. 5 (2009): 465–476.

25. Stanley Engerman and Kenneth Sokoloff, "Institutions, Factor Endowments and Paths of Development in the New World," in *How Latin America Fell Behind,* ed. Stephen Haber (Stanford: Stanford University Press, 1997).

26. Stanley Engerman and Kenneth Sokoloff, "Institutions, Factor Endowments and Paths of Development."

27. Daron Acemoglu and James Robinson, *Why Nations Fail: The Origins of Power, Prosperity, and Poverty* (New York: Random House, 2012).

28. Keefer and Knack, "Polarization, Politics and Property Rights"; William Easterly, "Inequality Does Cause Underdevelopment: Insights from a New Instrument," *Journal of Development Economics* 84, no. 2 (2007): 755–776; Ehro Eicher, Cecilia Garcia-Penalosa, and Tanguy van Ypersele, "Education, Corruption, and the Distribution of Income," *Journal of Economic Growth* 14, no. 3 (2009): 205–231; Roberto Perotti, "Growth, Income Distribution, and Democracy: What the Data Say," *Journal of Economic Growth* 1, no. 2 (1996): 149–187; Joel Hellman, Geraint Jones, and Daniel Kaufmann, "Seize the State, Seize the Day: State Capture and Influence in Transition Economies," *Journal of Comparative Economics* 31, no. 4

(2003): 751–773; Kwabena Gyimah-Brempong, "Corruptions, Economic Growth, and Income Inequality in Africa," *Economics of Governance* 3, no. 3 (2002): 183–209; Raghuram G. Rajan and Luigi Zingales, "The Persistence of Underdevelopment: Institutions, Human Capital or Constituencies?," Working Paper 12093 (National Bureau of Economic Research, 2006); James A. Robinson and Thierry Verdier, "The Political Economy of Clientelism," *Scandinavian Journal of Economics* 115, no. 2 (2013): 260–291. For a formal model making a similar argument, see Joan Esteban and Debraj Ray, "Inequality, Lobbying, and Resource Allocation," *American Economic Review* 96, no. 1 (2006): 257–279; Alberto Chong and Mark Gradstein, "Inequality and Institutions," *Review of Economics and Statistics* 89, no. 3 (2007): 454–465. See also Antonio Savoia, Joshy Easaw, and Andrew McKay, "Inequality, Democracy, and Institutions: A Critical Review of Recent Research," *World Development* 38, no. 2 (2010): 142–154; Norman Loayza, Jamele Rigolini, and Gonzalo Llorente, "Do Middle Classes Bring Institutional Reforms," Working Paper 6015 (World Bank, 2012); Eric M. Uslaner, *Corruption, Inequality, and the Rule of Law: The Bulging Pocket Makes the Easy Life* (New York: Cambridge University Press, 2010); Konstantin Sonin, "Why the Rich May Favor Poor Protection of Property Rights," *Journal of Comparative Economics* 31, no. 4 (2003): 715–731; Karla Hoff and Joseph E. Stiglitz, "After the Big Bang? Obstacles to the Emergence of the Rule of Law in Post-Communist Societies," *American Economic Review* 94, no. 3 (2004): 753–763; Lars-Erik Borge, Torberg Falch, and Per Tovmo, "Public Sector Efficiency: The Roles of Political and Budgetary Institutions, Fiscal Capacity, and Democratic Participation," *Public Choice* 136, nos. 3–4 (2008): 475–495; Alicia Adsera, Carles Boix, and Mark Payne, "Are You Being Served? Political Accountability and Quality of Government," *Journal of Law, Economics, & Organization* 19, no. 2 (2003): 445–490; William Easterly, "The Middle Class Consensus and Economic Development," *Journal of Economic Growth* 6, no. 4 (2001): 317–335. Note that some of these studies use instruments or other advanced statistical techniques to attempt to deal with endogeneity and to show that governance causes growth.

29. Easterly, "The Middle Class Consensus." In another article, Easterly writes, "Income inequality and ethnic fractionalization ... determine institutional quality, which in turn causally determines growth." William Easterly, Josef Ritzen, and Michael Woolcock, "Social Cohesion, Institutions, and Growth," *Economics and Politics* 18, no. 2 (2006): 103–120. Note that a number of other researchers have come to similar findings, including Jonas Gunnar Pontusson, *Inequality and Prosperity: Social Europe versus Liberal America* (Ithaca, NY: Cornell University Press, 2005); Guido Tabellini and Alberto Alesina, "Voting on the Budget Deficit," *American Economic Review* 80, no. 1 (1990): 37–49; Guillermo A. Calvo and Allan Drazen, "Uncertain Duration of Reform: Dynamic Implications," *Macroeconomic Dynamics* 2, no. 4 (1998): 443–455; Torsten Persson and Guido Tabellini, "Is Inequality Harmful for Growth?," *American Economic Review* 84, no. 3 (1994): 600–621.

30. You Jong-sung and Sanjeev Khagram, "A Comparative Study of Inequality and Corruption," *American Sociological Review* 70, no. 1 (2005): 136–157.

31. For evidence on Russia and Sierra Leone, see, among others, Earl Conteh Morgan and Mac Dixon-Fyle, *Sierra Leone at the End of the 20th Century* (New York: Peter Lang, 1999); Edward Glaeser, Jose Scheinkman, and Andrei Shleifer, "The Injustice of Inequality," *Journal of Monetary Economics* 50, no. 1 (2003): 199–222; Dinah Deckstein and others, "Promising but Perilous: German Firms Put Off by Russian Corruption," *Der Spiegel*, April 3, 2012, www.spiegel.de/international/europe/german-investors-discouraged-by-corruption-in-russia-a-892043.html.

32. For evidence on the value of slaves as a share of total wealth, see Thomas Piketty and Gabriel Zucman, "Capital Is Back: Wealth-Income Ratios in Rich Countries, 1700–2010" (Paris: Paris School of Economics, 2013).

33. Robin Einhorn, *American Taxation, American Slavery* (Chicago: University of Chicago Press, 2006).

34. Ibid.

35. Peter H. Lindert and Jeffrey G. Williamson, "American Incomes, 1774–1860," Working Paper 18396 (National Bureau of Economic Research, 2012). See also Branko Milanovic, Peter Lindert, and Jeffrey Williamson, "Pre-Industrial Inequality," *Economic Journal* 121 (March 2011): 255–272.

36. Sun Go and Peter Lindert, "The Uneven Rise of American Public Schools to 1850," *Journal of Economic History* 70, no. 1 (2010): 1–26.

37. Ibid.

38. Eric Zolt, "Inequality, Collective Action, and Taxing and Spending Patterns of State and Local Governments," *Tax Law Review* 62, no. 4 (2009): 445–504.

39. Go and Lindert, "The Curious Dawn of American Public Schools," NBER Working Paper No. 13335 (August 2007); Go and Lindert, "The Uneven Rise of American Public Schools to 1850."

40. Einhorn, *American Taxation, American Slavery*. This three-times figure only refers to taxes raised on white people in the South. If you include black persons, the North was collecting over six times as much.

41. Go and Lindert, "The Curious Dawn of American Public Schools"; Go and Lindert, "The Uneven Rise of American Public Schools to 1850."

42. Go and Lindert, "The Uneven Rise of American Public Schools to 1850."

43. In addition to those cited below, see also Rose Razaghian, "Financing the Civil War: The Confederacy's Financial Strategy," Working Paper 04–45 (Yale International Center for Finance, 2005), for more on the South's reluctance to tax.

44. Einhorn, *American Taxation, American Slavery*.

45. Ibid.

46. Ibid.; Zolt, "Inequality, Collective Action and Taxing and Spending Patterns"; Go and Lindert, "The Curious Dawn of American Public Schools."

47. Einhorn, *American Taxation, American Slavery*. Similarly, Go and Lindert argue, "Centralized restraints on political voice in the South held back the schooling of Southern white children of modest economic background." Go and Lindert, "The Curious Dawn of American Public Schools."

48. Claudia Goldin and Lawrence F. Katz, "Why the United States Led in Education: Lessons from Secondary School Expansion, 1910 to 1940," Working Paper 6144 (National Bureau of Economic Research, 1997). See also Oded Galor, Omer Moav, and Dietrich Vollrath, "Inequality in Landownership, the Emergence of Human-Capital Promoting Institutions, and the Great Divergence," Review of Economic Studies 76, no. 1 (2009): 143–179.

49. For statistic on percent of wealth owned by the top 12 percent, see Nell Irvin Painter, *Standing at Armageddon: A Grassroots History of the Progressive Era* (New York: W.W. Norton, 1987); James Davidson and Lord William Rees-Mogg, *The Sovereign Individual: Mastering the Transition to the Information Age* (New York: Simon & Schuster, 1999). For additional information on inequality in the Gilded Age, see Hugh Rockoff, "Great Fortunes of the Gilded Age," Working Paper 14555 (National Bureau of Economic Research, 2008); Sam Roberts, "As the Data Shows, There's a Reason the Wall Street Protestors Chose New York," *New York Times*, October 25, 2011, www.nytimes.com/2011/10/26/nyregion /as-data-show-theres-a-reason-the-wall-street-protesters-chose-new-york.html?_r = 3&&gwh = 0EDC81A362BA95B4BECBBD7BC4EC7F63&gwt = pay.

50. For information on how business interests dominated government, see Morton Keller, *Affairs of State: Public Life in Late Nineteenth Century America* (Cambridge, MA: Belknap

Press of Harvard University Press, 1977); Richard L. McCormick, *The Party Period and Public Policy: American Politics from the Age of Jackson to the Progressive Era* (New York: Oxford University Press, 1986); Mark Wahlgren Summers, *The Era of Good Stealings* (New York: Oxford University Press, 1993); Jack Beatty, *Age of Betrayal: The Triumph of Money in America, 1865–1990* (New York: Vintage, 2007). For a more contemporary review of this period, see Mathew Josephson, *The Robber Barons* (New York: Harcourt, Brace, 1934).

51. Kevin Phillips, *Wealth and Democracy* (New York: Broadway, 2002).

52. Glaeser, Scheinkman, and Shleifer, "The Injustice of Inequality." See also Edward Glaeser and Andrei Shleifer, "The Rise of the Regulatory State," *Journal of Economic Literature* 41, no. 2 (2003): 401–425.

53. For an overview of these practices, see Beatty, *Age of Betrayal*, 98–100.

54. Ibid. Note also that the Populist Party Platform of 1892—many of whose reforms were eventually adopted, including the direct election of senators, the progressive income tax, and wage and hour laws—stated: "Corruption dominates the ballot-box, the Legislatures, the Congress, and touches even the ermine of the bench." American Presidency Project, "Populist Party Platform of 1892," www.presidency.ucsb.edu/ws/?pid = 29616.

55. As cited in Bill Moyers, *Moyers on Democracy* (New York: Anchor, 2009).

56. Robert Gordon, "Is U.S. Economic Growth Over? Faltering Innovation Confronts the Six Headwinds," Working Paper 18315 (National Bureau of Economic Research, 2012); Rockoff, "Great Fortunes of the Gilded Age."

57. Glaeser, Scheinkman, and Shleifer, "The Injustice of Inequality."

58. Seymour Martin Lipset, "Some Social Requisites of Democracy: Economic Development, and Political Legitimacy," *American Political Science Review* 53, no. 1 (1959): 69–105. See also, for example, Robert Dahl, *Polyarchy* (New Haven, CT: Yale University Press, 1972); Francis Fukuyama, "The Future of History: Can Liberal Democracy Survive the Decline of the Middle Class?," *Foreign Affairs* 91, no. 1 (2012): 53–61; Barrington Moore, *The Social Origins of Dictatorship and Democracy* (Boston: Beacon, 1993). Note that even critics of Moore's argument give significant emphasis to the importance of the middle class's or working class's role in changing the power dynamics in society, such as Theda Skocpol, *States and Social Revolutions: A Comparative Analysis of France, Russia, and China* (Cambridge: Cambridge University Press, 1979); Theda Skocpol, "A Critical Review of Barrington Moore's *Social Origins of Dictatorship and Democracy*," *Politics & Society* 4, no. 1 (1973): 1–34; Goran Therborn, "The Rule of Capital and the Rise of Democracy," *New Left Review* 103 (1977): 3–41; Dietrich Rueschemeyer, Evelene Huber Stephens, and John D. Stephens, *Capitalist Development and Democracy* (Chicago: University of Chicago Press, 1992). And for a review of this critical literature, see Michael Bernhard, "The Moore Thesis: What's Left after 1989?," presented at 101st Annual Meeting of the American Political Science Association, 2005.

59. Aristotle, *The Politics and the Constitution of Athens* (Cambridge: Cambridge University Press, 1996).

60. Note that some modern observers still cling to the notion that if inequality reaches a certain level or the masses become so immiserated, then political revolt is inevitable. This Marxist view of social movements is not well supported in US history. Immiseration can help provide fuel for social movements, but objective conditions do not inevitably lead to revolt. Further, when the poor have made forceful political demands in US history, they have usually sought to be incorporated into the basic political and economic structures, rather than to do away with them.

61. Author's analysis of American National Election Studies survey. For the figure from 1964, see American National Election Studies, "The ANES Guide to Public Opinion

and Electoral Behavior: Table 5A.2," www.electionstudies.org/nesguide/toptable
/tab5a_2.htm. For the figure from 2012, see American National Election Studies, "Users'
Guide and Codebook for the Preliminary Release of the ANES 2012 Time Series Study"
(2013).

62. For an example of Dahl being referred to as the "dean of American political science," see John C. Campbell, "Controlling Nuclear Weapons: Democracy versus Guardi-
anship," *Foreign Affairs* 64, no. 1 (1985): 171.

63. Robert A. Dahl, *Who Governs? Democracy and Power in an American City* (New Haven,
CT: Yale University Press, 1974).

64. List of Woodrow Wilson Award winners available in American Political Science
Association, "Woodrow Wilson Foundation Award Recipients" (2013).

65. Raymond A Bauer, Ithiel de Sola Pool, and Lewis Anthony Dexter, *American Business and Public Policy: The Politics of Foreign Trade* (Cambridge, MA: MIT Press, 1963).

66. Samuel Eldersveld, *Political Parties: A Behavioral Analysis* (Skokie, IL: Rand
McNally, 1965).

67. For one example among many others, see Paul Pierson and Jacob Hacker, *Winner
Take All Politics* (New York: Simon & Shuster, 2011).

68. Martin Gilens and Benjamin Page, "Testing Theories of American Politics:
Elites, Interest Groups and Average Citizens," *Perspectives on Politics* (Fall 2014).

69. Larry Bartels, "Economic Inequality and Political Representation," in *The Unsustainable American State,* ed. Lawrence Jacobs and Desmond King (New York: Oxford University Press, 2009). Note also that Thomas Hayes, "Responsiveness in an Era of
Inequality," *Political Research Quarterly* 66, no. 3 (2012): 585–599, does a similar but more
updated analysis and finds senators' votes responsive only to upper-income constituents.

70. Martin Gilens, *Affluence and Influence* (Princeton, NJ: Princeton University Press,
2012).

71. Stephen Ansolabehere, James M. Snyder Jr., and Charles Stewart III, "Candidate
Positioning in U.S. House Elections," *American Journal of Political Science* 45, no. 1 (2001):
136–159; Alan D. Monroe, "Public Opinion and Public Policy, 1980–1993," *Public Opinion
Quarterly* 62, no. 1 (1998): 6–28; Lawrence Jacobs and Robert Shapiro, *Politicians Don't Pander:
Political Manipulation and the Loss of Democratic Responsiveness* (Chicago: University of Chi-
cago Press, 2000).

72. See Stephen Ansolabehere, John M. Figueiredo, and James M. Snyder Jr., "Why Is
There So Little Money in U.S. Politics," *Journal of Economic Perspectives* 17, no. 1 (2003): 105–
130, figure 1.

73. Center for Responsive Politics, "The Money behind the Elections," www.opense-
crets.org/bigpicture/. Nominal dollars doubled, but the figures here are inflation adjusted.

74. Athena Jones, "Political Newcomers Face High Costs and Difficult Odds," *CNN.
com,* January 22, 2012, www.cnn.com/2012/01/22/politics/newcomers-campaign-costs.

75. Gilens, *Affluence and Influence.*

76. See Kay Lehman Schlozman, Sidney Verba, and Henry Brady, *The Unheavenly
Chorus: Unequal Political Voice and the Broken Promise of American Democracy* (Princeton, NJ:
Princeton University Press, 2012), figure 5.2.

77. See, among others, Americans for Campaign Reform, "Money in Politics: Who
Gives," www.acrreform.org/research/money-in-politics-who-gives/. Similar results are
found in Michael J. Malbin and Sean A. Cain "The Ups and Downs of Small and Large
Donors" (Washington, DC: Campaign Finance Institute, 2007). See also Schlozman,
Verba, and Brady, *The Unheavenly Chorus,* chap. 9; Benjamin I. Page, Larry M. Bartels,
and Jason Seawright, "Democracy and the Policy Preferences of Wealthy Americans,"

Perspectives on Politics 11, no. 1 (2013): 51–73; Lee Drutman, "The Political One Percent of the One Percent," *Sunlight Foundation,* December 13, 2011, http://sunlightfoundation.com /blog/2011/12/13/the-political-one-percent-of-the-one-percent/.

78. Adam Bonica, and others, "Why Hasn't Democracy Slowed Rising Inequality?," *Journal of Economic Perspectives* 27, no. 3 (2013): 103–124. Note that Drutman, "The Political One Percent of the One Percent," shows similar trends, finding that donors contributing over $10,000, who accounted for just under 0.01 percent of the US population, gave over 44 percent of total itemized contributions in 2010, up from 28 percent in 1990.

79. For explanations on how relaxed spending limitations for Super PACs and 501(c)(4) organizations have enabled more money to enter elections via routes that require less disclosure, see John Dunbar, "The 'Citizens United' Decision and Why It Matters," *Center for Public Integrity,* October 18, 2012, www.publicintegrity.org/2012/10/18/11527/citizens-united-decision-and-why-it-matters; Center for Response Politics, "Outside Spending: Frequently Asked Questions About 501(c)(4) Groups," www.opensecrets.org/outsidespending /faq.php.

80. For the trend on lobbying dollars, see Center for Responsive Politics, "Lobbying Database," www.opensecrets.org/lobby/.

81. For the amount of money spent on lobbying being comparable to campaign spending, see Center for Responsive Politics, "Lobbying Database," which shows that $3.33 billion was spent on lobbying in 2011 and $3.31 billion in 2012, totaling over $6.6 billion for the election cycle. See also Jake Harper, "Total 2012 Election Spending: $7 Billion," *Sunlight Foundation,* January 31, 2013, http://reporting.sunlightfoundation.com/2013/total-2012-election-spending-7-billion/, which notes that total campaign spending for the 2012 election is estimated to have totaled over $7 billion, with $3.2 billion coming from spending by private candidate committees, $2 billion from party committees, and $2 billion or more from outside groups. For the skew of spending, approximately $2.9 billion of the $3.3 billion spent on lobbying was conducted by firms. Center for Responsive Politics, "Top Industries," www.opensecrets.org/lobby/top.php?showYear = 2012&indexType = i.

82. This can occur because some efforts to influence policy do not meet the legal requirements for disclosure: think of Newt Gingrich claiming he was not a lobbyist. It also occurs because state and local governments have different disclosure requirements. For more, see Public Citizen, "Lobbying Disclosure Act: A Brief Synopsis of Key Components" (2011).

83. Bonica and others, "Why Hasn't Democracy Slowed Rising Inequality?"

84. Ibid.

85. Lawrence Lessig, *Free Culture* (New York: Penguin, 2004). Other research in a similar vein indicates that campaign contributions function as a kind of gift exchange and establish a bond so that the politicians wants to help out the gift giver. See George A. Akerlof, "Labor Contracts as Partial Gift Exchange," *Quarterly Journal of Economics* 97, no. 4 (1982): 543–569; Ulrike Malmendier and Klaus Schmidt, "You Owe Me," Working Paper 4007 (CESifo Working Paper Series, 2012); Stacey B. Gordon, *Campaign Contributions and Legislative Voting: A New Approach* (New York: Routledge Taylor & Francis, 2005).

86. Center for Responsive Politics Communications, "Millionaires' Club: For First Time, Most Lawmakers Are Worth $1 Million-Plus," *Center for Responsive Politics,* January 9, 2014, www.opensecrets.org/news/2014/01/millionaires-club-for-first-time-most-lawmakers-are-worth-1-million-plus.html; Stephanie Condon, "Why Is Congress a Millionaires Club?," *CBS News,* March 27, 2012, www.cbsnews.com/news/why-is-congress-a-millionaires-club/.

87. The Congressional Management Foundation estimated members of Congress spend one-fifth of their time on campaign work, which mostly means fundraising. See Congressional Management Foundation and Society for Human Resource Management, "Life in Congress: The Member Perspective" (2013). For information on the specific guidance given by House Democratic leadership, see Ryan Grim and Sabrina Siddiqui, "Call Time for Congress Shows How Fundraising Dominates Bleak Work Life," *Huffington Post,* January 8, 2013, www.huffingtonpost.com/2013/01/08/call-time-congressional-fundraising_n_2427291.html.

88. For a review of the literature showing the influence of contributions and lobbying, see Craig and Madland, "How Campaign Contributions and Lobbying Can Lead to Inefficient Economic Policy." See Ansolabehere, Figuerodo, and Snyder, "Why Is There So Little Money in U.S. Politics?," for a skeptical take on the influence of campaign contributions and lobbying. Note that they are stuck in the framework that primarily focuses on measured roll call votes, and ignores many other ways that money can influence outcomes. See James M. Snyder, "Long-Term Investing in Politicians," *Journal of Law & Economics* 35, no. 1 (1992): 15–43, for a somewhat different take. For a skeptical take that acknowledges some degree of influence, see Tobin Project, "Preface," in *Preventing Regulatory Capture: Special Interests Influence and How to Limit It,* ed. Daniel Carpenter and David Moss (Cambridge: Cambridge University Press, 2013).

89. Lawrence Jacobs and others, "American Democracy in an Age of Rising Inequality," *Perspectives on Politics* 2, no. 4 (2004): 651–666.

90. Schlozman, Verba, and Brady, *The Unheavenly Chorus.*

91. While there is much academic debate concerning the impact of campaign contributions and lobbying on politician's voting and behavior, a number of studies have produced suggestive evidence of statistically significant relationships. See, for example, Robert E. Baldwin and Christopher S. Magee, "Is Trade Policy for Sale? Congressional Voting on Recent Trade Bills," *Public Choice* 105, nos. 1–2 (2000): 79–101; Thomas Stratmann, "Can Special Interests Buy Congressional Votes? Evidence from Financial Services Legislation," *Journal of Law and Economics* 45, no. 2 (2002): 345–373, both of which have found evidence of the impact of monetary contributions on congressional voting behavior. Gregory A. Caldeira and John R. Wright, "Lobbying for Justice: Organized Interests, Supreme Court Nominations, and the United States Senate," *American Journal of Political Science* 42, no. 2 (1998): 499–523, also found evidence of a link between interest group lobbying and senators' confirmation votes on Supreme Court nominees. Other studies have found that lobbying on behalf of universities can increase the earmarks they receive from lawmakers, while lobbying on behalf of corporations may help them reduce their tax burden in the following year. See John M. de Figueiredo and Brian S. Silverman, "Academic Earmarks and the Return to Lobbying," *Journal of Law and Economics* 49, no. 2 (2006); Brian K. Richter, Krislert Samphantharak, and Jeffrey F. Timmons, "Lobbying and Taxes," *American Journal of Political Science* 53, no. 4 (2009): 893–909. For alternative interpretations of the relationship between campaign contributions and lobbying and the political process, see Ansolabehere, Figueiredo, and Snyder, "Why Is There So Little Money in U.S. Politics."

92. Lesley Stahl, "Jack Abramoff: The Lobbyist's Playbook," *60 Minutes,* November 6, 2011, www.cbsnews.com/8301-18560_162-57459874/jack-abramoff-the-lobbyists-playbook/?pageNum = 2.

93. For information on increases in lobbying between the 1970s and 1990s, see Jeffrey Birnbaum, *The Money Men: The Real Story of Fund-Raising's Influence on Political Power in*

America (New York: Crown, 2000). For more recent lobbying figures, see Public Citizen, "Congressional Revolving Doors: The Journey from Congress to K Street" (2005).

94. Seymour Martin Lipset, *Political Man* (Baltimore: Johns Hopkins University Press, 1981). Similarly, MIT economist Daron Acemoglu and Harvard political scientist James Robinson argue in their book *Economic Origins of Dictatorship and Democracy* that the "role of the middle class is that of a buffer in the conflict between the elite and the citizens." Daron Acemoglu and James Robinson, *Economic Origins of Dictatorship and Democracy* (Cambridge: Cambridge University Press, 2006).

95. See, for example, Eric Uslaner, *The Decline of Comity in Congress* (Ann Arbor: University of Michigan Press, 1993). For more general information, see Robert Putnam, *Making Democracy Work: Civic Traditions in Modern Italy* (Princeton, NJ: Princeton University Press, 1994).

96. Thomas Mann and Norman Ornstein, *The Broken Branch: How Congress Is Failing America and How to Get It Back on Track* (New York: Oxford University Press, 2008).

97. Laura Meckler and Rebecca Ballhaus, "More than 800,000 Federal Workers Are Furloughed," *Wall Street Journal,* October 1, 2013, http://online.wsj.com/news/articles/SB10001424052702304373104579107480729687014; Steven Perlberg, "S & P: The Shutdown Took $24 Billion out of the US Economy," *Business Insider,* October 16, 2013, www.businessinsider.com/sp-cuts-us-growth-view-2013-10.

98. Jonathan Weisman, "House Vote Sidesteps an Ultimatum on Debt," *New York Times,* January 23, 2013, www.nytimes.com/2013/01/24/us/politics/house-passes-3-month-extension-of-debt-limit.html.

99. United States Senate, "Senate Action on Cloture Motions," www.senate.gov/pagelayout/reference/cloture_motions/clotureCounts.htm.

100. Nolan McCarthy, Keith Poole, and Howard Rosenthal, *Polarized America: The Dance of Ideology and Unequal Riches* (Cambridge, MA: MIT Press, 2008).

101. See Juan Linz, "The Perils of Presidentialism," *Journal of Democracy* 1, no. 1 (1990): 51–69. Note also that as inequality has risen, this status quo bias has increasingly benefited the wealthy, as Peter Enns, a government professor at Cornell University, and his coauthors find. Peter Enns and others, "Conditional Status Quo Bias and Top Income Shares: How US Political Institutions Benefit the Rich," Working Paper (University of Tennessee, 2012).

102. See, among others, Putnam, *Making Democracy Work;* Kay Schlozman, Benjamin Page, and Sidney Verba, "Inequalities of Political Voice" (Washington, DC: Task Force on Inequality and American Democracy, American Political Science Association, 2004).

103. Alexis de Tocqueville, *Democracy in America* (Cambridge, MA: Sever and Francis, 1863).

104. Carles Boix and Daniel Posner, "Social Capital: Explaining Its Origins and Effects on Government Performance," *British Journal of Political Science* 4 (1998): 686–693.

105. See, for example, Eliana La Ferrara, "Inequality and Group Participation: Theory and Evidence from Rural Tanzania," *Journal of Public Economics* 85, no. 2 (2002): 235–273; Frederick Solt, "Civics or Structure? Revisiting the Origins of Democratic Quality in the Italian Regions," *British Journal of Political Science* 34, no. 1 (2004): 123–135; Frederick Solt, "Economic Inequality and Democratic Political Engagement," *American Journal of Political Science* 52, no. 1 (2008): 48–60; Dora Costa and Matthew Kahn, "Civic Engagement and Community Heterogeneity: An Economist's Perspective," *Perspective on Politics* 1, no. 1 (2003): 103–111; Dora Costa and Matthew Kahn, "Understanding the American Decline in Social Capital, 1952–1998," *Kyklos* 56, no. 1 (2003): 17–4; Antonio M. Jaime-Castillo, "Economic Inequality and Electoral Participation: A Cross-Country Evaluation," Comparative Study of the Electoral Systems (CSES) Conference, Toronto, Ontario, Canada,

September 2009; Michael O'Connell, "Anti 'Social Capital': Civic Values versus Economic Equality in the EU," *European Sociological Review* 19, no. 3 (2003): 241–248; Eric M. Uslaner and Mitchell Brown, "Inequality, Trust, and Civic Engagement," *American Politics Research* 33, no. 6:868–894.

106. Boix and Posner, "Social Capital."

107. Putnam, *Making Democracy Work.* Note that Putnam largely ignores economic inequality in his analysis of social capital, though he does argue that "equality is an essential feature of the civic community" (105). Putnam's downplaying of the role of equality has been criticized by numerous scholars, and reexaminations of his argument have shown the importance of equality for civic engagement. See Solt, "Civics or Structure?"; O'Connell, "Anti 'Social Capital'"; Uslaner and Brown, "Inequality, Trust, and Civic Engagement"; Ichiro Kawachi and others, "Social Capital, Income Inequality, and Mortality," *American Journal of Public Health* 87, no. 9 (1997): 1491–1498.

108. Note that Boix and Posner also argue that social capital will produce good governance. Boix and Posner, "Social Capital."

109. Tom W. Rice, "Social Capital and Government Performance in Iowa Communities," *Journal of Urban Affairs* 23, no. 3–4 (2003): 375–389.

110. Christian Bjørnskov, "Combating Corruption," *Journal of Law and Economics* 54, no. 1 (2011): 135–159; Bjørnskov and Méon, "Is Trust the Missing Root of Institutions, Education, and Development?"; Uslaner, *Corruption, Inequality, and the Rule of Law.*

111. Stephen Knack, "Social Capital and the Quality of Government," *American Journal of Political Science* 46, no. 4 (2002): 772–785. Knack also found that trust was correlated with higher-quality governance, indicating another channel through which inequality affects the technocratic capability of governments.

112. Eric M. Uslaner, "Trust, Democracy and Governance: Can Government Policies Influence Generalized Trust," prepared for the European Consortium for Political Research, Copenhagen, Denmark, 2000.

113. Robert Putnam, *Bowling Alone* (New York: Simon & Shuster, 2001). Putnam has noted that the trend has not improved since he wrote *Bowling Alone* a decade ago. See Thomas H. Sander and Robert Putnam, "Still Bowling Alone? The Post 9/11 Split," *Journal of Democracy* 21, no. 1 (2010): 9–16.

114. For information on the decline between 1990 and 1997, see Putnam, *Bowling Alone.* For information on subsequent declines, see David Crary, "National PTA Tries to Increase Membership after Numbers Drop," *Huffington Post,* April 6, 2011, www.huffingtonpost.com/2012/04/07/national-pta-membership_n_1410102.html.

115. See National Conference on Citizenship, "America's Civic Health Index: Broken Engagement" (2006), figure 2.

116. United States Election Project, "National Turnout Rates, 1787–2012," www.electproject.org/home/voter-turnout/voter-turnout-data.

117. Note that even as overall education levels have increased over the past several decades—which has helped increase participation—participation for each level of education has actually decreased. For example, in the election in 1972 nearly 84 percent of people with a bachelor's degree or higher voted, but that figure fell over the years, reaching just under 72 percent by 2012. Similarly, over this same time period voting rates fell by 13 percentage points for those with some college, and by 16 percentage points for high school graduates. See US Census Bureau, "Voting and Registration," www.census.gov/hhes/www/socdemo/voting/publications/historical/, table A2.

118. Costa and Kahn, "Understanding the American Decline in Social Capital, 1952–1998." See also, Costa and Kahn, "Civic Engagement and Community Heterogeneity";

Alberto Alesina and Eliana La Ferrara, "Participation in Heterogeneous Communities," *Quarterly Journal of Economics* 115, no. 3 (2000): 847–904; Alesina and La Ferrara, "Who Trusts Others?"; Kawachi and others, "Social Capital, Income Inequality, and Mortality." For studies on political participation, see Solt, "Civics or Structure?"; Joe Soss and Lawrence Jacobs, "The Place of Inequality: Non-Participation in the American Polity," *Political Science Quarterly* 141, no. 1:95–125; James K. Galbraith and J. Travis Hale, "State Income Inequality and Presidential Election Turnout and Outcomes," *Social Science Quarterly* 89, no. 4 (2008): 887–901; Kim Nguyen and James Garand, "Income Inequality and Voter Turnout in the American States, 1960—2004," presented at American Political Science Association Annual Meeting, 2008. For studies with other measures of civicness, see Solt, "Civics or Structure?"; Daniel Horn, "Income Inequality and Voter Turnout," GINI Discussion Paper 16 (GINI Project Studies, 2011).

119. American Society of Civil Engineers, "2013 Report Card for America's Infrastructure," www.infrastructurereportcard.org/.

120. American Society of Civil Engineers, "Failure to Act: The Impact of Current Infrastructure Investment on America's Economic Future" (2013).

121. Steve James, "Bridge Collapse Could Cost Washington State Millions, Jobs," *NBC News*, May 24, 2013, www.nbcnews.com/business/bridge-collapse-could-cost-washington-state-millions-jobs-6C10066338.

122. David Shrank, Bill Eisele, and Tim Lomax, "2012 Urban Mobility Report," (College Station: Texas A & M Transportation Institute, 2012).

123. Ashley Halsey III, "Nation's Aging Electrical Grid Needs Billions of Dollars in Investment, Report Says," *Washington Post*, April 26, 2012, http://articles.washingtonpost.com/2012-04-26/news/35452037_1_electrical-system-electricity-costs-power-plants.

124. Susan Lund and others, "Game Changers: Five Opportunities for US Growth and Renewal" (New York: McKinsey Global Institute, 2013).

125. See, for example, Michael Gerson and Pete Wehner, who wrote, "The GOP could commit itself to ensuring a greater degree of social mobility across the board. At the center of any such effort lies a thoroughgoing reform of the federal role in education, focusing on public and private choice, charter schools, testing and accountability, and merit pay for teachers and principals." Michael Gerson and Pete Wehner, "How to Save the Republican Party," *Commentary*, March 2013, www.commentarymagazine.com/article/how-to-save-the-republican-party/.

126. Claudia Goldin and Lawrence Katz, "The Future of Inequality" (New York: Milken Institute, 2009).

127. Organisation for Economic Co-Operation and Development, "Education at a Glance 2013: OECD Indicators" (2013).

128. Ibid.

129. These figures refer to the United States's ranking in graduation rates from tertiary type-A programs (first-time graduates) among OECD and G20 member nations for whom there were rankings in 1995 and 2011. See Organisation for Economic Co-Operation and Development, ibid., table A3.2.a.

130. Calculating total public spending on higher education over time is extremely difficult for a number of reasons. Very few data sources contain comparable information on total appropriations made at the federal, state, and local levels while also keeping track of all types of grants made at all levels of government and all other forms of expenditure. While databases and reports available from the National Center for Education Statistics (NCES) do offer some summaries of total appropriations, grants, and other forms of funding and assistance provided over time, multiple changes in accounting standards over the

past several decades and differences in contemporary accounting standards between public and private institutions make producing any accurate continuous measure extremely difficult. That said, there is a good deal of evidence that indicates that total spending on higher education over time has remained relatively stagnant as a share of GDP for the past several decades. First, the Bureau of Economic Analysis provides measures of total government consumption expenditures and gross investment by function, as well as measures of current expenditures by function that go back to 1959. While these two measures are calculated in slightly different ways and show somewhat different spending totals year to year, when transformed into a share of annual GDP both show total US spending on higher education increasing as a share of the economy from the early 1960s until the mid-1970s, and then remaining relatively flat, just below 1 percent of GDP, until the late 2000s. Both measures appear to show a very slight uptick in spending as a share of GDP since the Great Recession, but even when this is taken into account, spending on higher education remains near 1 percent of GDP and overall has exhibited far less volatility than has spending on elementary and secondary education over the same time period. Author's calculations using data available in Bureau of Economic Analysis, "National Income and Product Accounts Tables," tables 1.1.5, 3.15.5, and 3.16, www.bea.gov/iTable/iTable.cfm?ReqID = 9&step = 1#reqid = 9&step = 1&isuri = 1.

Furthermore, while data available from the National Center for Education Statistics do not allow for the creation of a single time series for the reasons noted, looking at particular segments of time for which data appear to be somewhat comparable still appears to indicate that higher education spending has not increased significantly as a share of GDP over the past several decades. These figures appear to show total spending hovering just below 1 percent of GDP between the early 1980s and mid-1990s, during which time some forms of support such as Pell grants were not consistently included in spending totals, and then hovering just above 1 percent during the 2000s once some of these forms of financial support were factored in. Most importantly, however, in neither of these periods during which spending totals appeared relatively comparable did public spending on higher education appear to show any significant upward trend. Author's calculations using revenue data from table 328 in the NCES's 2000 Digest of Education Statistics, table 331 from the 2002 Digest of Education Statistics, Tables 340 and 342 from the 2003 Digest of Education Statistics, table 336 from the 2006 Digest of Education Statistics, table 350 from the 2008 Digest of Education Statistics, table 357 from the 2009 Digest of Education Statistics, and tables 333.10, 333.40, and 333.55 from the 2013 Digest of Education Statistics. All data can be found at National Center for Education Statistics, "Digest of Education Statistics," http://nces.ed.gov/programs/digest/index.asp. Finally, OECD figures also provide a measure of total public support for higher education in more recent decades, although they only go back to 1995. Nevertheless, they also show total public spending on higher education as having remained stagnant in recent years, with the US spending the equivalent of 1.1 percent of GDP in 1995 and 1.0 percent in 2010. This data can be found in 2013 National Digest of Education statistics at National Center for Education Statistics, "Digest of Education Statistics," table 605.20.

131. CollegeBoard, "TABLE 2. Average Tuition and Fee and Room and Board Charges, 1971–72 to 2013–14," http://trends.collegeboard.org/college-pricing/figures-tables/published-prices-national. Tuition and fees at a four-year public university (in 2013 dollars) were $2,470 in 1982–1983, and $8,816 in 2012–2013 for a percentage increase of 256.92 percent.

132. Median family incomes are the author's calculation based on data from table F-6 found in US Census Bureau, "Income: Families," www.census.gov/hhes/www/income

/data/historical/families/. The median family income in 1982 was $53,534 and in 2012 it was $62,241 (in 2012 dollars), meaning it had increased by approximately 16.26 percent.

133. State Higher Education Executive Officers, "State Higher Education Finance: FY 2012" (2013). Also for a similar trend, though based on a shorter period, see CollegeBoard, "RevenueSourcesatPublicInstitutionsoverTime,"http://trends.collegeboard.org/college-pricing/figures-tables/revenue-sources-public-institutions-over-time.

134. Organisation for Economic Co-Operation and Development, "Education at a Glance 2013: OECD Indicators."

135. Thomas Mortenson, "State Funding: A Race to the Bottom" (Washington, DC: American Council of Education, 2012).

136. For information on how state governments have become the primary source of public funding for many schools, see State Higher Education Executive Officers, "State Higher Education Finance FY 2012." For information on reductions in spending, see Phil Oliff and others, "Recent Deep State Higher Education Cuts May Harm Students and the Economy for Years to Come" (Washington, DC: Center on Budget and Policy Priorities, 2013).

137. Pew Charitable Trusts, "State Tax Revenue Up—but Short of Peak," www.pewstates.org/research/data-visualizations/fiscal-50-state-trends-and-analysis-85899523649#indo.

138. Oliff and others, "Recent Deep State Higher Education."

139. David Madland and Nick Bunker, "A Stronger Middle Class Leads to More Investment in Postsecondary Education" (Washington, DC: Center for American Progress, 2013).

140. Madland and Bunker, "A Stronger Middle Class."

141. Note that this ranking refers to spending that occurred in 2010, the most recent year for which data are publicly available. Ranking based on data available in Organisation for Economic Co-Operation and Development, "Education at a Glance 2013: OECD Indicators." Ranking of spending in 1995 based on data found at National Center for Education Statistics, "Advance Release of Selected 20113 Digest Tables: Table 605.20," http://nces.ed.gov/programs/digest/d13/tables/dt13_605.20.asp.

142. David Madland and Nick Bunker, "Middle-Class Societies Invest More in Public Education" (Washington, DC: Center for American Progress, 2011).

143. David De La Croix and Matthais Doepke, "To Segregate or to Integrate: Education Politics and Democracy," *Review of Economic Studies* 76, no. 2 (2009): 597–628. In contrast, Nora Gordon, "High School Graduation in the Context of Changing Elementary and Secondary Education Policy and Income Inequality: The Last Half Century," Working Paper 19049 (National Bureau of Economic Research, 2013), finds that state inequality is correlated with higher spending. However, her measure of spending is the combined value of federal, state, and local spending, which gives a distorted view of the politics at work. For example, based largely on policies that have existed since the 1960s, the federal government awards money to school districts because of their levels of poverty as well as other special needs. Thus it is not likely that the poor and the middle class are currently so politically powerful in the unequal states that they can pressure for higher levels of public spending; rather, it is likely that formulas or interactions between federal, state, and local spending are driving results. For more on the interactions between layers of government that impact education spending, see Bruce Baker, "America's Most Financially Disadvantaged School Districts and How They Got that Way," Center for American Progress, Washington, DC, July 2014.

144. Total current expenditures on public elementary and secondary education were equal to approximately 3.04 percent of GDP in 1979–1980 and had increased to roughly

3.60 percent of GDP by 2008–2009 before declining slightly in more recent years. Author's calculations using current expenditure data and GDP data that can be found at National Center for Education Statistics, "Advance Release of Selected 2013 Digest Tables: Table 236.10," http://nces.ed.gov/programs/digest/d13/tables/dt13_236.10.asp; Bureau of Economic Analysis, "National Data: Table 1.1.5 Gross Domestic Product," www.bea.gov/itable/. Note that spending per pupil has increased significantly. Total current expenditures per pupil in average daily attendance increased from approximately $6,770 in 1979–1980 to roughly $12,198 in 2009–2010 before falling very slightly to $11,948 in 2010–2011 (all figures in 2012–2013 dollars). Data can be found at National Center for Education Statistics, "Advance Release of Selected 2013 Digest Tables: Table 236.55," http://nces.ed.gov/programs/digest/d13/tables/dt13_236.55.asp. Note also that the study of the relationship between inequality and elementary and secondary education spending—especially at the local, as opposed to the state or national, level—is not conclusive and needs additional research. Sean Corcoran and William Evans, "Income Inequality, the Median Voter, and the Support for Public Education," Working Paper 16097 (National Bureau of Economic Research, 2010), find that inequality reduces state-level elementary and secondary education spending (though not to a statistically significant degree), but increases local spending. Further, note that Calin Archalean and Ioana Schiopu, "Inequality and Educational Funding," Working Paper 238 (ESADE, 2012), find that inequality's effect on local elementary and secondary education spending depends upon the level of income in the district. Combined, these mixed results on the relationship between inequality and elementary and secondary spending at the local level suggest that researchers have not adequately captured the relationship. It is likely that other variables that researchers have not factored in are also affecting results. One factor that has not been accounted for in the research is partisanship: large cities are often heavily Democratic and thus more supportive of public education spending, but are also often highly unequal. Thus, by ignoring partisanship, the research on local education spending and inequality could be missing much of the story. Further, historical policy legacies may also be impacting results. Finally, it is important to note that researchers suggesting that inequality increases local elementary and secondary education spending base their argument on the median-voter theorem, which claims the poor and the lower middle class have great political power. Unfortunately, the researchers present no evidence that they actually do have power, which suggests that other factors besides the political power of the poor may be driving their results. Still, it is possible that the poor and the middle class have more political power at the local level than they do at the state and national level—but again no evidence that this is the case is actually presented.

145. Note that this ranking refers to spending that occurred in 2010, the most recent year for which complete data are publicly available. Ranking based on data available in Organisation for Economic Co-Operation and Development, "Education at a Glance 2013: OECD Indicators." Note that other data from the World Bank using slightly different measures show the United States ranking even worse among OECD nations. According to the World Bank, in terms of per student spending as a share of per capita GDP, the United States ranks only sixteenth among OECD nations in public expenditures on primary education, and only eighteenth in public expenditures on secondary education.

146. Congressional Budget Office, "Public Spending on Transportation and Water Infrastructure" (2010). Note that the same trend is true using other measures of infrastructure spending such as the growth rate of public capital stock. See Bivens, "Public Investment," figure A.

147. Figure is in 2009 dollars. Author's calculations based on real GDP figures found at Bureau of Economic Analysis, "Gross Domestic Product," www.bea.gov/national/index.htm.

148. President's Economic Recovery Advisory Board, "Infrastructure Investment and the Creation of a National Infrastructure Bank" (2009). According to the report: "Infrastructure spending in real inflation adjusted dollars and adjusting for the depreciation of existing assets is about the same level now as it was in 1968 when the economy was one-third smaller."

149. David Madland and Nick Bunker, "Ties that Bind" (Washington, DC: Center for American Progress, 2012).

150. "Life in the Slow Lane," *Economist*, April 29, 2011, www.economist.com /node/18620944.

151. World Economic Forum, "The Global Competitiveness Index 2012–2013 Data Platform" (2012).

152. Keith Laing, "Lawmakers in House and Senate Exhale after Heavy Lift on Transportation Bill," *Hill's Transportation and Infrastructure Blog,* June 29, 2012, http://thehill.com /blogs/transportation-report/highways-bridges-and-roads/235683-lawmakers-exhale-after-heavy-lift-on-transportation-bill.

153. David Grant, "US Chamber to Congress on Transportation Bill: You're Doing It Wrong," *Christian Science Monitor,* May 21, 2012, www.csmonitor.com/USA/Politics /monitor_breakfast/2012/0521/US-Chamber-to-Congress-on-transportation-bill-You-re-doing-it-wrong.

154. As Representative Nick Rahall (D-W.Va.) put it, "This is a 27-month bill. It's the best we could get with the money we could find." Laing, "Lawmakers in House and Senate Exhale."

155. Tim Harlow, "Stopgap Funding for Highway Trust Fund Keeps MnDOT Projects on Track," *Star Tribune,* August 3, 2014, www.startribune.com/local/269760301 .html.

156. In the poll 70 percent said college education is very or extremely important for achieving the American Dream, with an additional 24 percent saying it is somewhat important. See Northeastern University, FTI Consulting, and Brookings Institution, "Innovation in Higher Education, Public Opinion Survey Results" (2012).

157. Tom W. Smith, "Trends in National Spending Priorities, 1973–2012" (Chicago: NORC at the University of Chicago, 2013).

158. For the percentage who feel making improvements to infrastructure is important, see Hart Research and Associates, "Rockefeller Foundation Transportation Survey" (2011). For the percentage who support increasing federal spending to build and repair roads, bridges, and schools, see CNN and ORC, "CNN/ORC Poll," http://i2.cdn.turner .com/cnn/2011/images/10/17/oct17.poll.economy.pdf. For the percentage prepared to pay more taxes to finance such projects, see Building American's Future Educational Fund, "Majority of Americans Ready to Pay for Better Infrastructure but Demand Accountability," press release, January 8, 2009, www.bafuture.org/news/press-release/poll-majority-americans-ready-pay-better-infrastructure-demand-accountability.

159. Joshua Holland, "Why Do the Rich Get to Go Through Airport Security Faster Than You?," *Alternet,* August 1, 2010, www.alternet.org/econo-my/147703/why_do_the_rich_get_to_go_through_airport_security_fast-er_than_you_/?page = entir.

160. Michael J. Sandel, "What Isn't for Sale?," *Atlantic,* April 2012, www.theatlantic .com/magazine/archive/2012/04/what-isnt-for-sale/308902/.

161. Dianne Stewart, "Buy the Right Car and You May Never Notice the Budget Holes," *Policy Shop,* September 19, 2011, http://policyshop.squarespace.com/home/2011 /9/19/buy-the-right-car-and-you-may-never-notice-the-budget-holes.html.

162. Martin Gilens, "Inequality and Democratic Responsiveness in the United States," *Public Opinion Quarterly* 69, no. 5 (2005): 778–796. For additional research on the preferences of the wealthy, see, for example, Leslie McCall and Jeff Manza, "Class Differences in Social and Political Attitudes in the United States," in *Oxford Handbook of American Public Opinion and the Media*, ed. Robert Shapiro and Lawrence Jacobs (New York: Oxford University Press, 2011); Benjamin Page and Cari Lynn Hennessy, "What Affluent Americans Want from Politics," paper presented at the annual American Political Science Association meeting, Washington DC, 2010; Gilens and Page, "Testing Theories of American Politics."

163. Page, Bartels, and Seawright, "Democracy and the Policy Preferences."

164. A study by the Society of General Internal Medicine found that using the Federal Supply Schedule like the VA, DOD, and other government agencies would yield $21.9 billion in annual savings. In other words, not using the FSS costs the federal government $21.9 billion per year. Walid F. Gellad and others, "What If the Federal Government Negotiated Pharmaceutical Prices for Seniors? An Estimate of National Savings," *Journal General Internal Medicine* 23, no. 9 (2008): 1435–1440.

165. A report from 2008 by the House Committee on Government Oversight and Reform found that pharmaceutical companies received a $3.7 billion windfall from just 100 drugs used by dual-eligibles in 2006 and 2007 alone. House Committee on Oversight and Government Reform, "Medicare Part D: Drug Prices and Manufacturing Windfalls" (Washington, DC: US House of Representatives Committee on Oversight and Government Reform, 2008).

166. Spending data from Center for Responsive Politics, "Pharmaceuticals/Health Products," www.opensecrets.org/industries/indus.php?ind = H04. Revolving door information from Michael Singer, "Under the Influence," *60 Minutes,* July 29, 2007, www.cbsnews.com/8301-18560_162-2625305.html.

167. Mike Stuckey, "Tauzin Aided Drug Firms, Then They Hired Him," *NBCNews. com,* March 22, 2006, www.nbcnews.com/id/11714763/t/tauzin-aided-drug-firms-then-they-hired-him/#.UeQHj215F3q.

168. Singer, "Under the Influence."

169. For the share of the economy, see Justin Lahart, "Number of the Week: Finance's Share of Economy Continues to Grow," *Wall Street Journal,* December 10, 2011, http://blogs.wsj.com/economics/2011/12/10/number-of-the-week-finances-share-of-economy-continues-to-grow/, who finds banking rose from 2.8 percent of the economy in 1950 to 8.4 percent in 2011. For profits, see Kathleen Madigan, "Like the Phoenix, U.S. Finance Profits Soar," *Wall Street Journal,* March 25, 2011, http://blogs.wsj.com/economics/2011/03/25/like-the-phoenix-u-s-finance-profits-soar/. Note the vast majority of that growth came from a few very large banks. Banks with assets exceeding $10 billion make up only 1.5 percent of US banks, but accounted for about 83 percent of the industry earnings in the first quarter of 2013. Marcy Gordon, "US Banks Report Record Earnings of $40.3B for Q1," *Associated Press,* May 29, 2013, http://bigstory.ap.org/article/us-banks-report-record-earnings-403b-q1.

170. The percentages here refer to the percentage of primary taxpayers in the top 0.1 percent of the income distribution (excluding capital gains) who are classified as working in "financial professions, including management." See Jon Bakija, Adam Cole, and Bradley Heim, "Jobs and Income Growth of Top Earners and the Causes of Changing Income Inequality: Evidence from U.S. Tax Return Data," Working Paper (Williams College, 2012). Other studies have also found financial professionals' representation among the top earners increasing. For example, see Steven N. Kaplan and Joshua Rauh, "Wall Street and

Main Street: What Contributes to the Rise in the Highest Incomes?," *Review of Financial Studies* 23, no. 3 (2010): 1004–1050.

171. Simon Johnson and James Kwak, *13 Bankers* (New York: Vintage, 2011).

172. Figures are adjusted for inflation and presented in 2012 dollars. Nominal figures at Center for Responsive Politics, "Finance/Insurance/Real Estate: Long-Term Contribution Trends," www.opensecrets.org/industries/totals.php?cycle = 2012&ind = F.

173. Figures are adjusted for inflation and presented in 2012 dollars. Nominal figures at Center for Responsive Politics, "Finance, Insurance & Real Estate: Sector Profile 2006," www.opensecrets.org/lobby/indus.php?id = F&year = 2006.

174. Center for Responsive Politics, "Finance, Insurance & Real Estate: Sector Profile 2012," www.opensecrets.org/lobby/indus.php?id = F&year = 2012.

175. See, for example, Deniz Igan, Prachi Mishra, and Thierry Tressel, "A Fistful of Dollars: Lobbying and the Financial Crisis," *NBER Macroeconomics Annual* 26, no. 1 (2012): 195–230.

176. Atif Mian, Amir Sufi, and Francesco Trebbi, "The Political Economy of the Subprime Mortgage Credit Expansion," *Quarterly Journal of Political Science* 8, no. 4 (2013): 373–408. Note they find constituent interests and Wall Street influence both played a role in the expansion of credit. Their research also indicates that Wall Street "contributions increasingly targeted US representatives from districts with a large fraction of subprime borrowers," a finding consistent with research cited in this chapter indicating that most citizens have relatively little independent political influence.

177. Johnson and Kwak, *13 Bankers*.

178. See, for example, "The Long Demise of Glass Steagall," *Frontline,* May 8, 2003, www.pbs.org/wgbh/pages/frontline/shows/wallstreet/weill/demise.html, where it is stated that "after 12 attempts in 25 years, Congress finally repeals Glass-Steagall, rewarding financial companies for more than 20 years and $300 million worth of lobbying efforts." See also "Looking Back at the Repeal of Glass-Steagall, or, How the Banks Caught Casino Fever," *Next New Deal: The Blog of the Roosevelt Institute,* November 12, 2009, www.rooseveltinstitute.org/new-roosevelt/looking-back-repeal-glass-steagall-or-how-banks-caught-casino-fever; Johnson and Kwak, *13 Bankers*.

179. Binyamin Appelbaum, "As Subprime Lending Crisis Unfolded, Watchdog Fed Didn't Bother Barking," *Washington Post,* September 27, 2009, http://articles.washingtonpost.com/2009-09-27/business/36805549_1_regulators-bank-affiliates-subprime-loans.

180. Binyamin Appelbaum, "Fed Held Back as Evidence Mounted on Subprime Loan Abuses," *Washington Post,* September 27, 2009, www.washingtonpost.com/wp-dyn/content/article/2009/09/26/AR2009092602706.html?hpid = topnews.

181. Corine Hegland, "Why The Financial System Collapsed," *National Journal,* April 11,2009,http://srkaufman72.wordpress.com/2009/04/20/corine-heglandwhy-the-financial-system-collap/.

182. US Securities and Exchange Commission, "SEC's Oversight of Bear Stearns and Related Entities: The Consolidated Supervised Entity Program" (2008). See also Roger Lowenstein, who wrote, "The investment banks, led by Goldman and its then-CEO, Hank Paulson, pleaded for a new regime to govern capital requirement." Roger Lowenstein, *The End of Wall Street* (New York: Penguin, 2010).

183. James Kwak, "Cultural Capture and the Financial Crisis," in *Preventing Regulatory Capture,* ed. Daniel Carpenter and David Moss (New York: Cambridge University Press, 2013).

184. Johnson and Kwak, *13 Bankers*; Peter Goodman, "Taking Hard New Look at a Greenspan Legacy," *New York Times,* October 9, 2008, www.nytimes.com/2008/10/09/business/economy/09greenspan.html.

185. For Warren Buffett's quotation, see Warren Buffett, "Berkshire Hathaway Annual Report, 2002" (Omaha, NE: Berkshire Hathaway, 2002).

186. For a detailed description of the role CDOs played in the crisis, see National Commission on the Causes of the Financial and Economic Crisis in the United States, "The Financial Crisis Inquiry Report" (2011).

187. Luigi Zingales, "Causes and Effects of the Lehman Brothers Bankruptcy," testimony before the Committee on Oversight and Government Reform, US House of Representatives, October 6, 2008, http://research.chicagobooth.edu/igm/docs/Zingales-Testimonies.pdf.

188. Mian, Sufi, and Trebbi, "The Political Economy of the US Mortgage Default Crisis."

189. Bob Ivry, "No Lehman Moments as Biggest Banks Deemed Too Big to Fail," *Bloomberg Markets Magazine*, May 10, 2013, www.bloomberg.com/news/2013-05-10/no-lehman-moments-as-biggest-banks-deemed-too-big-to-fail.html. Note that some estimates indicate that the discount large banks receive has been declining since Dodd-Frank regulations went into effect. Government Accountability Office, "Large Bank Holding Companies: Expectations of Government Support" (2014).

190. See, for example, Thomas Philippon and Ariell Reshef, "Wages and Human Capital in the U.S. Financial Industry, 1909–2006," *Quarterly Journal of Economics* 127, no. 4 (2012): 1551–1609; Madigan, "Like the Phoenix, U.S. Finance Profits Soar"; Anton Korinek and Jonathan Kreamer, "The Redistributive Effects of Financial Deregulation," Working Paper 19572 (National Bureau of Economic Research, 2013).

191. Johnson and Kwak, *13 Bankers.*

192. John Plender, "Capitalism in Crisis: The Code That Forms a Bar to Harmony," *Financial Times*, January 8, 2012, www.ft.com/intl/cms/s/0/fb95b4fe-3863-11e1-9d07-00144feabdc0.html#axzz2rpXnESoo.

193. Johnson and Kwak, *13 Bankers.*

194. Public Citizen, "The Best Energy Bill Corporations Could Buy: Summary of Industry Giveaways in the 2005 Energy Bill" (2005). Michael Grunwald and Juliet Eilperin, "Energy Bill Raises Fears about Pollution, Fraud," *Washington Post*, July 30, 2005, www.washingtonpost.com/wp-dyn/content/article/2005/07/29/AR2005072901128.html.

195. Government Accountability Office, "Energy Task Force: Process Used to Develop the National Energy Policy" (2003).

196. Jake Tapper, "Pro-Bush Pork in Medicare, Energy Bills?," *ABCNews.com*, November 23, 2003, http://abcnews.go.com/WNT/story?id=131465.

197. Ibid.

198. Jonathan Fahey, "Renewable Energy Growth Is Rising around the World, IEA Says," *Associated Press*, June 26, 2013, www.huffingtonpost.com/2013/06/26/renewable-energy-growth_n_3504265.html; Salvatore Lazzari, "Energy Tax Policy: History and Current Issues" (Washington, DC: Congressional Research Service, 2008), table 1.

199. Julius Genachowski, "Winning the Global Bandwidth Race: Opportunities and Challenges for the US Broadband Economy," September 25, 2012.

200. Benjamin Lennett and Sascha Meinrath, "Building a 21st Century Broadband Superhighway" (Washington, DC: New America Foundation, 2009). Edward Luce of the *Financial Times* echoes a similar theme: "In the late 1990s the US had the fastest speeds and widest penetration of almost anywhere—unsurprisingly given that it invented the platform. Today the US comes 16th, according to the OECD, with an average of 27 megabits per second, compared with up to quadruple that in countries such as Japan and the Netherlands." See Edward Luce, "Corporate Tie Binds US to a Slow Internet," *Financial Times*, February 24, 2013, www.ft.com/intl/cms/s/0/98e2a5fc-7c54-11e2-99f0-00144feabdc0

.html#axzz2WCgesEZS. And some rankings put us far lower. See Vernie G. Kopytoff, "America: Land of the Slow," *New York Times*, September 20, 2011, http://bits.blogs.nytimes.com/2011/09/20/america-land-of-the-slow/.

201. Luce, "Corporate Tie Binds US to a Slow Internet." For more on the lobbying, see Edward Wyatt, "F.C.C. Commissioner Leaving to Join Comcast," *New York Times*, May 11, 2011, http://mediadecoder.blogs.nytimes.com/2011/05/11/f-c-c-commissioner-to-join-comcast/.

202. Susan Crawford, "U.S. Internet Users Pay More for Slower Service," *Bloomberg News*, December 27, 2012, www.bloomberg.com/news/2012-12-27/u-s-internet-users-pay-more-for-slower-service.html. Zaid Jilani of *Republic Report* tells a similar story. Zaid Jilani, "ALEC Wants You to Pay 750 Percent More for High-Speed Internet," *Republic Report*, April 17, 2012, www.republicreport.org/2012/alec-wants-to-kill-cheap-broadband/.

203. For information on the extension of copyrights, see "Disney Lobbying for Copyright Extension No Mickey Mouse Effort," *Associated Press*, October 17, 1998, www.public.asu.edu/~dkarjala/commentary/ChiTrib10-17-98.html. For information on the "bankruptcy reform" bill, see Mike Simkovic, "The Effect of BAPCPA on Credit Card Industry Profits and Prices," *American Bankruptcy Law Journal* 83, no. 1 (2009): 1–26.

204. For David Stockman quotation, see Bill Moyers, "David Stockman on Crony Capitalism," *Moyers & Company*, March 9, 2012, http://billmoyers.com/segment/david-stockman-on-crony-capitalism/. Thomas E. Patterson made his statement when commenting on the book *Dollarocracy* by John Nichols and Robert McChesney. See "Nichols and McChesney at the First Congregational Church of Berkeley," *Nation Institute*, 2013, www.nationinstitute.org/events/nationbooks/3345/nichols_and_mcchesney_at_the_first_congregational_church_of_berkeley. For the Joseph Stiglitz quotation, see Stiglitz, *The Price of Inequality*.

205. Stanley S. Surrey and Paul R. McDaniel, *Tax Expenditures* (Cambridge, MA: Harvard University Press, 1985).

206. Seth Hanlon and Michael Ettlinger, "Cut Spending in the Tax Code" (Washington, DC: Center for American Progress, 2011).

207. Note the number of tax expenditures is the correct measure of whether rent seeking has become more successful. The value of tax expenditures fluctuates based on underlying tax rates, which themselves are subject to rent seeking. Further, even as tax rates have generally declined—making each individual tax expenditure less valuable—the overall amount spent on tax expenditures has increased at least since 1988, as is made clear in Allison Rogers and Eric Toder, "Trends in Tax Expenditures" (Washington, DC: Tax Policy Center, 2011).

208. Government Accountability Office, "Tax Expenditures Represent a Substantial Federal Commitment and Need to Be Reexamined" (2005).

209. See Pew reports from 2004 and 2013 containing data from the Treasury. The Pew Charitable Trusts, "Downloadable Tax Expenditure Datasets: Report Years 2001 Through 2013" (2013).

210. The famed tax reform in 1986 only eliminated 24 tax breaks and thus was but a slight interruption in the larger trend. Deloitte, "Resetting the Code: Issues in Corporate Tax Reform" (2011).

211. See, for example, Mark Koba, "End the Mortgage Interest Deduction? Expect a Fight," *CNBC*, February 28, 2013, www.cnbc.com/id/100506426.

212. See Congressional Budget Office "The Distribution of Major Tax Expenditures in the Individual Income Tax System" (2013), figure 1.

213. For information on the case involving former Washington, DC, city council member, see Andrea Noble, "Michael Brown Is Latest D.C. Lawmaker to Plead Guilty to Federal Charges," *Washington Times,* June 10, 2013, www.washingtontimes.com/news/2013 /jun/10/michael-brown-is-latest-dc-lawmaker-to-plead-guilt/?page = all. For information on the case involving the Louisiana congressman, see Allan Lengel, "FBI Says Jefferson Was Filmed Taking Cash," *Washington Post,* May 22, 2006, www.washingtonpost.com /wp-dyn/content/article/2006/05/21/AR2006052100167.html.

214. Terry Baynes, "Court Upholds Conviction of Jefferson County Official," *Reuters,* November 29, 2011, www.reuters.com/article/2011/11/29/us-jefferson-county-white-idUSTRE7AS2MC20111129.

215. *United States of America v Gary L. White,* Case No. 10–13654 (11th Cir 2011).

216. A survey of state house reporters' perceptions of public corruption lists Louisiana and Alabama as two of the most corrupt states. See Richard Boylan and Cheryl Long, "Measuring Public Corruption in the American States: A Survey of State House Reporters," *State Politics & Policy Quarterly* 3, no. 4 (2003): 420–438. For an example of a study that controls for other factors, see Nicholas Apergis, Oguzhan C. Dincer, James E. Payne, "The Relationship between Corruption and Income Inequality in U.S. States: Evidence from a Panel Cointegration and Error Correction Model," *Public Choice* 145, nos. 1–2 (2010): 125–135.

217. Edward Glaeser and Raven Saks, "Corruption in America," *Journal of Public Economics* 90, no. 6 (2006): 1053–1072.

218. Author's calculations based on United States Department of Justice, "Report to Congress on the Activities and Operations of the Public Integrity Section" (2012). The conviction figures from 1973 are contained in United States Department of Commerce, "Statistical Abstract of the United States: 1980" (1980), table 330. Population estimates are found at Federal Reserve Bank of St. Louis, "Total Population: All Ages Including Armed Forces Overseas," http://research.stlouisfed.org/fred2/series/POP/downloaddata?cid = 104. Population totals used are for December of each given year.

219. Glaeser and Saks, "Corruption in America."

220. Author's analysis of Worldwide Governance Indicators produced by Daniel Kauffman, Aart Kraay, and Massimo Mastruzzi. See World Bank, "Worldwide Governance Indicators," http://info.worldbank.org/governance/wgi/index.asp.

221. Author's analysis of American National Election Studies survey. For the figure from 1972, see American National Election Studies, "The ANES Guide to Public Opinion and Electoral Behavior: Table 5A.4," www.electionstudies.org/nesguide/toptable /tab5a_4.htm. For the figure from 2012, see American National Election Studies, "Users' Guide and Codebook."

CHAPTER FOUR

1. Daniel M.G. Raff and Lawrence H. Summers, "Did Henry Ford Pay Efficiency Wages?" *Journal of Labor Economics* 5, no. 4 (1987): S57–S86; Ford Motor Company, "Henry Ford's $5-a-Day Revolution," press release, http://corporate.ford.com/news-center /press-releases-detail/677-5-dollar-a-day.

2. Ford Motor Company, "Henry Ford's $5-a-Day Revolution." For more examples of the response to Ford's decision, see Steven Watts, *The People's Tycoon: Henry Ford and the American Century* (New York: A. Knopf, 2005).

3. "An Experiment, With Consequences," *Wall Street Journal,* January 7, 1914, 1.

4. See Ford R. Bryan, *Henry's Lieutenants* (Detroit: Great Lakes Books, 1993).

5. Raff and Summers, "Did Henry Ford Pay Efficiency Wages?"; Ford Motor Company, "Henry Ford's $5-a-Day Revolution." Note that Ford's business reasons for increasing wages included reducing turnover and absenteeism. Others maintain that the decision was partly an effort to prevent his company from becoming unionized.

6. The quotation is from an article from 1926 in *The World's Work* as quoted in Watts, *The People's Tycoon;* and William McGaughey Jr., "Henry Ford's Productivity Lesson," *Christian Science Monitor,* December 22, 1982. Note that some question whether demand was really much of Ford's rationale for raising wages. But note that during the same time period the businessman Edward Filene also made statements about the importance of paying workers well so they could purchase products. See, for example, Edward Filene, *The Way Out* (New York: Page, 1924).

7. San Francisco State University, "From the Statement of Facts in Dodge v. Ford Motor Co.," http://online.sfsu.edu/rdaniels/2008_804/The%20Rise%20of%20the%20Ford%20 Motor%20Company.pdf. Other sources provide similar sales figures. See, for example, "533,921 Fords Built in 1 Year," *Automobile* 35, no. 1 (1916): 212. Yet another site provides slightly different sales total in 1916. See "Model T Ford Sales," www.mtfca.com/encyclo/fdsales.htm. Sources consistently agree, however, that profits grew from $30.3 million in 1914 to $60 million. See M. Todd Henderson, "Everything Old Is New Again: Lessons from *Dodge v. Ford Motor Company,*" Working Paper 373 (University of Chicago Law School, 2007).

8. It is worth noting that a number of other leading thinkers link the weakness of the middle class to the severe crash, including Joseph Stiglitz, Robert Reich, Michael Kumhof and Romain Rancière, Raghuram Rajan, and many others. These scholars focus on slightly different mechanisms than those emphasized in this chapter, but the underlying story that they tell of middle-class struggles contributing to the severity of the Great Recession in the United States is similar. See Joseph Stiglitz, *The Price of Inequality* (New York: W.W. Norton, 2013); Robert Reich, *Aftershock: The Next Economy and America's Future* (New York: Vintage, 2010); Michael Kumhof and Romain Rancière, "Inequality, Leverage and Crises," Working Paper 10/268 (International Monetary Fund, 2010); Raghuram G. Rajan, *Fault Lines: How Hidden Fractures Still Threaten the World Economy* (Princeton, NJ: Princeton University Press, 2010). For other sources making similar arguments, see Barry Z. Cynamon and Steven M. Fazzari, "Inequality and Household Finance during the Consumer Age," Working Paper 752 (Levy Economics Institute of Bard College, 2013); Thomas Philippon and Virgiliu Midrigan, "Household Leverage and the Recession," Working Paper 16965 (National Bureau of Economic Research, 2011); Engelbert Stockhammer, "Rising Inequality as a Root Cause of the Present Crisis," Working Paper 282 (Political Economy Research Institute, 2012); Jeff Madrick, "The Case for Wage-Led Growth," in "Renewing the American Social Contract," by New America Foundation (2013); Matthieu Charpe and Stefan Kühn, "Inequality, Aggregate Demand and the Crisis" (Geneva, Switzerland: International Labour Organization, 2012); Mark Setterfield, "Real Wages, Aggregate Demand, and the Macroeconomic Travails of the US Economy: Diagnosis and Prognosis," Working Paper 10–05 (Hartford, CT: Trinity College Department of Economics, 2010); Özlem Onaran and Giorgos Galanis, "Is Aggregate Demand Wage-Led or Profit-Led? National and Global Effects" (Geneva, Switzerland: International Labour Organization, 2012); Christopher Brown, "Does Income Distribution Matter for Effective Demand? Evidence from the United States," *Review of Political Economy* 16, no. 3 (2004): 291–307; "2012: The Year in Graphs," *Washington Post Wonkblog,* December 27, 2012, www.washingtonpost.com/blogs/wonkblog /wp/2012/12/27/2012-the-year-in-graphs/. This chapter does not emphasize these other

explanations. Stiglitz and Reich, for example, base their argument on a claim that the middle class tends to consume a larger share of their income than the rich; that is, they have a higher marginal propensity to consume. This argument is supported by a number of studies—especially recent ones with better data on higher income earners and more thorough analysis—including Karen Dynan, Jonathan Skinner, and Stephen P. Zeldes, "Do the Rich Save More?," *Journal of Political Economy* 112, no. 2 (2004): 397–444; Jonathan Parker and others, "Consumer Spending and the Economic Stimulus Payments of 2008," *American Economic Review* 103, no. 6 (2013): 2530–2553; Saktinil Roy and David M. Kemme, "Causes of Banking Crises," *International Review of Economics & Finance* 24, no. 1 (2012): 270–294; Christopher D. Carroll, Jiri Slacalek, and Kiichi Tokuoka, "The Distribution of Wealth and the Marginal Propensity to Consume" (Baltimore: Johns Hopkins University, 2013); Christopher D. Carroll, "Why Do the Rich Save So Much?," Working Paper 6549 (National Bureau of Economic Research, 1998). Still, not all research or theory comes to similar conclusions as Stiglitz and Reich. See Milton Friedman, *A Theory of the Consumption Function* (Princeton, NJ: Princeton University Press, 1957); Bruce D. Meyer and James X. Sullivan, "Consumption and Income Inequality in the U.S. since the 1960s," Working Paper (University of Notre Dame, 2013); Paul Krugman, "Inequality and Crises: Coincidence or Causation?" (Princeton, NJ: Princeton University, 2010). Kumhof and Rancière have a mechanical view that inequality inevitably leads to debt, which leads to crises, even though inequality does not always lead to such high levels of household debt—many countries, especially those with stronger banking regulations that have limited the expansion of credit, have seen smaller increases in household debt—and not every country where households have high levels of debt suffers such a disastrous crash. For this debate, see Michael Bordo and Christopher Meissner, "Does Inequality Lead to a Financial Crisis?," *Journal of International Money and Finance* 31, no. 8 (2012): 2147–2161; A. B. Atkinson and Salvatore Morelli, "Inequality and Banking Crises: A First Look," report prepared for the Global Labour Forum (2011); Edward L. Glaeser, "Does Economic Inequality Cause Crises?," *New York Times,* December 14, 2010, http://economix.blogs.nytimes.com/2010/12/14/does-economic-inequality-cause-crises/; A. B. Atkinson and Salvator Morelli, "Economics Crises and Inequality," Human Development Research Paper 2011/05 (United Nations Development Programme, 2011). See also International Monetary Fund, "World Economic Outlook: Growth Resuming, Dangers Remain" (2012); Xinhua Gu and Bihong Huang, "An Empirical Examination of the Inequality, Leverage and Crisis Nexus" (Macau, China: University of Macau, 2012); Michael Kumhof and others, "Income Inequality and Current Account Imbalances," Working Paper 12/8 (International Monetary Fund, 2012); Virgina Maestri and Andrea Roventini, "Stylized Facts on Business Cycles and Inequality," Working Paper 30 (Amsterdam Institute for Advanced Labor Studies, 2012); Giovanni Dosi and others, "Income Distribution, Credit and Fiscal Policies in an Agent-Based Keynesian Model," *Journal of Economic Dynamics and Control* 37, no. 8 (2013): 1598–1625; Cristiano Perugini, Jens Hölscher, and Simon Collie, "Inequality, Credit Expansion and Financial Crises," MPRA Paper 51336 (Munich University Library, 2013). Finally, Rajan argues that politicians helped expand credit out of an attempt to help struggling Americans, rather than as a process largely driven by wealthy elites pushing for financial deregulation, an argument for which there is better evidence, as I explain in chapter 3 and Daron Acemoglu notes in Daron Acemoglu, "Thoughts on Inequality and the Financial Crisis," presentation, Denver, CO, January 7, 2011, http://economics.mit.edu/files/6348.

9. Nick Hanaeur, "Raise Taxes on the Rich to Reward True Job Creators," *Bloomberg,* November 30, 2011, www.bloombergview.com/articles/2011-12-01/raise-taxes-on-the-rich-to-reward-job-creators-commentary-by-nick-hanauer.

10. Bureau of Labor Statistics, "The Employment Situation—May, 2014," press release, June 6, 2014, www.bls.gov/news.release/pdf/empsit.pdf. For evidence of skill deterioration, see, for example, Per-Anders Edin and Magnus Gustavsson, "Time out of Work and Skill Depreciation," *Industrial and Labor Relations Review* 61, no. 2 (January 2008): 163–180.

11. See, among others, Lawrence H. Summers, "U.S. Economic Prospects: Secular Stagnation, Hysteresis, and the Zero Lower Bound," *Business Economics* 49, no. 2 (2014): 65–73. For more on the importance of demand to long-run growth, see, for example, Mark Setterfield, *The Economics of Demand-Led Growth: Challenging the Supply Side Vision of the Long Run* (Northampton, MA: Edward Elgar, 2002).

12. For a summary of the basic argument that investments are important to growth, see, for example, Roger A. Arnold, *Macroeconomics*, 8th ed. (Mason, OH: Thomson South-Western, 2008). See also Paul Davidson, *The Keynes Solution: The Path to Global Economic Prosperity* (New York: Palgrave Macmillan, 2009). As Davidson, emeritus professor at the University of Tennessee and a leading follower of Keynes, puts it, "Expectation of increasing sales provides the positive incentives for business firms to hire more workers to produce additional output to sell at a profitable price."

13. John Maynard Keynes, *The General Theory of Employment, Interest, and Money* (London: Macmillan, 1936).

14. Ibid. Italics in original.

15. Jude Wanniski, *The Way the World Works* (Washington, DC: Regnery, 1978).

16. John C. Williams, "The Economy and Fed Policy: Follow the Demand" (San Francisco: Federal Reserve Bank of San Francisco, 2013).

17. Justin Fox, "The Comeback Keynes," *Time,* November 3, 2008, 60.

18. In addition to the Bruce Bartlett quotation, see Greg Mankiw, a Harvard economist and 2012 Republican presidential nominee Mitt Romney's economic adviser, who wrote that the lack of demand has been the central problem in our economy: "The decline in the aggregate demand for goods and services led to the most severe recession in a generation or more." N. Gregory Mankiw and Matthew Weinzierl, "An Exploration of Optimal Stabilization Policy" (Washington, DC: Brookings Institution, 2011).

19. Bruce Bartlett, "It's the Aggregate Demand, Stupid," *New York Times,* August 16, 2011, http://economix.blogs.nytimes.com/2011/08/16/its-the-aggregate-demand-stupid/?_r = 1.

20. The phrase "supply creates its own demand" is often referred to as Say's Law, named after economist Jean-Baptiste Say. This particular phrasing of the rule is generally attributed to John Maynard Keynes, who rebutted Say's Law in *The General Theory of Employment, Interest, and Money.* For more on the debate over Say's law among modern economists, see Steven Kates, ed., *Two Hundred Years of Say's Law: Essays on Economic Theory's Most Controversial Principle* (Northampton, MA: Edward Elgar, 2003).

21. Joseph Stiglitz, "Macroeconomic Fluctuations, Inequality, and Human Development," *Journal of Human Development and Capabilities: A Multi-Disciplinary Journal for People-Centered Development* 13, no. 1 (2012): 31–58.

22. Christopher Brown, "Does Income Distribution Matter for Effective Demand? Evidence from the United States," *Review of Political Economy* 16, no. 3 (2004): 291–307.

23. See, for example, Brown, "Does Income Distribution Matter for Effective Demand?"; Robert Solow, "Building a Science of Economics for the Real World," testimony before the House Committee on Science and Technology, Subcommittee on Investigation and Oversight, July 20, 2010, https://web.archive.org/web/20110204034313/http://democrats.science.house.gov/Media/file/Commdocs/hearings/2010/Oversight/20july

/Solow_Testimony.pdf; Sarah Bloom Raskin's speech on the role economic inequality played in the Great Recession in Sarah Bloom Raskin, "Aspects of Inequality in the Recent Business Cycle," speech, New York, NY, April 18, 2013; or Joseph Stiglitz arguing that "economists who had looked at the *average* equity of a homeowner—ignoring the distribution—felt comfortable that the economy could easily withstand a large fall in housing prices," in Stiglitz, "Macroeconomics Fluctuations, Inequality, and Human Development." Note that there were other models of growth, such as those by Nicholas Kaldor, but they were generally abandoned in favor of mathematically cleaner representative agent models that converged on unique equilibrium rather than yielding multiple, intermediate equilibria.

24. See, for example, Joseph Stiglitz, "Rethinking Macroeconomics: What Failed, and How to Repair It," *Journal of the European Economic Association* 9, no. 4 (2011): 591–645; Joseph Stiglitz, "Rethinking Macroeconomics: What Went Wrong, and How to Fix It," *Global Policy* 2, no. 2 (2011): 165–175.

25. For a critique of this, see, for example, Christopher D. Carroll, "Representing Consumption and Saving without a Representative Consumer," in *Measuring Economic Sustainability and Progress,* ed. Dale Jorgenson, Steven Landefeld, and Paul Schreyer (Chicago: University of Chicago Press, 2014); Stiglitz, "Macroeconomic Fluctuations, Inequality, and Human Development."

26. See, for example, Robert Pollin, "Deeper in Debt: The Changing Financial Conditions of U.S. Households" (Washington, DC: Economic Policy Institute, 1990); Thomas Palley, "Economic Contradictions Coming to Roost? Does the U.S. Economy Long-Term Aggregate Demand Generation Problem?," *Journal of Post Keynesian Economics* 25, no. 1 (2002): 9–32; Heather Boushey and Christian E. Weller, "Has Growing Inequality Contributed to Rising Household Economic Distress?," *Review of Political Economy* 20, no. 1 (2008): 1–22; Matteo Iacoveillo, "Household Debt and Income Inequality, 1963–2003," *Journal of Money, Credit and Banking* 40, no. 5 (2008): 929–965.

27. Author's' analysis of Federal Reserve's Flow of Funds data on household and nonprofit liabilities. See also Cynamon and Fazzari, "Inequality and Household Finance during the Consumer Age."

28. Note also that the percentage of household income that went to servicing debt also increased sharply. Author's analysis of Federal Reserve's Flow of Funds Data and data from the Survey of Consumer Finances, as well as Kathleen W. Johnson and Geng Li, "Do High Debt Payments Hinder Household Consumption Smoothing?," Working Paper 52 (Federal Reserve Board, 2007).

29. Author's analysis of Federal Reserve's Flow of Funds data on household and nonprofit liabilities. See also Aldo Barba and Massimo Pivetti, "Rising Household Debt: Its Causes and Macroeconomic Implications—a Long-Period Analysis," *Cambridge Journal of Economics* 33, no. 1 (2008): 113–137. For further discussion of these trends, see Neil Bhutta, "Mortgage Debt and Household Deleveraging: Accounting for the Decline in Mortgage Debt Using Consumer Credit Record Data," Working Paper 14 (Federal Reserve Board, 2012); Karen Dynan and Donald Kohn, "The Rise in U.S. Household Indebtedness: Causes and Consequences," Working Paper 37 (Federal Reserve Board, 2007).

30. Bureau of Economic Analysis, "Alternative Measures of Personal Saving" (2012).

31. For example, Christian Weller, public policy professor at the University of Massachusetts, Boston, explains that "the debt boom was concentrated among middle-income families." See Christian Weller, "Unburdening America's Middle Class: Shrinking Families' Debt Burden Faster Is Imperative," *Challenge* 55, no. 1 (2012): 23–52. Note that Weller finds slightly different figures than those cited below, but his findings are quite similar.

32. Note that the rich did also take on additional debt in this period, but because their incomes increased rapidly, debt as a share of income didn't increase very much.

33. Barry Z. Cynamon and Steven M. Fazzari, "Inequality, the Great Recession, and Slow Recovery," Working Paper (Social Science Research Network, 2014). In this paper, which was last updated on January 23, 2014, Cynamon and Fazzari find that debt-to-income ratios for the bottom 95 percent increased by 71 percentage points between 1989 and 2007, but for the top 5 percent they only increased by 7 percentage points. Note that in a previous version of the paper they find similar but slightly different figures. Cynamon and Fazzari, "Inequality and Household Finance during the Consumer Age." Note also that Kumhof and Rancière come to very similar findings when analyzing the top 5 percent of wealth holders, rather than the top 5 percent of income earners. See Michael Kumhof and Romain Rancière, "Inequality, Leverage and Crises."

34. Atif Mian and Amir Sufi, *House of Debt: How They (and You) Caused the Great Recession, and How We Can Prevent It from Happening Again* (Chicago: University of Chicago Press, 2014).

35. See, for example, Barba and Pivetti, "Rising Household Debt."

36. Cynamon and Fazzari, "Inequality and Household Finance during the Consumer Age."

37. William R. Emmons, "Don't Expect Consumer Spending to Be the Engine of Economic Growth It Once Was," *Regional Economist,* January, 2012, www.stlouisfed.org /publications/re/articles/?id = 2201.

38. Juliet Schor provides some examples of such excessive spending in her book *The Overspent American.* For example, she describes how a small percentage of the population may suffer from psychological disorders that lead them to buy compulsively and spend well beyond their means. She also points out, however, that more innocuous forms of these compulsions may impact a significant share of Americans. See Juliet Schor, *The Overspent American: Why We Want What We Don't Need* (New York: Harper Perennial, 1998).

39. Board of Governors of the Federal Reserve System, "Report to the Congress on Practices of the Consumer Credit Industry in Soliciting and Extending Credit and Their Effects on Consumer Debt and Insolvency" (2006); Cynamon and Fazzari, "Inequality and Household Finance during the Consumer Age."

40. See, for example, Atif Mian and Amir Sufi, "The Consequences of Mortgage Credit Expansion: Evidence from the U.S. Mortgage Default Crisis," *Quarterly Journal of Economics* 124, no. 4 (2009): 1449–1496. Mian and Sufi find, for example, that "the expansion in mortgage credit from 2002 to 2005 to subprime ZIP codes occurs despite sharply declining relative (and in some cases absolute) income growth in these neighborhoods." See also Cynamon and Fazzari, "Inequality and Household Finance during the Consumer Age"; Barry Z. Cynamon and Steven M. Fazzari, "Household Debt in the Consumer Age: Source of Growth—Risk of Collapse," *Capitalism and Society* 3, no. 2 (2008): 3–30.

41. Cynamon and Fazzari, "Household Debt in the Consumer Age"; Barba and Pivetti, "Rising Household Debt"; Christian Weller, "Need or Want: What Explains the Run-Up in Consumer Debt?" *Journal of Economic Issues* 41, no. 2 (2007): 583–591.

42. United States Senate Health, Education, Labor and Pensions Committee, "Saving the American Dream: The Past, Present, and Uncertain Future of America's Middle Class" (2011).

43. In this period inflation-adjusted prices increased by 89 percent according to Federal Reserve researchers. This figure reflects the change in the S & P/Case-Shiller index between 1998 and 2006. See Jeffrey P. Cohen, Cletus C. Coughlin, and David A. Lopez, "The Boom and Bust of U.S. Housing Prices from Various Geographic Perspectives,"

Federal Reserve Bank of St. Louis Review 94, no. 5 (September/October 2012): 341–367. Evidence for the relationship between housing prices and debt can be found in Karen Dynan, "Is a Household Debt Overhang Holding Back Consumption?," *Brookings Papers on Economic Activity* (Spring 2012). Dynan writes, "As of 2007 homeowners in states that had experienced the most pronounced housing booms tended to have considerably more mortgage debt than homeowners in other states."

44. Elizabeth Warren and Amelia Warren Tyagi, "What's Hurting the Middle Class," *Boston Review,* September 1, 2005, https://bostonreview.net/forum/what%E2%80%99s-hurting-middle-class.

45. Atif Mian and Amir Sufi, "House Prices, Home Equity-Based Borrowing, and the U.S. Household Leverage Crisis," *American Economic Review* 101, no. 5 (2011): 2132–2156.

46. James Duesenberry, *Income, Saving, and the Theory of Consumer Behavior* (Cambridge, MA: Harvard University Press, 1949); building on Thorstein Veblen, *The Theory of the Leisure Class* (New York: Macmillan, 1899). See also David Moss, Anant Thaker, and Howard Rudnick, "Inequality and Decision Making: Imagining a New Line of Inquiry," Working Paper 13–099 (Harvard Business School, 2013); Schor, *The Overspent American;* Markus Christen and Ruskin M. Morgan, "Keeping Up with the Joneses: Analyzing the Effect of Income Inequality on Consumer Borrowing," *Quantitative Marketing and Economics* 3, no. 2 (2003): 145–173; Robert H. Frank, *Falling Behind: How Rising Inequality Harms the Middle Class* (Berkeley: University of California Press, 2007); Adam S. Levine, Robert H. Frank, and Oege Dijk, "Expenditure Cascades," Working Paper (Social Science Research Network, 2010).

47. Marianne Bertrand and Adair Morse, "Trickle-Down Consumption," Working Paper 18883 (National Bureau of Economic Research, 2013); Schor, *The Overspent American;* Frank, *Falling Behind;* Levine, Frank, and Dijk, "Expenditure Cascades"; Christen and Morgan, "Keeping Up with the Joneses."

48. Housing price peak referred to here is the peak in the S & P/Case-Schiller House Price Index, which peaked in the second quarter of 2006. See Cohen, Coughlin, and Lopez, "The Boom and Bust of U.S. Housing Prices from Various Geographic Perspectives." Unemployment numbers taken from Bureau of Labor Statistics, "Labor Force Statistics from the Current Population Survey: Seasonally Adjusted Unemployment Rate," http://data.bls.gov/timeseries/LNS14000000. For information on the tightening of the credit market, see Markus K. Brunnermeier, "Deciphering the Liquidity and Credit Crunch, 2007–2008," *Journal of Economic Perspectives* 23, no. 1 (2009): 77–100.

49. For stock market loss figures, see "Dow Jones Industrial Average All-Time Largest One Day Gains and Losses," http://wsj.com/mdc/public/page/2_3024-djia_alltime.html; "Dow Jones Industrial Fast Facts," www.cnn.com/2013/05/31/us/dow-jones-industrial-average-fast-facts/index.html. For job loss figures, see Bureau of Labor Statistics, "Employment, Hours, and Earning from the Current Employment Statistics Survey," http://data.bls.gov/timeseries/CES0000000001?output_view = net_1mth. For information on the collapse of housing prices, see Cohen, Coughlin, and Lopez, "The Boom and Bust of U.S. Housing Prices from Various Geographic Perspectives." For information on the credit market freeze, see Gretchen Morgenson, "U.S. Lenders Freeze Home Equity Credit Lines," *New York Times,* April 13, 2008, www.nytimes.com/2008/04/13/business/worldbusiness/13iht-morgen14.1.11930277.html?pagewanted = all; Kirk Shinkle, "America's Credit Catastrophe," *U.S. News and Report,* October 3, 2008, http://money.usnews.com/money/business-economy/articles/2008/10/03/americas-credit-catastrophe?page = 2; US Department of the Treasury, "The Financial Crisis Response in Charts" (2012).

50. Note that changes in mortgage lending significantly exacerbated the crash. See, for example, Marc Jarsulic, "The Origins of the U.S. Financial Crisis of 2007: How a

House-Price Bubble, a Credit Bubble, and Regulatory Failure Caused the Greatest Economic Disaster since the Great Depression," in *The Handbook of the Political Economy of Financial Crises*, ed. Martin H. Wolfson and Gerald A. Epstein (New York: Oxford University Press, 2013).

51. Ivaylo Petev, Luigi Pistaferri, and Itay Saporta Eksten, "Consumption and the Great Recession: An Analysis of Trends, Perceptions, and Distributional Effects," in *The Great Recession*, ed. David B. Grusky, Bruce Western, and Christopher Wimer (New York: Russell Sage, 2011).

52. Raskin, "Aspects of Inequality in the Recent Business Cycle."

53. Mian and Sufi, "House Prices, Home Equity-Based Borrowing, and the U.S. Household Leverage Crisis."

54. Mian and Sufi, *House of Debt*. Other evidence of the disproportionate wealth impact on the middle class comes from Fabian T. Pfeffer, Sheldon Danziger, and Robert F. Schoeni, "Wealth Disparities before and after the Great Recession," *Annals of the American Academy of Political and Social Science* 650, no. 1 (2013): 98–123; Edward N. Wolff, Lindsay A. Owens, and Esra Burak, "How Much Wealth Was Destroyed in the Great Recession?," in Grusky, Western, and Wimer, *The Great Recession*.

55. Mian and Sufi, *House of Debt*.

56. Daniel Hartley, "Distressed Sales and Housing Prices" (Cleveland, OH: Federal Reserve Bank of Cleveland, 2012).

57. Mian and Sufi, *House of Debt*.

58. Pfeffer, Danziger, and Schoeni, "Wealth Disparities before and after the Great Recession."

59. Atif Mian and Amir Sufi, "What Explains High Unemployment? The Aggregate Demand Channel," Working Paper 17830 (National Bureau for Economic Research, 2012). Note that in a separate paper, they and a coauthor also find that housing net worth shocks negatively impact consumption and that consumption is more adversely affected in zip codes where households were more leveraged entering the Great Recession. See Atif Mian, Kamalesh Rao, and Amir Sufi, "Household Balance Sheets, Consumption, and the Economic Slump," *Quarterly Journal of Economics* 128, no. 4 (2013): 1687–1726.

60. Dynan, "Is a Household Debt Overhang Holding Back Consumption?"

61. Linda Levine, "The Increase in Unemployment since 2007: Is It Cyclical or Structural?" (Washington, DC: Congressional Research Service, 2013).

62. John H. Makin, "The Global Financial Crisis and American Wealth Accumulation: The Fed Needs a Bubble Watch" (Washington, DC: American Enterprise Institute, 2013).

63. The housing price index being referenced here is the S & P/Case-Shiller house price index. Alternative price indices produce different estimates of the percentage decline in housing prices, although all illustrate the same general trend. For both the figure cited here and alternative measures, see Cohen, Coughlin, Lopez, "The Boom and Bust of U.S. Housing Prices from Various Geographic Perspectives."

64. Raskin, "Aspects of Inequality in the Recent Business Cycle."

65. See, for example, Dynan, "Is a Household Debt Overhang Holding Back Consumption?"

66. Author's analysis of Federal Reserve's Flow of Funds data on household and nonprofit liabilities. Other sources have documented this deleveraging process as well, such as Bhutta, "Mortgage Debt and Household Deleveraging." See also Federal Reserve Bank of New York, "Quarterly Report on Household Debt and Credit" (2013).

67. The saving rate referred to here is the NIPA saving rate taken from Bureau of Economic Analysis, "Comparison of Personal Saving in the National Income and Product

Accounts (NIPAs) with Personal Saving in the Flow of Funds Accounts (FFAs)," www.bea
.gov/national/nipaweb/Nipa-Frb.asp. Note that the FFA saving rate available from the
same source also shows an overall similar trend, although it has appeared to recover by a
greater amount following the Great Recession than the NIPA saving rate. For more information on different measures of person saving over time, see Bureau of Economic Analysis, "Alternative Measures of Personal Saving." For disaggregated savings rates, see
Cynamon and Fazzari, "Inequality and Household Finance during the Consumer Age";
Mustafa Akcay and Christopher Cornell, "Scared Straight, U.S. Households Boost Saving," *Moody's Analytics,* December 2, 2009, www.economy.com/dismal/article_free.asp?cid
= 119772&src = msnbc.

68. Cynamon and Fazzari use multiple methods for illustrating how trends in consumption behavior have differed between the bottom 95 percent and the top 5 percent.
They show that while total personal consumption expenditures for the top 5 percent have
surpassed their prerecession levels and are trending upward once again, total personal
consumption expenditures for the bottom 95 percent remain below their 2008 levels.
When looking at consumption expenditures as a share of disposable income, they illustrate how the recession forced households in the bottom 95 percent to significantly
decrease their spending as a percentage of income, while this measure actually increased
significantly for households in the top 5 percent. This is because affluent households were
able to smooth their consumption by temporarily spending a greater percentage of their
income while waiting for their earnings to recover. Households in the bottom 95 percent,
on the other hand, did not have the financial capabilities to smooth their consumption to
this extent because much of their prerecession consumption was fueled by debt accumulation and they lacked the financial assets to continue funding their spending. See Cynamon
and Fazzari, "Inequality, the Great Recession, and Slow Recovery." For additional supporting evidence, see Mustafa Akcay and Christopher Cornell, "Scared Straight, U.S.
Households Boost Saving," and Jesse Bricker and others, "Changes in U.S. Family
Finances from 2007 to 2010: Evidence from the Survey of Consumer Finances," *Federal
Reserve Bulletin* 98, no. 2 (2012): 1–80, table 17.

69. Cynamon and Fazzari, "Inequality, the Great Recession, and Slow Recovery." See
note 68 for a more detailed explanation of their findings.

70. Neil Shah, "U.S. Wealth Rises, But Not All Benefit," *Wall Street Journal,* March 7,
2014, http://online.wsj.com/news/articles/SB20001424052702303824204579423183397213204.

71. See, among others, Raskin, "Aspects of Inequality in the Recent Business Cycle";
Dynan, "Is Household Debt Overhang Holding Back Consumption?"; Cynamon and Fazzari, "Inequality and Household Finance during the Consumer Age."

72. Kevin J. Lansing, "Gauging the Impact of the Great Recession" (San Francisco:
Federal Reserve Bank of San Francisco, 2011); Petev, Pistaferri, and Eksten, "Consumption
and the Great Recession."

73. Weller, "Unburdening America's Middle Class."

74. William C. Dunkelberg and Holly Wade, "Small Business Economic Trends"
(Nashville, TN: National Federation of Independent Business Research Foundation, 2013).
Note that other polls of business leaders have similar findings, including Gallup, "Small
Business Survey Topline" (2013); Sage North America, "Sage SMB Hiring Outlook Survey"
(2013); McKinsey & Company, "Economic Conditions Snapshot, June 2013: McKinsey Global Survey Results" (2013); American Sustainable Business Council, Main Street Alliance,
and Small Business Majority, "Opinion Survey: Business Owners' Opinions on Regulations
and Job Creation" (2012). Additionally, Dennis Jacobe, "Health Costs, Gov't Regulations
Curb Small Business Hiring," *Gallup Economy,* February 15, 2012, www.gallup.com

/poll/152654/Health-Costs-Gov-Regulations-Curb-Small-Business-Hiring.aspx, finds that of small businesses that were not planning to hire additional workers, 71 percent said they weren't doing so in part because they were "worried revenues or sales won't justify adding employees."

75. Phil Izzo, "Dearth of Demand Seen behind Weak Hiring," *Wall Street Journal*, July 18, 2011, http://online.wsj.com/news/articles/SB10001424052702303661904576452181063763332.

76. Brendan Duke and Ike Lee, "Retailer Revelations: Why America's Struggling Middle Class Has Businesses Scared" (Washington, DC: Center for American Progress, 2014).

77. Juan M. Sánchez and Emircan Yurdagul, "Why Are Corporations Holding So Much Cash?," *Regional Economist*, January, 2013, www.stlouisfed.org/publications/re/articles/?id = 2314.

78. Board of Governors of the Federal Reserve System, "Financial Accounts of the United States" (2013).

79. For example, UMass's Christian Weller argues: "High household indebtedness also contributed to slow business investment." See Weller, "Unburdening America's Middle Class." See also Lee Pinkowitz, Rene M. Stulz, and Rohan Williamson, "Is There a U.S. High Cash Holdings Puzzle after the Financial Crisis?," Working Paper 2013–03–07 (Fisher College of Business, 2013); John Melloy, "Firms Have Record $800 Billion of Cash But Still Won't Hire," *CNBC*, June 22, 2011, www.cnbc.com/id/43499606; Chris Burritt, "Cash Piles Up as U.S. CEOs Play Safe with Slow-Growth Economy," *Bloomberg*, May 23, 2013, www.bloomberg.com/news/2013-05-23/cash-piles-up-as-u-s-ceos-play-safe-with-slow-growth-economy.html. For alternative explanations, see Laurie Simon Hodrick, "Are U.S. Firms Really Holding Too Much Cash" (Stanford: Stanford Institute for Economic Policy Research, 2013); Sánchez and Yurdagul, "Why Are Corporations Holding So Much Cash?"

80. Justin Lahart, "Companies Cling to Cash," *Wall Street Journal*, December 10, 2010, http://online.wsj.com/article/SB10001424052748703766704576009501161973480.html.

81. Adam Hersh, "Resilient Jobs Market Needs More Policy Help," *Market Watch*, December7,2012,www.marketwatch.com/story/resilient-jobs-market-needs-more-policy-help-2012-12-07. Job creation started to pick up as this book went to print, but even estimates from this most recent period still indicate that full employment is still several years off. Dean Baker, "Three Paths to Full Employment," *Aljazeera America*, July 8, 2014, http://america.aljazeera.com/opinions/2014/7/full-employment-jobsnumberseconomics.html; International Monetary Fund, "2014 Article IV Consultation with the United States of America Concluding Statement of the IMF Mission," June 2014; Elise Gould, "Much Stronger Job Growth Is Needed If We're Going to See a Healthy Economy Any Time Soon" (Washington, DC: Economic Policy Institute, 2015).

82. In addition to those quoted or cited, see International Monetary Fund, "World Economic Outlook"; Antonio Spilimbergo and others, "Fiscal Policy for the Crisis" (Washington, DC: International Monetary Fund, 2008); Richard Kopcke and Anthony Webb, "How Has the Financial Crisis Affected the Consumption of Retirees?" (Chesnutt Hill, MA: Center for Retirement Research at Boston College, 2013); Veronica Guerrieri and Guido Lorenzoni, "Credit Crises, Precautionary Savings and the Liquidity Trap," Working Paper 17583 (National Bureau of Economic Research, 2011); Gauti Eggertsson and Paul Krugman, "Debt, Deleveraging, and the Liquidity Trap," *Quarterly Journal of Economics* 127, no. 3 (2012): 1469–1518. Furthermore, John T. Harvey, a Texas Christian University professor of economics and Forbes contributor, has stated, "In reality, the reason we are stuck where we are is because the middle class lacks jobs and incomes." See John T.

Harvey, "The Real Job Creators: Consumers," *Forbes,* June 17, 2012, www.forbes.com/sites /johntharvey/2012/06/17/job-creators/.

83. Alan B. Krueger, "The Rise and Consequences of Inequality in the United States," speech, Washington, DC, January 12, 2012.

84. Makin, "The Global Financial Crisis and American Wealth Accumulation."

85. Hanaeur, "Raise Taxes on the Rich to Reward True Job Creators."

86. Stiglitz, *The Price of Inequality.* Elsewhere Stiglitz argues, "Our middle class is too weak to support the consumer spending that has historically driven our economic growth." See Joseph Stiglitz, "Inequality Is Holding Back the Recovery," *New York Times,* January 19, 2013, http://opinionator.blogs.nytimes.com/2013/01/19/inequality-is-holding-back-the-recovery/.

CHAPTER FIVE

1. Steve Jobs, interview with Daniel Morrow, *Smithsonian Institution,* April 20, 1995, http://americanhistory.si.edu/comphist/sj1.html; Scott Gillam, *Steve Jobs: Apple iCon* (Minneapolis: ABDO, 2012).

2. Jobs, interview with Daniel Morrow; Gillam, *Steve Jobs: Apple iCon.*

3. Jobs, interview with Daniel Morrow. Of the college classes he attended, he notes a calligraphy class.

4. Entrepreneur Staff, "Steve Jobs: An Extraordinary Career," *Entrepreneur,* www .entrepreneur.com/article/197538; Walter Isaacson, *Steve Jobs* (New York: Simon & Schuster, 2011).

5. As Gary S. Becker, a Nobel Prize–winning economist and one of the leading scholars of human capital, explained in a speech, "To most of you, capital means a bank account, one hundred shares of IBM, assembly lines or steel plants.... [But] schooling, a computer training course, expenditures on medical care, and lectures on the virtues of punctuality and honesty are capital too in the sense that they … raise earnings." Gary S. Becker, "Human Capital Revisited," in *Human Capital: A Theoretical and Empirical Analysis with Special Reference to Education,* ed. Gary S. Becker (Chicago: University of Chicago Press, 1994). Similarly, as an academic review of the term put it, "The essence of the human capital approach is that people make conscious investments in themselves in the form of education, on-the-job training, health, and migration." Bruce A. Weinberg, "Which Labor Economists Invested in Human Capital? Geography, Vintage, and Participation in Scientific Revolutions," Working Paper (Ohio State University, 2006).

6. World Economic Forum, "The Human Capital Report" (2013).

7. See, for example, Gary M. Galles, "Supply-Side Economics in One Lesson," *Freeman,* July 25, 2013.

8. US Department of the Treasury, "The President's Agenda for Tax Relief," press release, February 9, 2001, www.treasury.gov/press-center/press-releases/Documents /report30652.pdf. Note also that Bush argued more generally that "over the long haul, tax relief will encourage work and innovation." George W. Bush, "Remarks on Signing the Economic Growth and Tax Relief Reconciliation Act of 2001," speech, Washington, DC, June 7, 2001. Note also that Edward Conard, among others, claims that people are more likely to be entrepreneurial when they see other people getting rich because the desire to make more money and have higher status is the "most powerful" motivation for people to take economic risks like starting a businesses or working for a start-up. Edward Conard, *Unintended Consequences: Why Everything You've Been Told about the Economy Is Wrong* (New York: Penguin, 2012).

9. See, for example, Finis Welch, "In Defense of Inequality," *American Economic Review* 89, no. 2 (1999): 1–17; Gary S. Becker, "How Can Inequality Be Good?," *Hoover Digest* 3 (2011), www.hoover.org/publications/hoover-digest/article/83976; Gary S. Becker and Kevin M. Murphy, "The Upside of Income Inequality," *American,* May/June 2007, www.american. com/archive/2007/may-june-magazine-contents/the-upside-of-income-inequality/#FN2. Note that these authors do recognize some downsides to inequality, but still feel it promotes human capital development.

10. For research on credit constraints hindering educational attainment, see, for example, Pedro Carneiro and James J. Heckman, "The Evidence on Credit Constraints in Post-Secondary Schooling," *Economic Journal* 112, no. 482 (2002): 705–734; Bas Jacobs and Sweder J.G. van Wijnbergen, "Capital-Market Failure, Adverse Selection, and Equity Financing of Higher Education," *Public Finance Analysis* 63, no. 1 (2007): 1–32; Lance Lochner and Alexander Monge-Naranjo, "Credit Constraints in Education," *Annual Review of Economics* 4, no. 1 (2012): 225–256; Karnit Flug, Antonio Spilimbergo, and Erik Wachtenheim, "Investment in Education: Do Economic Volatility and Credit Constraints Matter?," *Journal of Development Economics* 55, no. 2 (1998): 465–481. For examples of research that does consider how inequality can hinder growth, see, for example, Oded Galor and Omer Moav, "From Physical to Human Capital Accumulation: Inequality and the Process of Development," *Review of Economic Studies* 71, no. 4 (2004): 1001–1026; Oded Galor, "Inequality, Human Capital Formation and the Process of Development," Working Paper 17058 (National Bureau of Economic Research, 2011); Philippe Aghion, Eve Caroli, and Cecilia Garcia-Penalosa, "Inequality and Economic Growth: The Perspective of the New Growth Theories," *Journal of Economic Literature* 37, no. 4 (1999): 1615–1660; Roberto Perotti, "Growth, Income Distribution, and Democracy: What the Data Say," *Journal of Economic Growth* 1, no. 2 (1996): 149–187; Klaus Deininger and Lyn Squire, "New Ways of Looking at Old Issues: Inequality and Growth," *Journal of Development Economics* 57, no. 2 (1998): 259–287.

11. For empirical research on the importance of increasing education levels to economic performance, see, for example, Robert J. Barro, "Economic Growth in a Cross Section of Countries," *Quarterly Journal of Economics* 106, no. 2 (1991): 407–443; Alwyn Young, "The Tyranny of Numbers: Confronting the Statistical Realities of the East Asian Growth Experience," *Quarterly Journal of Economics* 110, no. 3 (1995): 641–680; Ellis W. Tallman and Ping Wang, "Human Capital and Endogenous Growth Evidence from Taiwan," *Journal of Monetary Economics* 34, no. 1 (1994): 101–124; Eric A. Hanushek and Dongwook Kim, "Schooling, Labor Force Quality, and Economic Growth," Working Paper 5399 (National Bureau of Economic Research, 1995); Yan Wang and Yudong Yao, "Sources of China's Economic Growth, 1952–1999: Incorporating Human Capital Accumulation," *China Economic Review* 14, no. 1 (2003): 32–52; Edward F. Denison, *Trends in American Growth, 1929–1982* (Washington, DC: Brookings Institution, 1985); Alan B. Krueger and Mikael Lindahl, "Education for Growth: Why and for Whom?," *Journal of Economic Literature* 39, no. 4 (2001): 1101–1136; David Card, "The Causal Effect of Education on Earnings," *Handbook of Labor Economics* 3 (1999): 1801–1863; Anna Bernasek, "What's the Return on Education?," *New York Times,* December 11, 2005, www.nytimes.com/2005/12/11/business/yourmoney/11view.html.

12. Theodore W. Schultz, "The Economic Importance of Human Capital in Modernization," *Education Economics* 1, no. 1 (1993): 13–19.

13. Theodore Shultz, for example, has stated that "since human capital invents new forms of physical capital, the former is the key to economic progress." See ibid. Oded Galor and Omer Moav have also worked to develop a theory of economic growth that is premised on the "replacement of physical capital accumulation by human capital accumulation as a prime engine of growth." See Galor and Moav, "From Physical to Human Capi-

tal Accumulation." Similarly, Peter Drucker argued, "Increasingly, the true investment in the knowledge society is not in machines and tools but in the knowledge of the knowledge worker." Peter Drucker, "The Age of Social Transformation," *Atlantic Monthly,* November, 1994. See also Gregory Mankiw, David Romer, and David N. Weil, "A Contribution to the Empirics of Economic Growth," *Quarterly Journal of Economics* 107, no. 2 (1992): 407–437; Jess Benhabib and Mark M. Spiegel, "The Role Of Human Capital in Economic Development Evidence from Aggregate Cross-Country Data," *Journal of Monetary Economics* 34, no. 2 (1994): 143–173.

14. Michael Hout and Alexander James, "Educational Mobility in the United States since the 1930s," in *Whither Opportunity? Rising Inequality, Schools and Children's Life Chances,* ed. Greg J. Duncan and Richard J. Murnane (New York: Russell Sage, 2011).

15. Claudia Goldin and Lawrence F. Katz, *The Race between Education and Technology* (Cambridge, MA: Harvard University Press, 2009); Claudia Goldin and Lawrence F. Katz, "Why the United States Led in Education: Lessons from Secondary School Expansion, 1910 to 1940," Working Paper 6144 (National Bureau of Economic Research, 1997); Claudia Goldin and Lawrence Katz, "The Future of Inequality" (Washington, DC: Milken Institute, 2009), describe how the United States used to be a leader in high school achievement. According to Organisation for Economic Co-Operation and Development, "Education at a Glance 2013: OECD Indicators" (2013), table A3.2.a, the United States was tied for first in graduation rates from tertiary type-A programs (first-time graduates) among OECD and G20 member nations for whom there were values in 1995. Another indicator of how the United States used to outperform the world in terms of college graduation is the percentage of the population age 55–64 holding a college degree. According to table A1.3.a of the same source, when looking at tertiary type-A degrees, the percentage of American 55- to 64-year-olds holding a degree is 31 percent, which is highest among all nations measured.

16. For example, less than half of men now have more education than their fathers and almost 20 percent of men now have less education than their fathers, a figure that is up sharply from the late 1970s. Hout and James, "Educational Mobility in the United States since the 1930s."

17. For US high school graduation rates over time, see Thomas D. Snyder and Sally A. Dillow, "Digest of Education Statistics 2012" (Washington, DC: Department of Education, 2013), table 122. The graduation rate only very recently surpassed its highest previous point of 74.9 percent measured in 1974–1975 and 1975–1976 in the 2008–2009 school year when it reached 75.5 percent. While the measured rate for 1969–1970 was technically even higher at 78.7 percent, the Department of Education will not vouch for that figures accuracy. See "National Study: High School Graduation Rate Highest since 1976," *Associated Press,* January 21, 2013, http://blog.al.com/live/2013/01/national_study_high_school_gra .html. For the most recent international comparisons of upper secondary graduation rates, see Organisation for Economic Co-Operation and Development, "United States—Country Note—Education at a Glance 2013: OECD Indicators" (2013).

18. These figures refer to the United States's ranking in graduation rates from tertiary type-A programs (first-time graduates) among OECD and G20 member nations for whom there were rankings in 1995 and 2011. See Organisation for Economic Co-Operation and Development, "Education at a Glance 2013: OECD Indicators," table A3.2.a.

19. Organisation for Economic Co-Operation and Development, "PISA 2012 Results in Focus: What 15-Year-Olds Know and What They Can Do with What They Know" (2013); National Center for Education Statistics, "Highlights from PISA 2009: Performance of U.S. 15-Year-Old Students in Reading, Mathematics, and Science Literacy in an International Context" (2010).

20. Compared to the top performing countries on the international PISA exams, the United States has both more poor performers and fewer high achievers. See Dennis J. Condron, "Egalitarianism and Educational Excellence: Compatible Goals for Affluent Societies?," *Educational Researcher* 40, no. 2 (2011): 47–55; Organisation for Economic Co-Operation and Development, "PISA 2012 Results in Focus."

21. See Joseph J. Merry, "Tracing the U.S. Deficit in PISA Reading Skills to Early Childhood: Evidence from the United States and Canada," *Sociology of Education* 86, no. 3 (2013): 234–252, table 2. For similar results, see also J. Douglas Willms, "Reading Achievement in Canada and the United States: Findings from the OECD Programme for International Student Assessment" (Quebec, Canada: Human Resources Skills and Development Canada Publications Center, 2004).

22. See Gosta Esping-Andersen's unpublished paper "Equal Opportunities in an Increasingly Hostile World" for similar findings. About 12 percent of American students performed at an "elite" level, compared to 19 percent of students in Finland, while 18 percent of US students scored below minimum proficiency standards, compared to just 7 percent of Finish students. Gosta Esping-Andersen, "Equal Opportunities in an Increasingly Hostile World" (2006).

23. Merry, "Tracing the U.S. Deficit in PISA Reading Skills to Early Childhood."

24. Organisation for Economic Co-Operation and Development, "OECD Skills Outlook 2013: First Results from the Survey of Adult Skills" (2013).

25. According to the Organisation for Economic Co-Operation and Development, in 2011 workers in the United States between the ages of 25 and 64 who possessed a tertiary degree could expect to earn 77 percent more than those with only an upper-secondary education. This compares to an average tertiary education premium of only 64 percent among OECD nations. See Organisation for Economic Co-Operation and Development, "Education at a Glance 2013." See also Organisation for Economic Co-Operation and Development, "United States—Country Note—Education at a Glance 2012: OECD Indicators" (2012); Organisation for Economic Co-Operation and Development, "United States—Country Note—Education at a Glance 2013." For information on how tertiary education premiums have grown over time, see Johnathan James, "The College Wage Premium" (Cleveland, OH: Federal Reserve Bank of Cleveland, 2012), www.clevelandfed.org/research/commentary/2012/2012-10.cfm.

26. John Schmitt and Heather Boushey, "Why the Benefits of a College Education May Not Be So Clear, Especially to Men" (Washington, DC: Center for American Progress, 2010).

27. Though the research indicates that family effects are especially important, it also finds that schools and neighborhoods can matter as well. Richard Kahlenberg, *All Together Now: Creating Middle-Class Schools through Public School Choice* (Washington, DC: Brookings Institution Press, 2001); Amita Chudgar and Thomas F. Luschei, "National Income, Income Inequality, and the Importance of Schools: A Hierarchical Cross-National Comparison," *American Educational Research Journal* 46, no. 3 (2009): 626–658; Anne C. Case and Lawrence F. Katz, "The Company You Keep: The Effects of Family and Neighborhood on Disadvantaged Youths," Working Paper 3705 (National Bureau of Economic Research, 1991); Heather Schwartz, "Housing Policy and School Policy: Economically Integrative Housing Promotes Academic Success in Montgomery County, Maryland" (Washington, DC: Century Foundation, 2010). According to the National Center for Education Statistics's Digest of Education Statistics from 2012, the average yearly tuition charged by private elementary schools in the school year 2007–2008 was $6,733, and the average tuition charged by private high schools was $10,549: amounts that many nonwealthy families may

struggle to pay. See Snyder and Dillow, "Digest of Education Statistics 2012," table 71. For a discussion of these trends, see, for example, Robert Reich, "Private Gain to a Few Trumps Public Good for the Many," *Robert Reich's Blog*, August 22, 2013, http://robertreich .org/post/59021478207.

28. White House Task Force on Middle-Class Families, "Financing the Dream: Securing Affordability for the Middle Class" (2009); White House Task Force on Middle-Class Families, "Barriers to Higher Education" (2009).

29. Neeraj Kaushal, Katherine Magnuson, and Jane Waldfogel, "How Is Family Income Related to Investments in Children's Learning?," in Duncan and Murnane, *Whither Opportunity?*; Kahlenberg, *All Together Now*.

30. Meghan Casserly, "10 Jobs That Didn't Exist 10 Years Ago," *Forbes*, May 11, 2012, www.forbes.com/sites/meghancasserly/2012/05/11/10-jobs-that-didnt-exist-10-years-ago/; Roopika Risam, "Kids Plus Pressure Equals Careers: Independent College Counseling Industry Booms," *Washington Post*, August 9, 2010, www.washingtonpost.com/express /wp/2010/08/09/independent-college-admissions-counselors-capitalize-fay-college- counseling/.

31. Kaushal, Magnuson, and Waldfogel, "How Is Family Income Related to Investments in Children's Learning?"

32. Glenn C. Loury, "Intergenerational Transfers and the Distribution of Earnings," *Econometrica* 49, no. 4 (1981): 843–867; W. Henry Chiu, "Income Inequality, Human Capital Accumulation and Economic Performance," *Economic Journal* 108, no. 466 (1998): 44–59; Oded Galor and Joseph Zeira, "Income Distribution and Macroeconomics," *Review of Economic Studies* 60, no. 1 (1993): 35–52; Flavio Cunha and James J. Heckman, "The Technology of Skill Formation," *American Economic Review* 97, no. 2 (2007): 31–47.

33. Heather Boushey and Alexandra Mitukiewicz, "Job Quality Matters" (Washington, DC: Washington Center for Equitable Growth, 2014).

34. For information on how inequality may result in people living in areas mostly with people of similar incomes, see Richard Fry and Paul Taylor, "The Rise of Residential Segregation by Income" (Washington, DC: Pew Research, 2013); Paul A. Jargowsky, "Take the Money and Run: Economic Segregation in U.S. Metropolitan Areas," *American Sociological Review* 61, no. 6 (1996): 984–998; Tara Watson, "Inequality and the Measurement of Residential Segregation by Income in American Neighborhoods," *Review of Income and Wealth* 55, no. 3 (2009): 820–844; Susan Meyers, "How the Growth in Income Inequality Increased Economic Segregation," Working Paper 0117 (Harris School of Public Policy Studies, 2001); Kjetil Bjorvatn and Andrew W. Cappelen, "Inequality, Segregation, and Redistribution," *Journal of Public Economics* 87, nos. 7–8 (2003): 1657–1679. For information on how residential segregation may harm educational performance, see Jeffrey R. Kling, Jeffrey B. Liebman, and Lawrence F. Katz, "Experimental Analysis of Neighborhood Effects," *Econometrica* 75, no. 1 (2007): 83–119; Schwartz, "Housing Policy and School Policy"; Case and Katz, "The Company You Keep"; Sean F. Reardon, "The Widening Academic Achievement Gap between the Rich and the Poor: New Evidence and Possible Explanations," in Duncan and Murnane, *Whither Opportunity?*; Joseph G. Altonji and Richard K. Mansfield, "The Role of Family, School and Community Characteristics in Inequality in Education and Labor-Market Outcomes," in Duncan and Murnane, *Whither Opportunity?*; Julia Burdick-Will and others, "Converging Evidence for Neighborhood Effects on Children's Test Scores: An Experimental, Quasi-Experimental, and Observational Comparison," in Duncan and Murnane, *Whither Opportunity?*

35. Rob Reich, "Not Very Giving," *New York Times*, September 4, 2013, www.nytimes .com/2013/09/05/opinion/not-very-giving.html?_r = 0.

36. According to the OECD, "The United States is one of only three OECD countries in which, for example, socio-economically disadvantaged schools have to cope with less favourable student-teacher ratios than socio-economically advantaged schools," from Organisation for Economic Co-Operation and Development, "Viewing Education in the United States through the Prism of PISA" (2010). For more details on the various factors that lead to inequality in school spending, see Bruce D. Baker and Sean P. Corcoran, "Stealth Inequities of School Funding: How State and Local School Finance Systems Perpetuate Inequitable Student Spending" (Washington, DC: Center for American Progress, 2012); Diana Epstein, "Measuring Inequity in School Funding" (Washington, DC: Center for American Progress, 2010). For examples of states that have prioritized cutting taxes for businesses and wealthy individuals over investing in education, see David Callahan and J. Mijin Cha, *Stacked Deck: How the Dominance of Politics by the Affluent & Business Undermines Economic Mobility in America* (New York: Demos, 2013).

37. Phillip B. Levine and Diane Schanzenbach, "The Impact of Children's Public Health Insurance Expansions on Educational Outcomes," *Forum for Health Economics & Policy* 12, no. 1 (2009): 1–26.

38. For more theoretical development of this underinvestment argument, see, for example, Thomas Gall, Patrick Legros, and Andrew F. Newman, "A Theory of Re-Match and Aggregate Performance," Working Paper (Boston University, 2013); Ming Ming Chiu and Lawrence Khoo, "Effects of Resources, Inequality, and Privilege Bias on Achievement: Country, School, and Student Level Analyses," *American Educational Research Journal* 42, no. 4 (2005): 575–603; Ming Ming Chiu, "Effects of Inequality, Family and School on Mathematics Achievement: Country and Student Differences," *Social Forces* 88, no. 4 (2010): 1645–1676; Gosta Esping-Andersen, "Equal Opportunities and the Welfare State," *Contexts* 6, no. 3 (2007): 23–27. Note also that some researchers such as Sean Reardon argue that increasing inequality per se has not caused the income achievement gap; rather, he argues that "a dollar of income (or factors correlated with income) appears to buy more academic achievement than it did several decades ago." Reardon, "The Widening Academic Achievement Gap."

39. For more on noneconomic factors, see, among others, Duncan and Murnane, *Whither Opportunity?*; V.J. Roscigno and J.W. Ainsworth-Darnell, "Race, Cultural Capital and Educational Resources: Persistent Inequalities and Achievement Returns," *Sociology of Education* 72, no. 3 (1999): 158–178; Pamela E. Davis-Kean, "The Influence of Parent Education and Family Income on Child Achievement: The Indirect Role of Parental Expectations and the Home Environment," *Journal of Family Psychology* 19, no. 2 (2005): 294–304; Charles Murray, *Coming Apart: The State of White America, 1960–2010* (New York: Crown, 2012); Annette Lareau, *Unequal Childhoods: Class, Race, and Family Life* (Berkeley: University of California Press, 2011).

40. See Reardon, "The Widening Academic Achievement Gap," figures 5.7 and 5.8. Note that some skeptics maintain that because the income achievement gap was growing before economic inequality started rising, inequality is not a factor in these trends. Evidence casts great doubt on this counterargument. For example, the gap between students at the ninetieth income percentile and those at the fiftieth in both reading and math increased ever so slightly between the 1940s and the 1970s, but then as inequality started rising, it jumped sharply. Similarly, but to a lesser degree, the 90/10 achievement gap grew at a slower rate between the 1940s and the 1970s than it did afterward—and in fact during the 1950s and 1960s appeared to flatten out. Finally, the 50/10 achievement gap on reading shrunk slightly over recent decades, as the poor and middle class have suffered more similar economic fates.

41. Ibid. Note also that international comparisons show that the affluent in the United States score slightly below the affluent in other countries, but middle-class and especially poor students score much below their international peers. For example, see Willms, "Reading Achievement in Canada and the United States."

42. Reardon, "The Widening Academic Achievement Gap."

43. Ibid. Author's analysis of the figures in this paper.

44. Ibid.

45. Sean F. Reardon, "No Rich Child Left Behind," *New York Times,* April 27, 2013, http://opinionator.blogs.nytimes.com/2013/04/27/no-rich-child-left-behind/?_php = true &_type = blogs&_r = 0.

46. Martha J. Bailey and Susan M. Dynarski, "Gains and Gaps: Changing Inequality in U.S. College Entry and Completion," Working Paper 17633 (National Bureau of Economic Research, 2011); Anthony P. Carnevale and Stephen J. Rose, "Socioeconomic Status, Race/Ethnicity, and Selective College Admissions," in *America's Untapped Resource: Low Income Students in Higher Education,* ed. Richard D. Kahlenberg (New York: Century Foundation Press, 2004); Caroline Hoxby and Christopher Avery, "The Missing 'One-Offs': The Hidden Supply of High-Achieving Low-Income Students" (Washington, DC: Brookings Institution, 2013); Emmeline Zhao, "Fewer Low-Income Students Going to College," *Wall Street Journal,* July 7, 2010, http://blogs.wsj.com/economics/2010/07/07/fewer-low-income-students-going-to-college/; Daron Acemoglu and J.-S. Pischke, "Changes in the Wage Structure, Family Income, and Children's Education," *European Economic Review* 45, nos. 4–6 (2001): 890–904.

47. Bailey and Dynarski, "Gains and Gaps."

48. Martha J. Bailey and Susan M. Dynarski, "Inequality in Postsecondary Education," in Duncan and Murnane, *Whither Opportunity?*

49. See Mary Ann Fox, Brooke A. Connolly, and Thomas D. Snyder, "Youth Indicators 2005: Trends in the Well-Being of American Youth" (Washington, DC: US Department of Education, 2005), for underlying data. For analysis of this data, see White House Task Force on Middle-Class Families, "Barriers to Higher Education"; Elise Gould, "High-Scoring, Low-Income Students No More Likely to Complete College Than Low-Scoring, Rich Students," *Economic Policy Institute,* March 9, 2012, www.epi.org/blog /college-graduation-scores-income-levels/. For another paper arguing that cognitive differences don't explain the gap, see Bailey and Dynarski, "Gains and Gaps."

50. Alexandria Walton Radford, *Top Student, Top School? How Social Class Shapes Where Valedictorians Go to College* (Chicago: University of Chicago Press, 2013).

51. This figure refers to the percentage of the entering classes of the top 146 highly selective colleges coming from the bottom three income quartiles, which was found to be 26 percent by Anthony Carnevale and Stephen Rose. See Carnevale and Rose, "Socioeconomic Status, Race/Ethnicity, and Selective College Admissions." For more on class-based differences at elite colleges, see John Jerrim, "Family Background and Access to 'High Status' Universities" (London: Sutton Trust, 2013).

52. Thomas Piketty, *Capital in the Twenty-First Century* (Cambridge, MA: Harvard University Press, 2014).

53. Harvard University Center on the Developing Child, "InBrief: The Science of Early Childhood Development" (2011); David Edie and Deborah Schmid, "Brain Development and Early Learning: Research on Brain Development" (Madison: Wisconsin Council on Children and Families, 2013).

54. Michael Greenstone and others, "Thirteen Economic Facts about Social Mobility and the Role of Education" (Washington, DC: Hamilton Project, 2013). In this report the

authors state, "At the earliest ages, there is almost no difference in cognitive ability between high- and low-income individuals. Figure 4 shows the impact of a family's socio-economic status—a combination of income, education, and occupation—on the cognitive ability of infants between eight and twelve months of age, as measured in the Early Child-hood Longitudinal Survey." Other studies that examine similar questions from a different perspective find that only a relatively small degree of cognitive skills are inherited. See also Samuel Bowles and Herbert Gintis, "The Inheritance of Economic Status," *Journal of Economic Perspectives* 16, no. 3 (2002): 3–30; Anders Björklund, Markus Jäntti, and Gary Solon, "Influences and Nurture on Earnings Variation: A Report on a Study of Various Sibling Types in Sweden," in *Unequal Chances: Family Background and Economic Success,* ed. Samuel Bowles, Herbert Gintis, and Melissa Osborne Groves (Princeton, NJ: Princeton University Press, 2005). Note that even cognitive abilities at a very young age may be due not solely to genetics, but also to health differences during pregnancy, which are corre-lated with income. See Janet Currie, "Inequality at Birth: Some Causes and Conse-quences," *American Economic Review* 101, no. 3 (2011): 1–22.

55. Note that some try to make claims that the children of the wealthy are genetically smarter. For example, Gregory Mankiw, when commenting on graphs showing the corre-lation between student test scores and parental wealth, has stated that one likely explana-tion for these trends is parental genetics. See Gregory Mankiw, "The Least Surprising Correlation of All Time," *Greg Mankiw's Blog,* August 28, 2009, http://gregmankiw .blogspot.com/2009/08/least-surprising-correlation-of-all.html. Among the best-known works attempting to explain such relationships between performance, intelligence, and genetics is *The Bell Curve,* written by Richard Herrnstein and Charles Murray. See Richard Herrnstein and Charles Murray, *The Bell Curve: Intelligence and Class Structure* (New York: First Free Press, 1996).

56. The labor force participation rate of women with children under the age of six increased from 39.0 percent in 1975 to 65.3 percent in 2000, and has hovered around that level ever since. As of 2011, it stood at 64.2 percent according to the Bureau of Labor Statis-tics. See Bureau of Labor Statistics, "Women in the Labor Force: A Databook" (2013). For additional information on the increasing importance of working mothers as breadwinners and their need for affordable child care, see Sarah Jane Glynn, Jane Farrell and Nancy Wu, "The Importance of Preschool and Child Care for Working Mothers" (Washington, DC: Center for American Progress, 2013); Sarah Jane Glynn, "The New Breadwinners: 2010 Update" (Washington, DC: Center for American Progress, 2012). See also Lynda Laughlin, "Who's Minding the Kids? Child Care Arrangements: Spring 2011" (Washing-ton, DC: US Department of Commerce, 2011).

57. Author's calculation based on Census Bureau figures. According to the Census Bureau, after adjusting for inflation, average weekly child care costs paid by families with employed mothers grew from $84 per week in 1985 to $143 per week in 2011. Laughlin, "Who's Minding the Kids?"

58. US Census Bureau, "Who's Minding the Kids? Child Care Arrangements: 2011—Detailed Tables: Table 6," www.census.gov/hhes/childcare/data/sipp/2011/tables.html.

59. Jane Waldfogel, "The Role of Family Policies in Antipoverty Policy," *Focus* 26, no. 2 (2009): 50–55; Sarah Jane Glynn and Jane Farrell, "The United States Needs to Guaran-tee Paid Maternity Leave" (Washington, DC: Center for American Progress, 2013); Juliana Herman, Sasha Post, and Scott O'Halloran, "The United States Is Far Behind Other Countries on Pre-K" (Washington, DC: Center for American Progress, 2013).

60. Organisation for Economic Co-Operation and Development, "Education at a Glance 2013: OECD Indicators."

61. Greg J. Duncan and Katherine Magnuson, "The Nature and Impact of Early Achievement Skills, Attention Skills, and Behavior Problems," in Duncan and Murnane, *Whither Opportunity?*; Sean F. Reardon, "The Widening Income Achievement Gap," *Faces of Poverty* 70, no. 8 (2013): 10–16.

62. Reardon, "No Rich Child Left Behind."

63. For information on the wealthy reading more to their children, see Richard J. Coley, "An Uneven Start: Indicators of Inequality in School Readiness" (Princeton, NJ: Educational Testing Service, 2002). For the importance of preschool, see Greg J. Duncan and Aaron J. Sojourner, "Can Intensive Early Childhood Intervention Programs Eliminate Income-Based Cognitive and Achievement Gaps?," *Journal of Human Resources* 48, no. 4 (2013): 945–968; James J. Heckman, "Policies to Foster Human Capital," *Research in Economics* 54, no. 1 (2000): 1–48; James J. Heckman, "The Economics of Inequality: The Value of Early Childhood Education," *American Educator* 35, no. 1 (2011): 31–35.

64. Merry, "Tracing the U.S. Deficit in PISA Reading Skills to Early Childhood."

65. Ibid.

66. Chiu and Khoo, "Effects of Resources, Inequality, and Privilege Bias"; Condron, "Egalitarianism and Educational Excellence"; Richard Wilkinson and Kate Pickett, *The Spirit Level: Why Greater Equality Makes Societies Stronger* (London: Bloomsbury, 2009); Dennis J. Condron, "Affluence, Inequality, and Educational Achievement: A Structural Analysis of 97 Jurisdictions across the Globe," *Sociological Spectrum: Mid-South Sociological Association* 33, no. 1 (2013): 73–97; Ming Ming Chiu and Zeng Xihua, "Family and Motivation Effects on Mathematics Achievement: Analyses of Students in 41 Countries," *Learning and Instruction* 18, no. 4 (2008): 321–336; Ming Ming Chiu and Lawrence Khoo, "A New Method for Analyzing Sequential Processes: Dynamic Multilevel Analysis," *Small Group Research* 36, no. 5 (2005): 600–631; Chiu, "Effects of Inequality, Family and School on Mathematics Achievement."

67. Condron, "Egalitarianism and Educational Excellence."

68. Ibid.; Chiu and Xihua, "Family and Motivation Effects on Mathematics Achievement"; Chiu and Khoo, "Effects of Resources, Inequality, and Privilege Bias on Achievement"; Chiu, "Effects of Inequality, Family and School on Mathematics Achievement"; Wilkinson and Pickett, *The Spirit Level;* Pantelis Kammas, Anastasia Litina, and Theodore Palivos, "The Quality of Public Education in Unequal Societies: The Role of Tax Institutions," MPRA Paper 52193 (Munich University Library, 2013).

69. Chiu, "Effects of Inequality, Family and School on Mathematics Achievement."

70. David Madland and Nick Bunker, "The Middle Class Is Key to a Better-Educated Nation: A Stronger Middle Class Is Associated with Better Educational Outcomes" (Washington, DC: Center for American Progress, 2011).

71. McKinsey & Company, "The Economic Impact of the Achievement Gap in America's Schools" (2009). For more general research on the relationship between educational inequality and economic growth, see Amparo Castelló and Rafael Doménech, "Human Capital Inequality and Growth: Some New Evidence," *Economic Journal* 112, no. 478 (2002): C187–C200; Amparo Castello-Climent, "Channels through which Human Capital Inequality Influences Economic Growth," *Journal Of Human Capital* 4, no. 4 (2010): 394–450.

72. Eric A. Hanushek and Ludger Woessman, "How Much Do Educational Outcomes Matter in OECD Countries?" *Economic Policy* 26, no. 67 (2011): 427–491.

73. Ibid.

74. United Nations, "Development of Health Systems in the Context of Enhancing Economic Growth towards Achieving the Millennium Development Goals in Asia and the Pacific" (2007).

75. Specific figure is from Kwabena Gyimah-Brempon, "Health Human Capital and Economic Growth in Sub-Saharan African and OECD Countries," *Quarterly Review of Economics and Finance* 44, no. 2 (2004): 298–320. For other estimates of the impact of health on the economy, see also David E. Bloom, David Canning, and Jaypee Sevilla, "The Effect of Health on Economic Growth: A Production Function Approach," *World Development* 32, no. 1 (2004): 1–13; Anne Case, Angela Fertig, and Chirstina Paxson, "From Cradle to Grave? The Lasting Impact of Childhood Health and Circumstance," Working Paper 9788 (National Bureau of Economic Research, 2003); Levine and Schanzenbach, "The Impact of Children's Public Health Insurance on Educational Outcomes"; Anne Case and Christina Paxson, "Stature and Status: Height, Ability and Labor Market Outcomes," *Journal of Political Economy* 116, no. 3 (2008): 499–532. Amar A. Hamoudi and Jeffrey D. Sachs "Economic Consequences of Health Status: A Review of the Evidence," Working Paper 30 (Harvard University Center for International Development, 1999); Paolo C. Belli, Flavio Bustreo, and Alexander Preker, "Investing in Children's Health: What Are the Economic Benefits?," *Bulletin of the World Health Organization* 83, no. 10 (2005): 777–784; Robert J. Barro, "Health and Economic Growth," *Annals of Economics and Finance* 14, no. 2 (2013): 329–366.

76. For a review, see, for example, Barbara Wolfe, John Mullahy, and Stephanie Robert, "Health, Income, and Inequality: Review and Redirection" (New York: Russell Sage, 2003). For increased income-based differences, see Hilary Waldron, "Trends in Mortality Differentials and Life Expectancy for Male Social Security-Covered Workers, by Socioeconomic Status," *Social Security Bulletin* 67, no. 3 (2007): 1–28; Barry P. Bosworth and Kathleen Burke, "Differential Mortality and Retirement Benefits in the Health and Retirement Study" (Washington, DC: Brookings Institution, 2014).

77. Richard Wilkinson and Kate Pickett, "Income Inequality and Population Health: A Review and Explanation of the Evidence," *Social Science and Medicine* 62, no. 7 (2006): 1768–1784; Richard Wilkinson, "Income Distribution and Life Expectancy," *British Medical Journal* 34, no. 6820 (1992): 165–168; G.A. Kaplan and others, "Inequality in Income and Mortality in the United States: Analysis of Mortality and Potential Pathways," *British Medical Journal* 312, no. 7037 (1996): 999–1003; Bruce P. Kennedy, Ichiro Kawachi, and Deborah Prothrow-Stith, "Income Distribution and Mortality: Cross Sectional Ecological Study of the Robin Hood Index in the United States," *British Medical Journal* 312, no. 7037 (1996): 1004–1007; Robert S. Kahn and others, "State Income Inequality, Household Income, and Maternal Mental and Physical Health: Cross Sectional National Survey," *British Medical Journal* 321, no. 7272 (2000): 1311–1315; Tony Blakely and Alistair Woodward, "Income Inequality and Mortality in Canada and the United States: Third Explanation Is Plausible," *British Medical Journal* 321, no. 7275 (2000): 1532–1533; Nancy A. Ross and others, "Relation between Income Inequality and Mortality in Canada and in the United States: Cross Sectional Assessment Using Census Data and Vital Statistics," *British Medical Journal* 320, no. 7239 (2000): 898–902; Susan E. Meter and Ankur Sarin, "Some Mechanisms Linking Economic Inequality and Infant Mortality," *Social Science and Medicine* 60, no. 3 (2005): 439–455; Norman J. Waitzman and Ken R. Smith, "Separate but Lethal: The Effects of Economic Segregation on Mortality in Metropolitan America," *Milbank Quarterly* 76, no. 3 (1998): 341–373; Andrew Steptoe and others, "Depressive Symptoms, Socio-Economic Background, Sense of Control, and Cultural Factors in University Students from 23 Countries," *International Journal of Behavioral Medicine* 14, no. 2 (2007): 97–107.

78. National Research Council of the National Academies, "Explaining Divergent Levels of Longevity in High-Income Countries" (2011).

79. See ibid., figures 1.5 and 1.6.

80. See Steven H. Wolf and Laudan Aron, eds., "U.S. Health in International Perspective: Shorter Lives, Poorer Health" (Washington, DC: National Academy of Sciences, 2013), esp. figures 1.5 and 1.6.

81. S. Jay Olshansky and others, "Differences in Life Expectancy Due to Race and Educational Differences Are Widening, and Many May Not Catch Up," *Health Affairs* 31, no. 8 (2012): 1803–1803. For reporting on this, see Monica Potts, "What's Killing Poor White Women?," *American Prospect*, September 3, 2013, http://prospect.org/article/whats-killing-poor-white-women. For a critical take, see John Bound and others, "The Implications of Differential Trends in Mortality for Social Security Policy," Paper for the 16th Annual Joint Meeting of the Retirement Research Consortium, August 7–8, 2014.

82. Josh Zumbrun, "The Richer You Are the Older You'll Get," *Wall Street Journal*, April 18, 2014, http://blogs.wsj.com/economics/2014/04/18/the-richer-you-are-the-older-youll-get/; Barry P. Bosworth, and Kathleen Burke, "Differential Mortality and Retirement Benefits in the Health and Retirement Study" (Washington: Brookings, 2014), www.brookings.edu/research/papers/2014/04/differential-mortality-retirement-benefits-bosworth.

83. Sarah Donahue and others, "Trends in Birth Weight and Gestational Length Among Singleton Term Births in the United States: 1990s," *Obstetrics and Gynecology* 115, no. 2 (2010): 357–364.

84. Angus Deaton, *The Great Escape: Health, Wealth and the Origins of Inequality* (Princeton, NJ: Princeton University Press, 2013).

85. For some of the debate, see Wolfe, Mullahy, and Robert, "Health, Income, and Inequality"; Andrew Leigh, Christopher Jencks, and Timothy M. Smeeding, "Health and Economic Equality," in *The Oxford Handbook of Economic Inequality*, ed. Wiemer Salvera, Brian Nolan, and Timothy Smeeding (Oxford: Oxford University Press, 2011); Karen Rowlingston, "Does Income Inequality Cause Health and Social Problems?" (York, UK: Joseph Rowntree Foundation, 2011); Ichiro Kawachi and others, "Social Capital, Income Inequality, and Mortality," *American Journal of Public Health* 87, no. 9 (1997): 1491–1498; Timothy M. Smeeding and Peter Gottschalk, "Cross-National Income Inequality: How Great Is It and What Can We Learn from It?," *International Journal of Health Services* 29, no. 4 (1999): 733–741; Leiyu Shi and others, "Income Inequality, Primary Care, and Health Indicators," *Journal of Family Practice* 48, no. 4 (1999): 275–84; S.V. Subramanian and Ichiro Kawachi, "Income Inequality and Health: What Have We Learned So Far?," *Epidemiologic Reviews* 26, no. 1 (2004): 78–91; Peter Lobmayer and Richard G. Wilkinson, "Inequality, Residential Segregation by Income, and Mortality in US Cities," *Journal of Epidemiology and Community Health* 56, no. 3 (2002): 183–187; Jennifer M. Mellor and Jeffrey Milyo, "Income Inequality and Health Status in the United States: Evidence from the Current Population Survey," *Journal of Human Resources* 37, no. 3 (2002): 510–539; Zhuo Chen and Carol Gotway Crawford, "The Role of Geographic Scale in Testing the Income Inequality Hypothesis as an Explanation of Health Disparities," *Social Science and Medicine* 75, no. 6 (2012): 1022–1031; Rand D. Conger and M. Brent Donnellan, "An Interactionist Perspective on the Socioeconomic Context of Human Development," *Annual Review of Psychology* 58, no. 1 (2007): 175–199.

86. For example, a review in 2009 of the debate by Andrew Leigh, an economist at the Australian National University, and his coauthors explained, "Achieving more consensus will require more work with better data and better methods than have been usual in the past." Leigh, Jencks, and Smeeding, "Health and Economic Inequality." Note that this review finds little evidence for a causal relationship, but, as it acknowledges, can't observe long-term effects. Many of the studies it cites are also subject to the criticism described in this chapter.

87. For international comparisons, see Elise Gould, and Hilary Wething, "U.S. Poverty Rates Higher, Safety Net Weaker Than in Peer Countries" (Washington, DC: Economic Policy Institute, 2012). For trends over time in the United States, see Center on Budget and Policy Priorities, "Chart Book: The War on Poverty at 50" (Washington, DC: Center on Budget and Policy Priorities, 2014); and Elise Gould, Lawrence Mishel, and Heidi Shierholz, "Already More than a Lost Decade" (Washington, DC: Economic Policy Institute, 2013).

88. National Research Council of the National Academies, "Explaining Divergent Levels of Longevity in High-Income Countries."

89. Rowlingston, "Does Income Inequality Cause Health and Social Problems?"

90. As University of Wisconsin economist Barbara Wolfe and her coauthors write, "We suspect that there are complex causal links between income inequality, income level, racial distribution, residential segregation, and social and political decision-making that provide a more complete picture of how and why income and income inequality are related to health." Wolfe, Mullahy and Robert, "Health, Income and Inequality." See also John W. Lynch and others, "Income Inequality and Mortality: Importance to Health of Individual Income, Psychosocial Environment, or Material Conditions," *British Medical Journal* 320, no. 7243 (2000): 1200–1204. In addition, it is important to note that some studies have inconclusive findings because of the methods they use. For example, economic inequality shapes the political environment, and political decisions determine government policies on healthcare and hospital regulations, which in turn affect health outcomes. But studies critical of the direct connection between inequality and health are often designed in a way that makes them likely to miss these kinds of longer-term, indirect impacts. One element of this methodological debate that is not highlighted much in the reviews, such as the one by Wolfe, Mullahy, and Robert, is that the emphasis on certain kinds of statistical methods may be leading some researchers to discount the impact of inequality. For example, Andrew Leigh, Christopher Jencks, and Timothy M. Smeeding, in "Health and Economic Equality," only review estimates that include country and year fixed effects and ignore other kinds of studies. Yet this may bias them against finding any impact. Some articles on the use of fixed effects caution that there is no hard and fast rule for using fixed effects and note that fixed effects can soak up most of the explanatory power of slowly changing variables such as inequality or political systems. See Nathaniel Beck and Jonathan N. Katz, "Throwing Out the Baby with the Bath Water: A Comment on Green, Kim, and Yoon," *International Organization* 55, no. 2 (2001): 487–495; Nathaniel Beck, "Time-Series Cross-Section Data: What Have We Learned in the Last Few Years?," *Annual Review of Political Science* 4 (2001): 271–293. Further, several very recent studies that attempt to address the data and methodological concerns raised by skeptics provide support for the argument that inequality leads to worse health outcomes. As Naoki Kondo, a professor at the University of Tokyo's Graduate School of Medicine, and her coauthors wrote in an article from 2012, "Studies having higher average income inequality, using more recent data, and incorporating a time lag between income inequality and health outcomes are likely to show a more consistent association between income inequality and poor health." Naoki Kondo and others, "Income Inequality and Health: The Role of Population Size, Inequality Threshold, Period Effects and Lag Effects," *Journal of Epidemiology and Community Health* 66, no. 6 (2012). See also Tse-Chuan Yang and others, "Using Quantile Regression to Examine the Effects of Inequality across the Mortality Distribution in the U.S. Counties," *Social Science and Medicine* 74, no. 12 (2012): 1900–1910; Terese J. Lund and Eric Dearing, "Is Growing Up Affluent Risky for Adolescents or Is the Problem Growing Up in an Affluent Neighborhood?," *Journal of Research on Adolescence* 23, no. 2 (2013): 267–282;

Martin Karlsson, Therese Nilsson, Carl H. Lyttkens, and George Lesson, "Income Inequality and Health: Importance of a Cross-Country Perspective," *Social Science & Medicine* 70, no. 6 (2010): 875–885; Roberta Torre and Mikko Myrskylä, "Income Inequality and Population Health: A Panel Data Analysis on 21 Developed Countries," Working Paper 2011–006 (Max Planck Institute for Demographic Research, 2011); Roman Pabayo, Ichiro Kawachui, and Stephen E. Gilman, "Income Inequality among American States and the Incidence of Major Depression" (Boston, MA: Harvard School of Public Health, 2013).

91. National Research Council of the National Academies, "Explaining Divergent Levels of Longevity in High-Income Countries."

92. André van Stel, Martin Carree, and Roy Thurik, "The Effect of Entrepreneurial Activity on National Economic Growth," *Small Business Economics* 24, no. 3 (2005): 311–321; William J. Baumol, "Entrepreneurship and Innovation: The (Micro) Theory of Price and Profit," presented at 2008 American Economic Association Conference (2008); David B. Audretsch, Max C. Keilbach, and Erik E. Lehrman, *Entrepreneurship and Economic Growth* (Oxford: Oxford University Press, 2006); David B. Audretsch, Max C. Keilbach, and Erik E. Lehrman, "The Knowledge Spillover Theory of Entrepreneurship and Economic Growth," *Economia e Politica Industriale* 33, no. 3 (2006): 25–45.

93. Paul A. Geroski, "Entry, Innovation, and Productivity Growth," *Review of Economics and Statistics* 71, no. 4 (1989): 572–578; Stephen J. Nickell, "Competition and Corporate Performance," *Journal of Political Economy* 104, no. 4 (1996): 724–746; Stephen J. Nickell, Daphne Nicolitsas, and Neil Dryen, "What Makes Firms Perform Well?," *European Economic Review* 41, no. 3 (1997): 783–796. The term "creative destruction" is most often identified with the work of economist Joseph Schumpter, who best described his vision of the process in his book *Capitalism, Socialism, and Democracy,* published in 1942. Joseph Schumpter, *Capitalism, Socialism, and Democracy* (New York: Routledge, 1976).

94. John C. Haltiwanger, Ron S. Jarmin, and Javier Miranda, "Who Creates Jobs? Small vs. Large vs. Young," Working Paper 16300 (National Bureau of Economic Research, 2010).

95. Van Stel, Carree, and Thurik, "The Effect of Entrepreneurial Activity." Their results are for wealthy countries like the United States. Similarly, University of Chicago economist Kevin Murphy and his coauthors explain that entrepreneurs "improve the technology in the line of business they pursue, and as a result, productivity and income grow." Kevin M. Murphy, Andrei Shleifer, and Robert W. Vishny, "The Allocations of Talent: Implications for Growth," *Quarterly Journal of Economics* 106, no. 2 (1991): 503–530.

96. For example, measurement of self-employment can capture people who are really just nonstandard employees of a larger firm, rather than entrepreneurs. Similarly, measurement of new establishments may reflect not just entrepreneurial activity, but also new activity by divisions of larger firms.

97. Barry C. Lynn and Lina Khan, "Out of Business: Measuring the Decline of American Entrepreneurship" (Washington, DC: New America Foundation, 2012).

98. Ian Hathaway and Robert E. Litan, "Declining Business Dynamism in the United States: A Look at States and Metros" (Washington, DC: Brookings Institution, 2014). For media accounts of trends, see, for example, Sarah Stodola, "The American Entrepreneur: A Dying Breed?," *Fiscal Times,* May 3, 2012, www.thefiscaltimes.com/Articles/2012/05/03/The-American-Entrepreneur-A-Dying-Breed; Ben Casselman, "Risk-Averse Culture Infects U.S. Workers, Entrepreneurs," *Wall Street Journal,* June 2, 2013, http://online.wsj.com/article/SB10001424127887324031404578481162903760052.html.

99. Lynn and Khan, "Out of Business"; John Haltiwanger, Ron Jarmin, and Javier Miranda, "Business Dynamics Statistics Briefing: Where Have All the Young Firms

Gone?" (Kansas City, MO: Kauffman Foundation, 2012); Camilo Mondragón-Vélez, "How Does Middle-Class Financial Health Affect Entrepreneurship in America" (Washington, DC: Center for American Progress, forthcoming), comes to similar results. Other analysis shows a decline in self-employment over a longer time period. For example, see David G. Blanchflower, "Entrepreneurship in the United States," Working Paper 3130 (Institute for the Study of Labor, 2007). For evidence on the scale of employee misclassification, a route some large employers have chosen to cut down on healthcare costs and taxes, see Government Accountability Office, "Employee Misclassification: Improved Coordination, Outreach, and Targeting Could Better Ensure Detection and Prevention" (2009).

    100. Haltiwanger, Jarmin, and Miranda, "Business Dynamics Statistics Briefing."

    101. Ibid.

    102. John Schmitt and Nathan Lane, "An International Comparison of Small Business Employment" (Washington, DC: Center for Economic and Policy Research, 2009). See also David G. Blanchflower, "Entrepreneurship in the United States," *Annals of Finance 5*, nos. 3–4 (2009): 361–396 and Jordan Weissmann, "Think We're the Most Entrepreneurial Country in the World? Not So Fast," *Atlantic,* October 2 2012, www.theatlantic.com/business/archive/2012/10/think-were-the-most-entrepreneurial-country-in-the-world-not-so-fast/263102/.

    103. In addition to the citations previously mentioned, see Jose Ernesto Amoros and Niels Bosma, "Global Entrepreneurship Monitor: 2013 Global Report" (Global Entrepreneurship Monitor, 2014), www.gemconsortium.org/docs/download/3106. Similarly, the Organisation for Economic Co-Operation and Development, "Entrepreneurship at a Glance 2013" (2013), finds that the United States fares fairly well in new enterprise creations, but is near the bottom in the percentage of its workforce employed by very small businesses.

    104. For literature on the correlates of entrepreneurship, see David G. Blanchflower, "Self-Employment in OECD Countries," *Labour Economics* 7, no. 5 (2000): 471–505; Mondragón-Vélez, "How Does Middle-Class Financial Health Affect Entrepreneurship in America"; Heather Boushey and Adam Hersh, "Middle Class Series: The American Middle Class Series, Income Inequality, and the Strength of Our Economy: New Evidence in Economics" (Washington, DC: Center for American Progress, 2012); Stanley Cromie, "Assessing Entrepreneurial Inclinations: Some Approaches and Empirical Evidence," *European Journal of Work and Organizational Psychology* 9, no. 1 (2000): 7–30. And for an alternative argument on the decline of entrepreneurship, see explanations offered by Scott Shane in Stodola, "The American Entrepreneur." But note that part of his explanation—rising healthcare costs—is related to the financial weakness of the middle class. And for additional alternative explanations, see Casselman, "Risk-Averse Culture Infects U.S. Workers, Entrepreneurs."

    105. Lori Ioannou, "Small Business Still Reeling from Credit Crunch," *CNBC,* September 5, 2013, www.cnbc.com/id/101009116; Ami Kassar, "The State of Small-Business Lending," *New York Times,* January 8, 2013, http://boss.blogs.nytimes.com/2013/01/08/the-state-of-small-business-lending/?_r = 0. Note that some in the banking industry argue that there is no lack of supply when it comes to loans for small businesses, but others contend that while this may be true for more established and middle-sized firms, credit availability is still lacking for very small businesses and start-ups. See J.D. Harrison, "Bankers, Business Owners Offer Starkly Different Takes on Loan Availability," *Washington Post,* June 11, 2013, http://articles.washingtonpost.com/2013–06–11/business/39910264_1_bank-loan-lending-jeanne-hulit.

106. David S. Evans and Boyan Jovanovic, "An Estimated Model of Entrepreneurial Choice under Liquidity Constraints," *Journal of Political Economy* 97, no. 4 (1989): 808–827; Frank H. Knight, *Risk, Uncertainty and Profit* (Chicago: University of Chicago Press, 1921); Blanchflower, "Entrepreneurship in the United States"; Robert W. Fairlie and Harry A. Krashinsky, "Liquidity Constraints, Household Wealth, and Entrepreneurship Revisited," *Review of Income and Wealth* 58, no. 2 (2012): 279–306; Robert Shiller, *Macro Markets: Creating Institutions for Managing Society's Largest Economic Risks* (Oxford: Clarendon Press, 1993). See also the results in Alicia Robb and E.J. Reedy, "An Overview of the Kauffman Firm Survey: Results from 2009 Business Activities" (Kansas City, MO: Ewing Marion Kauffman Foundation, 2011). Finally, note that Samuel Bowles, *Microeconomics: Behavior, Institutions and Evolution* (Princeton, NJ: Princeton University Press, 2004), argues that those with higher levels of wealth also get better terms on their loans.

107. Francisco J. Buera, "A Dynamic Model of Entrepreneurship with Borrowing Constraints: Theory and Evidence," *Annals of Finance* 5, no. 3 (2009): 443–464; Camilo Mondragón-Vélez, "The Probability of Transition to Entrepreneurship Revisited: Wealth, Education and Age," *Annals of Finance* 5, no. 3 (2009): 421–441; Camilo Hernan Mondragon, "Entrepreneurship, Human Capital and Wealth," mimeo (Georgetown University, 2007); Mondragón-Vélez, "How Does Middle-Class Financial Health Affect Entrepreneurship in America." Note also that Evans and Jovanovic, "An Estimated Model of Entrepreneurial Choice under Liquidity Constraints," find that wealth has diminishing returns for promoting entrepreneurship, though they do not elaborate on their finding.

108. Buera, "A Dynamic Model of Entrepreneurship."

109. Mondragón-Vélez, "The Probability of Transition to Entrepreneurship Revisited." See also Mondragón-Vélez, "How Does Middle-Class Financial Health Affect Entrepreneurship in America."

110. Vivek Wadhwa and others, "Anatomy of an Entrepreneur: Family Background and Motivation" (Kansas City, MO: Ewing Marion Kauffman Foundation, 2009).

111. Mondragón-Vélez, "How Does Middle-Class Financial Health Affect Entrepreneurship in America." For more anecdotal evidence that middle-class incomes and debt are harming entrepreneurship, see Meera Louis, "Student Debt Puts Young Entrepreneurs on Hold," *Business Insider,* June 20, 2013, www.businessweek.com/articles/2013–06–20/student-debt-puts-young-entrepreneurs-on-hold; Meera Louis, "$1 Trillion Debt Crushes Business Dreams of U.S. Students," *Bloomberg,* June 6, 2013, www.bloomberg.com/news/2013–06–06/-1-trillion-debt-crushes-business-dreams-of-u-s-students.html.

112. Barry C. Lynn and Lina Khan, "The Slow-Motion Collapse of American Entrepreneurship," *Washington Monthly,* July/August 2012, http://newamerica.net/node/69385.

113. For example, the evidence presented in Barry C. Lynn and Lina Khan, "Out of Business: Measuring the Decline of American Entrepreneurship" (Washington, DC: New America Foundation, 2012); Hathaway and Litan, "Declining Business Dynamism in the United States"; and Haltiwanger, Jarmin, and Miranda, "Business Dynamics Statistics Briefing" all show a slight increase in entrepreneurship in the early 2000s, but long-term downward trends.

114. Atif Mian and Amir Sufi, "House Prices, Home Equity-Based Borrowing, and the U.S. Household Leverage Crisis," *American Economic Review* 101, no. 5 (2011): 2132–2156.

115. For information on entrepreneurs generally having higher levels of education, see Mondragón-Vélez, "The Probability of Transition to Entrepreneurship Revisited."

116. Sanjay Goel and Ranjan Karri, "Entrepreneurs, Effectual Logic, and Over-Trust," *Entrepreneurship Theory and Practice* 30, no. 4 (2006): 477–493; Marko Kohtamäki, Tauno

Kekäle, and Riitta Viitala, "Trust and Innovation: from Spin-Off Idea to Stock Exchange," *Creativity and Innovation Management* 13, no. 2 (2004): 75–88; Friederike Welter and others, "Trust Environments and Entrepreneurial Behavior—Exploratory Evidence from Estonia, Germany, and Russia," *Journal of Enterprising Culture* 12, no. 4 (2004): 327–349; David Smallbone and Fergus Lyon, "A Note on Trust, Networks, Social Capital, and Entrepreneurial Behavior," Working Paper 37 (Forschungsstelle Osteuropa, 2002).

117. Lynn and Khan, "The Slow-Motion Collapse of American Entrepreneurship." See also Barry C. Lynn, "Killing the Competition: How the New Monopolies Are Destroying Open Markets," *Harper's*, February 2012, http://harpers.org/archive/2012/02 /killing-the-competition/?single = 1; Stodola, "The American Entrepreneur."

118. Of course, other factors are at work as well, including the influence of Robert Bork. Dylan Matthews, "Antitrust Was Defined by Robert Bork: I Cannot Understate His Influence," *Washington Post*, December 20, 2012, www.washingtonpost.com/blogs /wonkblog/wp/2012/12/20/antitrust-was-defined-by-robert-bork-i-cannot-overstate-his-influence/.

119. Robert W. Fiarlie, Kanika Kapur, and Susan M. Gates, "Is Employer-Based Health Insurance a Barrier to Entrepreneurship?," Working Paper 637 (Rand Corporation, 2010); David Leonhardt, "Opposition to Health Law Is Steeped in Tradition," *New York Times*, December 14, 2010, www.nytimes.com/2010/12/15/business/economy/15leonhardt. html.

120. Herbert McClosky and John Zaller, *The American Ethos: Public Attitudes toward Capitalism and Democracy* (Cambridge, MA: Harvard University Press, 1984); Seymour Martin Lipset, *American Exceptionalism: A Double-Edged Sword* (New York: W. W. Norton, 1996).

121. For information on Steven Jobs, see Edwin J. Feulner, "How Did Steve Jobs Represent American Exceptionalism?," *Heritage Foundation*, October 6, 2011, www.askheritage.org /how-did-steve-jobs-represent-american-exceptionalism/; Cavan Sieczkowski, "Steve Jobs: Innovation, Capitalism, and the American Dream," *International Business Times*, October 12, 2011, www.ibtimes.com/steve-jobs-innovation-capitalism-american-dream-322991. For more on the more modest American Dream, see Sandra L. Hanson and John Zogby, "The Polls—Trends: Attitudes about the American Dream," *Public Opinion Quarterly* 74, no. 3 (2010): 570–584. See also Celinda Lake and others, "Findings from a Survey of Registered Voters" (Washington, DC: Lake Research Partners, 2007); Carol Morello, Peyton M. Craighill, and Scott Clement, "Portrait of the American Dream," *Washington Post*, September 28, 2013, www.washingtonpost.com/local/portraits-of-the-american-dream/2013/09/28 /d13eb892–289c-11e3-bae5-e0807a60a6aa_graphic.html; Sarah Robinson, "Talking about the American Dream: Drew Westen and Celinda Lake," *Campaign for America's Future Blog*, October 4, 2011, http://ourfuture.org/20111004/Talking_About_the_American_Dream_Drew_ Westen_and_Celinda_Lake.

122. James T. Adams, *The Epic of America* (Piscataway, NJ: Little, Brown, 1931).

123. Tom Hertz, "Understanding Mobility in America" (Washington: Center for American Progress, 2006), www.americanprogress.org/wp-content/uploads/issues/2006 /04/Hertz_MobilityAnalysis.pdf.

124. Greenstone and others, "Thirteen Economics Facts on Social Mobility and the Role of Education."

125. Daniel Aaronson and Bhash Mazumder, "Intergenerational Economic Mobility in the U.S., 1940 to 2000," Working Paper 2005–12 (Federal Reserve Bank of Chicago, 2005); Bhashkar Mazumder, "Is Intergenerational Economic Mobility Lower Now Than in the Past?" (Chicago: Federal Reserve Bank of Chicago, 2012); David I. Levine and Bhashkar Mazumder, "Choosing the Right Parents: Changes in the Intergenerational

Transmission of Inequality—between 1980 and the Early 1990s," Working Paper 2002–08 (Federal Reserve Bank, 2002); for additional estimates, see Gary Solon, "Intergenerational Income Mobility in the United States," *American Economic Review* 82, no. 3 (1992): 393–408; Bhashkar Mazumder, "Fortunate Sons: New Estimates of Intergenerational Mobility in the United States Using Social Security Earnings Data," *Review of Economics and Statistics* 87, no. 2 (2005): 235–255. Bhashkar Mazumder and David I. Levine, "The Growing Importance of Family and Community: An Analysis of Changes in the Sibling Correlation in Earnings," Working Paper 2003–24 (Federal Reserve Bank of Chicago, 2003); Bashkhar Mazumder "Sibling Similarities and Economic Inequality in the US," *Journal of Population Economics* 21, no. 3 (2008): 685–701.

126. Raj Chetty, Nathaniel Hendren, Patrick Kline, Emmanuel Saez, and Nicholas Turner, "Is the United States Still a Land of Opportunity? Recent Trends in Intergenerational Mobility," Working Paper 19844 (National Bureau of Economic Research, 2014).

127. Alan B. Krueger, "The Rise and Consequences of Inequality in the United States," speech, Washington, DC, January 12, 2012. Note also that Mazumder, "Sibling Similarities and Economic Inequality in the United States," found that income is "inherited" to an even greater degree than height. Though see also Bruce Sacerdote, "How Large Are the Effects from Changes in Family Environment? A Study of Korean American Adoptees," *Quarterly Journal of Economics* 122, no. 1 (2007): 119–157.

128. Daniel P. McMurrer, Mark Condon, and Isabel V. Sawhill, "Intergenerational Mobility in the United States" (Washington, DC: Urban Institute, 1997). But for a different take, see Gregory Mankiw, "Defending the One Percent," *Journal of Economic Perspectives* 27, no. 3 (2013): 21–34. Note also that even if the amount of inherited ability to have a high income is higher than these estimates, the point remains that a significant degree of income inheritance is not due to abilities.

129. See, for example, Hertz, "Understanding Mobility in America"; Miles Corak, "Do Poor Children Become Poor Adults? Lessons from a Cross Country Comparison of Generational Earnings Mobility," Working Paper 1993 (Institute for the Study of Labor, 2006); Miles Corak, "Chasing the Same Dream, Climbing Different Ladders: Economic Mobility in the United States and Canada" (Washington, DC: Economic Mobility Project, 2010); Jo Blanden, "Cross-Country Rankings in Intergenerational Mobility: A Comparison of Approaches from Economics and Sociology," *Journal of Economic Surveys* 27, no. 1 (2013): 38–73.

130. Jason DeParle, "Harder for Americans to Rise From Lower Rungs," *New York Times,* January 4, 2012, www.nytimes.com/2012/01/05/us/harder-for-americans-to-rise-from-lower-rungs.html.

131. For a summary of these studies, see ibid.

132. See, for example, Miles Corak, "How to Slide Down the 'Great Gatsby Curve'" (Washington, DC: Center for American Progress, 2012); Esping-Andersen, "Equal Opportunities in an Increasingly Hostile World."

133. In addition to those cited, see, for example, Dan Andrews and Andrew Leigh, "More Inequality, Less Social Mobility," *Applied Economics Letters* 16, no. 15 (2009): 1489–1492; Aaronson and Mazumder, "Intergenerational Economic Mobility in the U.S., 1940 to 2000."

134. Organisation for Economic Co-Operation and Development, "Divided We Stand: Why Inequality Keeps Rising" (2011).

135. Corak, "How to Slide Down the 'Great Gatsby Curve.'"

136. Raj Chetty, Nathaniel Hendren, Patrick Kline, and Emmanuel Saez, "Where Is the Land of Opportunity? The Geography of Intergenerational Mobility in the United States," Working Paper 19843 (National Bureau of Economic Research, 2014). See also Ben

Olinsky and Sasha Post, "Middle-Out Mobility: Regions with Larger Middle Classes Have More Economic Mobility" (Washington: Center for American Progress, 2013).

137. As University of Michigan economist Justin Wolfers has written, the Great Gatsby curve "will launch a thousand papers, as economists try to sort out just what these linkages are." Justin Wolfers, "Is Higher Income Inequality Associated with Lower Intergenerational Mobility?," *Freakonomics Blog*, January 1, 2012, http://freakonomics.com/2012/01/19/is-higher-income-inequality-associated-with-lower-intergenerational-mobility/. Note that some such as Scott Winship maintain that the data do not show or show only a very weak relationship between inequality and mobility. But his critiques have been rebutted on numerous occasions, including in Miles Corak, "The Economics of the Great Gatsby Curve," *Miles Corak Blog*, January 17, 2012, http://milescorak.com/2012/01/17/the-economics-of-the-great-gatsby-curve/; and Carter C. Price, "A Mathematical Response to Scott Winship's Analysis of The Great Gatsby Curve" (Washington, DC: Washington Center for Equitable Growth, 2014), http://equitablegrowth.org/2014/01/23/a-mathematical-response-to-scott-winships-analysis-of-the-great-gatsby-curve/.

138. See, for example, John E. Roemer, "Equal Opportunity and Intergenerational Mobility: Going beyond Intergenerational Income Transition Matrices," in *Generational Income Mobility in North America and Europe*, ed. Miles Corak (New York: Cambridge University Press, 2004). See also Murray, *Coming Apart*; Corak, "How to Slide Down the 'Great Gatsby Curve'"; Jo Blanden, "Cross-Country Rankings in Intergenerational Mobility"; DeParle, "Harder for Americans to Rise From Lower Rungs"; Mazumder, "Sibling Similarities and Economic Inequality in the United States."

139. Note that Lane Kenworthy argues that government policy is likely behind much of the relationship between inequality and mobility, finding that the overall relationship is weaker if the Nordic countries are not included in comparisons. Lane Kenworthy, "Inequality, Mobility, Opportunity," *Lane Kenworthy Blog*, January 31, 2012, http://lanekenworthy.net/2012/01/31/inequality-mobility-opportunity/. There is reason to doubt that government policy is the only thing that matters because inequality harms many of the channels of mobility, as discussed in this chapter; but even if government policy were the primary driver of mobility, inequality shapes government policy, as discussed at length in chapter 3.

140. Note that while there is some debate about Head Start's long-run impact on mobility, a significant body of research indicates it has a positive effect. See, for example, Chloe Gibbs, Jens Ludwig, and Douglas L. Miller, "Does Head Start Do Any Lasting Good?," Working Paper 17452 (National Bureau of Economic Research, 2011); David Deming, "Early Childhood Intervention and Life-Cycle Skill Development: Evidence from Head Start," *American Economic Journal: Applied Economics* 1, no. 3 (2009): 111–134; Jens Ludwig and Douglas L. Miller, "Does Head Start Improve Children's Life Chances? Evidence from a Regression Discontinuity Design," Working Paper 11702 (National Bureau of Economic Research, 2005); Eliana Garces, Duncan Thomas, and Janet Currie, "Longer-Term Effects of Head Start," *American Economic Review* 92, no. 4 (2002): 999–1012.

141. See Adam Carasso, Gillian Reynolds, and C. Eugene Steuerle, "How Much Does the Federal Government Spend to Promote Economic Mobility and for Whom?" (Washington, DC: Pew Research, 2008), figure 7. Note that spending on tax breaks (as opposed to direct government spending) to promote mobility has increased since 1980, but these tax breaks overwhelmingly benefit more affluent households, rather than lower- and middle-income families, as explained in chapter 3.

142. Ibid. Note that there are no official measures of mobility spending, so it is fair to quibble with some of their categories, but the differences are so stark that the results won't change.

143. Corak, "How to Slide Down the 'Great Gatsby Curve.'"

144. Pew/Greenberg Quinlan Rosner Research, "Pew Economic Mobility Survey, January 27-February 8, 2009" (2009).

145. Melvin M. Tumin, "Some Principles of Stratification," *American Sociological Review* 18, no. 4 (1953): 387–394.

146. Organisation for Economic Co-Operation and Development, *Divided We Stand*. For a more theoretical examination, see, for example, Tumin, "Some Principles of Stratification."

147. See, for example, Gall, Legros, and Newman, "A Theory of Re-Match and Aggregate Performance"; Ann L. Owen and David N. Weil, "Intergenerational Earnings Mobility, Inequality and Growth," *Journal of Monetary Economics* 41, no. 1 (1998): 71–104; Richard Breen, "Inequality, Economic Growth and Social Mobility," *British Journal of Sociology* 48, no. 3 (1997): 429–449; Roland Benabou, "Heterogeneity, Stratification, and Growth," *American Economic Review* 86, no. 3 (1996): 584–609; Oded Galow and Daniel Tsiddon, "Technological Progress, Mobility, and Economic Growth," *American Economic Review* 87, no. 3 (1997): 363–382.

148. Chaing-Tai Hseih and others, "The Allocation of Talent and U.S. Economic Growth," Working Paper 18693 (National Bureau of Economic Research, 2013).

149. Ibid.

150. Paul Krugman, "Inequality Is a Drag," *New York Times,* August 7, 2014, www .nytimes.com/2014/08/08/opinion/paul-krugman-inequality-is-a-drag.html.

CHAPTER SIX

1. For detailed policy agendas to rebuild the middle class, see, among others, David Madland, "Making Our Middle Class Stronger: 35 Policies to Revitalize America's Middle Class" (Washington, DC: Center for American Progress, 2012); Karla Walter and others, "States at Work: Progressive State Policies to Rebuild the Middle Class" (Washington, DC: Center for American Progress, 2013); Jennifer Erickson and Michael Ettlinger, "300 Million Engines of Growth: A Middle-Out Plan for Jobs, Business, and a Growing Economy" (Washington, DC: Center for American Progress, 2013); Jennifer Erickson, "The Middle-Class Squeeze" (Washington, DC: Center for American Progress, 2014); Josh Bivens and Lawrence Mishel, "The Pay of Corporate Executives and Financial Professional as Evidence of Rents in Top 1 Percent Incomes," *Journal of Economic Perspectives* 27, no. 3 (2013): 57–78; Michael Kumhof and Romain Rancière, "Leveraging Inequality," *Finance and Development* 4, no. 47 (2010): 28–31; Trade Union Congress, "How to Boost the Wage Share" (2013); Robert Kuttner, "The Task Rabbit Economy," *American Prospect,* October 10, 2013, http://prospect.org/article/task-rabbit-economy; Jacob S. Hacker and Nate Leowentheil, "Prosperity Economics: Building an Economy for All" (Washington, DC: Economic Policy Institute, 2012); Eric Liu and Nick Hanauer, "The True Origins of Prosperity," *Democracy: A Journal of Ideas* 29 (2013): 10–17; Thomas Kochan, "The American Jobs Crisis and Implications for Employment Policy: A Call for a Jobs Compact," *Industrial & Labor Relations Review* 66, no. 2 (2013): 291; Dean Baker, *The Loser End of Liberalism* (Washington, DC: Center for Economic and Policy Research, 2011); Samuel Bowles, *The New Economics of Inequality and Redistribution* (New York: Cambridge University Press, 2012).

2. For a synopsis of theories that emphasize skill-biased technological change, globalization, and superstar incomes, see Paul Krugman, "For Richer," *New York Times,* October 20, 2002, www.nytimes.com/2002/10/20/magazine/for-richer.html. For examples of

analyses that emphasize these factors to a strong degree, see Sherwin Rosen, "The Economics of Superstars," *American Economic Review* 71, no. 5 (1981): 845–858; Florence Jaumotte, Subir Lall, and Chris Papageorgiou, "Rising Income Inequality: Technology, or Trade and Financial Globalization?," *IMF Economic Review* 61, no. 2 (2013): 271–309; David Leonhart, "Standard of Living Is in the Shadows as Election Issue," *New York Times*, October 23, 2012, www.nytimes.com/2012/10/24/us/politics/race-for-president-leaves-income-slump-in-shadows.html?ref = politics&_r = 2&.

3. David Leonhardt and Kevin Quealy, "The American Middle Class Is No Longer the World's Richest," *New York Times*, April 22, 2014, www.nytimes.com/2014/04/23/upshot/the-american-middle-class-is-no-longer-the-worlds-richest.html?_r = o. See also Glenn Phelps and Steve Crabtree, "Worldwide Median Household Income about $10,000," *Gallup*, December 16, 2013, www.gallup.com/poll/166211/worldwide-median-household-income-000.aspx.

4. According to a report by the OECD from 2011, growth in real median income in the United States lagged behind that of many other nations between the mid-1980s and the mid-2000s, including Norway, Finland, Sweden, and the Netherlands, among others. See Organisation for Economic Co-Operation and Development, "Society at a Glance 2011: OECD Social Indicators" (2011), figure GE1.1.

5. John Schmitt, "Low-Wage Lessons" (Washington, DC: Center for Economic and Policy Research, 2012).

6. Facundo Alvaredo and others, "The Top 1 Percent in International and Historical Perspective," *Journal of Economic Perspectives* 27, no. 3 (2013): 3–20. Note that other measures of inequality show similar patterns of inequality rising less in other advanced countries. For example, see Organisation for Economic Co-Operation and Development, "An Overview of Growing Income Inequalities in OECD Countries: Main Findings" (2011). Note also that some countries have reduced inequality. See, for example, Nora Lustig, Luis F. Lopez-Calva, and Eduardo Ortiz-Juarez, "Declining Inequality in Latin America in the 2000s: The Cases of Argentina, Brazil and Mexico," *World Development* 44 (2013): 129–141.

7. Note that this stat refers to pretax income. Organization for Economic Co-Operation and Development, "Focus on Top Incomes and Taxation in OECD Countries: Was the Crisis a Game Changer?" (2014).

8. Alvaredo and others, "The Top 1 Percent."

9. Allstate/National Journal, "Heartland Monitor Poll XVI" (2013).

10. "Poll: United We Stand on Wealth Gap," *USA Today*, January 23, 2014, www.usatoday.com/story/news/nation/2014/01/23/pew-poll-obama-wealth-gap-sotu/4777385/.

11. See, for example, Timothy Noah, "Can Bill Clinton Defend His Record on Inequality," MSNBC, May 2, 2014, www.msnbc.com/msnbc/bill-clinton-defends-his-record; and Jim Lindgren, "If We Want More Income Equality, Should We Return to the Economy of George W. Bush?," *Washington Post*, January 28, 2014, figure 2, www.washingtonpost.com/news/volokh-conspiracy/wp/2014/01/28/if-we-want-more-income-equality-should-we-return-to-the-economy-of-george-w-bush/.

12. Alex DeMots, "How to Address Corporate Political Spending" (Washington, DC: Center for American Progress, 2010); Bill Corriher, "Campaign Finance Laws Fails as Corporate Money Floods Judicial Races" (Washington, DC: Center for American Progress, 2013); Azmat Khan, "What's the Future for Campaign Finance Reform?," *Frontline*, November 19, 2012, www.pbs.org/wgbh/pages/frontline/government-elections-politics/big-sky-big-money/whats-the-future-for-campaign-finance-reform/; Michael Beckel, "After

'Citizens United,' Is Constitutional Amendment Needed?," *Center for Public Integrity,* May 23, 2013, www.publicintegrity.org/2012/05/23/8941/after-citizens-united-constitutional-amendment-needed; *Amendment to the Constitution of the United States Relating to Contributions and Expenditures Intended to Affect Elections,* S.J. Res. 29, 112 Cong., 1 sess. (Government Printing Office, 2011).

13. Scott Keyes and others, "Voter Suppression 101" (Washington, DC: Center for American Progress, 2012); Scott Keyes, "Strengthening Our Democracy by Expanding Voter Rights" (Washington, DC: Center for American Progress, 2012); Norman J. Ornstein, "No Need for Election Holiday; Vote on the Weekend," *New York Times,* May 8, 3013, www.nytimes.com/roomfordebate/2013/02/17/which-holidays-should-government-recognize/election-day-should-be-on-the-weekend.

14. Juliana Herman, Sasha Post, and Scott O'Halloran, "The United States Is Far Behind Other Countries on Pre-K" (Washington, DC: Center for American Progress, 2013); Cyntia G. Brown and others, "Investing in Our Children" (Washington, DC: Center for American Progress, 2013).

15. Brown and others, "Investing in Our Children"; Sarah Jane Glynn, Jane Farrell, and Nancy Wu, "The Importance of Preschool and Child Care for Working Mothers" (Washington, DC: Center for American Progress, 2013).

16. Sarah Jane Glynn, "Working Parents Lack of Access to Paid Leave and Workplace Flexibility" (Washington, DC: Center for American Progress, 2012).

17. John Griffith, "Time to Make an Offer FHFA Can't Refuse" (Washington, DC: Center for American Progress, 2012); John Griffith and Jordan Eizenga, "Sharing the Pain and Gain in the Housing Market" (Washington, DC: Center for American Progress, 2012); Sarah Edelman and Julia Gordon, "Why the Nation's Housing Market Needs Mel Watt" (Washington, DC: Center for American Progress, 2013).

18. Atif Mian and Amir Sufi, *House of Debt: How They (and You) Caused the Great Recession, and How We Can Prevent It from Happening Again* (Chicago: University of Chicago Press, 2014).

19. Sarah Audelo and Gurwin Ahuja, "Refinancing Student Loans 101" (Washington, DC: Generation Progress, 2014).

20. David Madland, "Making Our Middle Class Stronger"; David Madland and Karla Walter, "Growing the Wealth" (Washington, DC: Center for American Progress, 2013).

21. Joseph Blasi, Richard Freeman, and Douglas Kruse, "Do Workers Gain by Sharing? Employee Outcomes under Employee Ownership, Profit Sharing and Broad Based Stock Options," in *Shared Capitalism at Work: Employee Ownership, Profit and Gain Sharing, and Broad-Based Stock Options,* ed. Douglas L. Kruse, Richard B. Freeman, and Joseph R. Blasi (Chicago: National Bureau of Economic Research, 2010); Robert Buchele and others, "Show Me the Money: Does Shared Capitalism Share the Wealth?," in Kruse, Freeman, and Blasi, *Shared Capitalism at Work;* Joseph Blasi and Douglas Kruse, "Employee Ownership, Employee Attitudes and Firm Performance: A Review of the Evidence," in *Handbook of Human Resources Management,* ed. Daniel Mitchell, David Lewin, and Mahmood Zaidi (Greenwich, CT: JAI Press, 1997); Rhokeun Park, Douglas Kruse, and James Sesil, "Does Employee Ownership Enhance Firm Survival?," in *Employee Participation, Firm Performance and Survival: Advances in the Economic Analysis of Participatory and Labor Managed Firms,* vol. 8, ed. Virginie Perotin and Andrew Robinson (Greenwich, CT: JAI Press, 2004); Margaret Blair, Douglas Kruse, and Joseph Blasi, "Is Employee Ownership an Unstable Form or a Stabilizing Force?," in *New Relationship: Human Capital and the American Corporation,* ed. Thomas Kochan and Margaret Blair (Washington, DC: Brookings Institution, 2000); Douglas

Kruse, "Research Evidence on the Prevalence and Effects of Employee Ownership," testimony before the Subcommittee on Employer-Employee Relations, House Committee on Education and the Workforce, February 13, 2002, www.ownershipassociates.com/kruse .shtm; Eric Kaarsemaker, "Employee Ownership and Human Resources Management: A Theoretical and Empirical Treatise with a Digression on the Dutch context," PhD diss., Radbound University, 2006; Steven F. Freeman, "Effects of ESOP Adoption and Employee Ownership: Thirty Years of Research and Experience," Working Paper 07–01 (University of Pennsylvania, 2007); Douglas Kruse, Joseph Blasi, and Richard Freeman, "Does Linking Worker Pay to Firm Performance Help the Best Firms Do Even Better?," Working Paper 17745 (National Bureau for Economic Research, 2012).

22. For examples of some similar proposals that seek to expand national service, see Stanley McChrystal, "Lincoln's Call to Service—and Ours: A Proposal That Would Help Young Americans Understand That Civic Duty Is Not Restricted to the Military," *Wall Street Journal,* May 29, 2013; Shirley Sagawa and John Bridgeland, "National Service 2.0," *Huffington Post,* June 25, 2013, www.huffingtonpost.com/shirley-sagawa/national-service-20_b_3490919.html; Shirley Sagawa, "Serving America: A National Service Agenda for the Next Decade" (Washington, DC: Center for American Progress, 2007); Aspen Institute's Franklin Project, "A 21st Century National Service System: Plan of Action" (2013). For more on the GI Bill and its effect on higher education, see Suzanne Mettler, *Soldiers to Citizens: The G.I. Bill and the Making of the Greatest Generation* (New York: Oxford University Press, 2005); John Bound and Sarah Turner, "Going to War and Going to College: Did World War II and the G.I. Bill Increase Educational Attainment for Returning Veterans?," *Journal of Labor Economics* 20, no. 4 (2002): 784–815; Marcus Stanley, "College Education and the Midcentury GI Bills," *Quarterly Journal of Economics* 118, no. 2 (2003): 671–708.

23. John Schmitt, "The Minimum Wage is Too Damn Low" (Washington, DC: Center for Economic and Policy Research, 2012); John Schmitt, "Minimum Wage: Catching Up to Productivity," *Democracy: A Journal of Ideas* 29 (Summer 2013): 35–39.

24. For information on how frequently labor laws are violated, see, among others, National Employment Law Project, "Broken Laws, Unprotected Workers: Violations of Employment and Labor Laws in America's Cities" (2009).

25. For more information on this proposal, see Madland, "Making Our Middle Class Stronger." For more on enforcement, see David Madland and Karla Walter, "Enforcing Change" (Washington, DC: Center for American Progress Action Fund, 2008).

26. David Madland and Karla Walter, "The Employee Free Choice Act 101: A Primer and a Rebuttal" (Washington, DC: Center for American Progress Action Fund, 2009); David Madland and Karla Walter, "The Bottom Line in Labor Law Negotiations" (Washington, DC: Center for American Progress Action Fund, 2009).

27. For a summary of the problems with current law that prevent workers from being able to join unions, see Madland, "Making Our Middle Class Stronger."

28. For some ideas about how to modernize union law, see, for example, Madland, "Making Our Middle Class Stronger." See also Rich Yeselson, "Fortress Unionism," *Democracy: A Journal of Ideas* 29 (Summer 2013): 68–81; Stephen Lerner, "Hope, Love and Strategy in the Time of the Zombie Apocalypse," *Truthout,* April 14, 2013, http://truth-out.org/opinion /item/15610-hope-love-and-strategy-in-the-time-of-the-zombie-apocalypse; Janice Fine, "Why Labor Needs a Plan B: Alternatives to Conventional Trade Unionism," *New Labor Forum* 16, no. 2 (2007): 35–44. For an example of a type of union policy that can benefit both firms and workers, see the description of work councils in David Madland, "Labor and Management Working Together" (Washington, DC: Center for American Progress, 2013).

See also this description of how unions are more integrated into the business arrangements of firms in Germany, for example, Knut Panknin, "Germany's Lessons for a Strong Economy" (Washington, DC: Center for American Progress, 2012).

29. Richard B. Freeman and James L. Medoff, *What Do Unions Do?* (New York: Basic Books, 1984); Barry T. Hirsch and Edward J. Schumacher, "Union Wages, Rents, and Skills in Health Care Labor Markets," *Journal of Labor Research* 19, no. 1 (1998): 125–147; Lawrence Mishel and Matthew Walters, "How Unions Help All Workers" (Washington, DC: Economic Policy Institute, 2003); Robert Johansson and Jay Coggins, "Union Density Effects in the Supermarket Industry," *Journal of Labor Research* 23, no. 4 (2002): 673–684.

30. For a review of this, see David Madland, Karla Walter, and Nick Bunker, "Unions Make the Middle Class" (Washington, DC: Center for American Progress Action Fund, 2011).

31. David Madland and Nick Bunker, "Unions Make Democracy Work for the Middle Class" (Washington, DC: Center for American Progress Action Fund, 2012).

32. See, for example, Vincent A. Mahler, David K. Jesuit, and Piotr R. Paradowski, "The Political Sources of Government Redistribution in the Developed World: A Focus on the Middle Class," presented at Inequality and the Status of the Middle Class: Lessons from the Luxembourg Income Study Conference (2010); Jonas Pontusson, David Rueda, and Christopher Way, "Comparative Political Economy of Wage Distribution: The Role of Partisanship and Labour Market Institutions," *British Journal of Political Science* 32, no. 2 (2002): 281–308; Richard Freeman, "Labor Market Institutions around the World," Discussion Paper 844 (Centre for Economic Performance, 2008).

33. David Madland and Keith Miller, "Middle Classes Are Stronger in States with Greater Union Membership" (Washington, DC: Center for American Progress Action Fund, 2013).

34. In addition to studies discussed in this section, see Madland, Walter, and Bunker, "Unions Make the Middle Class." See also David Jacobs and Lindsey Myers, "Union Strength, Neoliberalism, and Inequality: Contingent Political Analyses of U.S. Income Differences since 1950," American Sociological Review, June 9, 2014.

35. Bruce Western and Jake Rosenfeld, "Unions, Norms, and the Rise in American Earnings Inequality," *American Sociological Review* 76, no. 4 (2011): 513–537.

36. Daron Acemoglu and James Robinson, "Economics versus Politics: Pitfalls of Policy Advice," *Journal of Economic Perspectives* 27, no. 2 (2013): 173–192.

37. For a summary of this literature, see Freeman and Medoff, *What Do Unions Do?*

38. Acemoglu and Robinson, "Economics versus Politics."

39. For a review of the literature on the potential impacts of raising the minimum wage, see T. William Lester, David Madland, and Nick Bunker, "An Increased Minimum Wage Is Good Policy Even during Hard Times" (Washington, DC: Center for American Progress Action Fund, 2011); T. William Lester, David Madland, and Nick Bunker, "The Facts on Raising the Minimum Wage When Unemployment Is High" (Washington, DC: Center for American Progress Action Fund, 2012); T. William Lester, David Madland, and Jackie Odum, "Raising the Minimum Wage Would Help, Not Hurt, Our Economy" (Washington, DC: Center for American Progress Action Fund, 2013). Note also that many economists now recognize the benefits of a higher minimum wage. See Economic Policy Institute, "Prominent Economists Endorse $10 Minimum Wage," press release, January 14, 2014, www.epi.org/press/prominent-economists-endorse-10-10-minimum/.

40. Daniel Aaronson, Sumit Agarwal, and Eric French, "The Spending and Debt Response to Minimum Wage Hikes," Federal Reserve Bank of Chicago, February 2011.

41. Dean Baker and John Schmitt, "The Bogus Case against the Minimum Wage Hike," *Salon,* January 4, 2012, www.salon.com/2012/01/04/the_bogus_case_against_the_minimum_wage_hike/; Daniel Aaronson, Sumit Agarwal, and Eric French, "The Spending and Debt Response to Minimum Wage Hikes," *American Economic Review* 102, no. 7 (2012): 3111–3139; John Schmitt, "San Francisco Becomes First in Nation with $10 Minimum Wage (and the Sky Isn't Going to Fall)," *AlterNet,* December 29, 2011, www.alternet.org/story/153620/san_francisco_becomes_first_in_nation_with_%2410_minimum_wage_%28and_the_sky_isn%27t_going_to_fall%29; Arindrajit Dube, T. William Lester, and Michael Reich, "Do Frictions Matter in the Labor Market? Accessions, Separations and Minimum Wage Effects," Working Paper 5811 (IZA Discussion Paper Series, 2011).

42. Note that Acemoglu and Robinson also make this argument. See Acemoglu and Robinson, "Economics versus Politics."

43. Jane Gravelle and Donald Marple, "Tax Rates and Economic Growth" (Washington, DC: Congressional Research Service, 2011); Thomas Hungerford, "Taxes and the Economy: An Analysis of the Top Tax Rates, since 1945" (Washington, DC: Congressional Research Service, 2012). For a review of much of the current literature on this topic, see Andrew Fieldhouse, "A Review of the Economic Research on the Effects of Raising Ordinary Income Tax Rates" (Washington, DC: Economic Policy Institute, 2013). For a claim of potential positive impacts of raising taxes, see Benjamin Lockwood, Charles Nathanson, and E. Glen Weyl, "Taxation and the Allocation of Talent," Working Paper (Social Sciences Research Network, 2014). Some key steps toward ensuring that our tax code is more progressive include adding new brackets on very high earners, taxing very large estates at a higher rate when they are passed down to heirs, making sure that income from capital is taxed at a similar rate as income from labor, and getting rid of loopholes such as those that allow hedge fund managers to pay a lower rate on their taxes, make taxpayers subsidize excessive CEO compensation, and enable some profitable corporations to escape paying any taxes for years.

44. For research on the relationship between taxation and inequality, see Hungerford, "Taxes and the Economy"; Thomas Piketty, Emmanuel Saez, and Stefanie Stantcheva, "Optimal Taxation of Top Labor Incomes: A Tale of Three Elasticities," Working Paper 17616 (National Bureau of Economic Research, 2011); Thomas Piketty and Emmanuel Saez, "How Progressive Is the US Federal Tax System? A Historical and International Perspective," *Journal of Economic Perspectives* 21, no. 1 (2007): 3–24; Peter Diamond and Emmanuel Saez, "The Case for a Progressive Tax: From Basic Research to Policy Recommendations," *Journal of Economic Perspectives* 25, no. 4 (2011): 165–190.

45. Jonathan D. Ostry, Andrew Berg, and Charalambos G. Tsangarides, "Redistribution, Inequality and Growth" (International Monetary Fund, 2014).

46. For more information on achieving full employment, see Erickson and Ettlinger, "300 Million Engines of Growth"; Ruy Teixeira and John Halpin, "The Origins and Evolution of Progressive Economics" (Washington, DC: Center for American Progress, 2011); Dean Baker and Jared Bernstein, "Getting Back to Full Employment: A Better Bargain for Working People" (Washington, DC: Center for Economic and Policy Research, 2013). For more information on trade policies that encourage companies to employ American workers, see Erickson and Ettlinger, "300 Million Engines of Growth"; Sam Ungar and Donna Cooper, "Buy America Works" (Washington, DC: Center for American Progress, 2011). For information on more effective antitrust enforcement, see David Balto, "Reinvigorating Antitrust Enforcement" (Washington, DC: Center for American Progress, 2011); Barry Lynn, "Estates of Mind," *Washington Monthly,* July/August 2013, www.washingtonmonthly.com/magazine/july_august_2013/features/estates_of_mind045639.php.

47. S & P Capital IQ, "Economic Research: How Increasing Income Inequality Is Dampening U.S. Economic Growth, and Possible Ways to Change the Tide" (New York: S & P Capital IQ, 2014), www.globalcreditportal.com/ratingsdirect/renderArticle.do?arti cleId=1351366&SctArtId=255732&from=CM&nsl_code=LIME&sourceObjectId=8741033 &sourceRevId=&fee_ind=N&exp_date=20240804–19:41:13. Similarly, in September 2014, Morgan Stanley cautioned that "stronger growth in wages and salaries is essential to the macro outlook." Morgan Stanley, "US Economics, Inequality, and Consumption" (New York: Morgan Stanley, 2014). In addition, a majority of economists surveyed by the AP in 2013 said that inequality was harming the US economy. Christopher S. Rugaber, "AP Survey: US Income Gap Is Holding Back Economy," *Associated Press*, December 17, 2013, http://bigstory.ap.org/article/ap-survey-us-income-gap-holding-back-economy-0.

INDEX

Abramoff, Jack, 78
Acemoglu, Daron, 65, 164–65, 197n19, 204n94, 217n8, 248n42
Adams, James Truslow, 147
advanced countries, 44, 88, 129, 137, 139, 140, 142, 144, 146, 149, 151, 178n49, 190n64, 244n6. *See also* developed countries; rich countries
Affordable Care Act, 140
American Dream, 93, 147, 210n156
American Revolution, 9, 56
Argentina, 63, 65
Aristotle, 72
Arrow, Kenneth, 42
Aschauer, David, 59
Ashenfelter, Orley, 45
Australia, 39, 131, 157
Austria, 89

Bahrain, 92
Banfield, Edward, 28–29, 55
banks, 28, 98–102, 120, 144, 146, 156, 160, 211n169, 213n189. *See also* megabanks; Wall Street

Barbados, 92
Bartels, Larry, 74, 95
Bartlett, Bruce, 114, 184n92
Belgium, 89, 187n36
Berg, Andrew, 14, 166, 197n19
Bivens, Josh, 59
Bloom, David, 45
Bloomberg, Michael, 21
Boix, Carles, 82, 205n108
Bosnia, 92
Boushey, Heather, 15, 132, 178n53
Boyd, Robert, 33
Brazil, 13, 65
Brownback, Sam, 22, 183n84
Buera, Francisco, 145
Buffett, Warren, 100
Bush, George H. W., 114
Bush, George W., 26, 97, 103, 225n8; tax cuts 20, 22, 129, 181n74, 182nn75,81, 183n85, 225n8
business cycle, 53

campaign contributions, 76–78, 96, 99, 101, 108, 202n85, 203nn88,91
campaign finance, 71, 76, 102